LEAVING JUSTICEVILLE:

A Life Behind

By

ERIC DRAIN

…Based on a true story…

ERIC WALTER

Leaving Justiceville: A Life Behind

FOREWORD

Here is the novelization of a true story about a young boy who knew he was different from everyone else, even if he didn't understand how or why. He craved his parents' affection, but instead received only mental cruelty and physical abuse from his mother and father, the people who were supposed to love him unconditionally. Finally, shunned by his family, he lived on his own from the age of eleven, facing challenges with which no child should have to cope. This is the author's interpretation of actual events that occurred in the life of one innocent gay child who defied the odds and became the successful and happy man he longed to be.

Leaving Justiceville: A Life Behind

CHAPTER ONE

"You little bastard! I never wanted you anyway!" his mother shouted at him.
Eleven year old Ricky picked himself up off the ground and glared at the angry woman.
"That's fine with me!" he retorted. He was determined not to show the hurt her words had caused him. "You'll never have to worry about it again!"

With that declaration, Ricky stormed into the shabby, green, two-bedroom bungalow that was situated on the edge of town. He ran into the small room he shared with his sister and two brothers. Naturally, his selfish parents had taken the larger bedroom for themselves, leaving their four children to make do with the cramped space next door.
Ricky was a diminutive child of less than average height and undernourished appearance, who took after his father's side of the family. His thinness had more to do with the fact that he ate very little rather than his genetics. His mother rarely cooked, and when she did, the food was largely tasteless and poorly prepared. As a result, he lived mostly on peanut butter sandwiches and potato chips.
He gathered up his few clothes, most of which had come from the thrift store or rummage sales in the small town of Justiceville, Texas, and stuffed them into a worn and soiled duffel bag. It wasn't the first time his parents had spoken to him so harshly; almost

Leaving Justiceville: A Life Behind

every interaction with the hateful pair was unpleasant, to say the least. He should be accustomed to it by now, and yet the hurtfulness always managed to find its way into his young, tender heart.
It was an ironic name for a town, Ricky thought, because there was no justice for him or his brothers and sister. If there had been, they would be living in a comfortable home with loving parents who doted on each of them. His biggest worry should have been whether his pearl necklace wearing mother was fixing chicken or pork for supper. Instead he was more concerned about avoiding another scolding or beating for whatever infraction for which his detestable parents had decided he was guilty.

The final straw had come that morning. He had accompanied his mother, Stella, to the local grocery store. She was a slovenly woman with broad hips, black cat-eye plastic glasses, missing teeth, and short curly hair. She wore overly tight polyester pedal-pushers and ill fitting blouses that only made her pear shaped body appear even more distorted. Ricky had watched her on several occasions flirting with the mailman, store clerks, and some of the neighbor men. What does she think these guys see in her, he wondered? Even at his young age, he realized that she was unattractive and none too clean. He thought it rather humorous to observe her acting like a femme fatale whenever there was a man around. The exception to that behavior was when her husband Deed was around. His real name was Edgar but, for

reasons that Ricky never understood, he went by the unusual nickname. He was a stocky man with a beer-belly that his stained and greasy tee shirts usually failed to cover completely. The thinning brown hair that he grew long on one side was a futile attempt to cover his balding and speckled pate. He wasn't fooling anyone, Ricky thought disdainfully; if a small child could see through his charade, anybody could. His father was rarely home; when he wasn't at work as a welder, he spent most of his free time at one of the local bars, where he engaged in his own inappropriate flirting with any woman who would give him the time of day. The times that Deed and Stella were together, they were usually fighting. There were never any words of love or kindness spoken between them, Ricky noted, only expressions of cruelty and disgust. Often they would take their anger and unhappiness with each other out on their children, either verbally or physically.

This morning had been another example of that, and this time, Ricky decided he had had enough. He had grudgingly accompanied his mother to the store, knowing full well that she didn't want his company, merely someone to load the grocery bags into the back of their 1964 green Chevrolet Impala sedan and then carry them into the house, while she sat down in front of the television with a glass of iced Coke and a cigarette.

While they were in the store Stella took the opportunity to flirt with a tall, gangly stock boy, who

couldn't have been more than sixteen or seventeen years old.

"I love the way you can reach all the way to the top shelf like that, Eddy," she smiled coyly at him.

"Uh, thanks," the youth said uncomfortably.

"He doesn't think you're pretty," Ricky rolled his eyes. "You're wasting your time."

Without warning his mother turned and slapped him across the face with her hand. Eddy backed away and then turned and hurried awkwardly from the aisle, leaving mother and son alone.

"You shut the fuck up!" she seethed. "Don't you never talk like that to me again."

"I was just –" Ricky began.

"Shut up!" she yelled.

With that she began hitting him with her hands, her purse, even items in the grocery cart. Ricky covered his head and face and knelt down in a protective stature to shield himself from the worst of the blows.

"Ya goddammed little bastard," she cried. "Talking to your mother like that in public. Just you wait 'til I tell your father what you did."

She grabbed him by the arm and yanked him roughly to his feet before shaking him as hard as she could. She gave him a shove and pointed to the cans and boxes of food scattered around them.

"Now pick up this shit!" she said coldly. "Eddy shouldn't have to clean up the mess you made."

Ricky bit back a sharp retort, knowing that it would only enrage his mother further and make the situation worse. He looked around, and his face turned even

redder with humiliation as he noticed the curious expressions on the other shoppers' faces. Several people were standing at the ends of the aisle and had observed the angry woman hitting and berating her son. None of them offered to intervene in any way or come to his assistance. They seemed unconcerned that an innocent child was being attacked right in front of their eyes.

How could they be that way, Ricky wondered for the hundredth time? All of his life, he had lived with the inaction of neighbors, the police, social workers, and teachers when they heard the cries coming from their house or when they observed the bruises on his and his sibling's bodies. Once when his sister was being brutally spanked, and her screams could be heard a couple of blocks away, Ricky had actually seen the next door neighbor close his window and pull the drapes.

No one ever offered to help or get involved. It was as if they all thought it was perfectly normal, like he and his brothers and sister deserved to be beaten and called horrible names for merely existing.

But he didn't deserve it, did he? He wasn't a bad person; he did as he was told, never caused anyone any trouble, didn't lie or steal. But in his mind, even if he did lie and steal, he didn't deserve to be treated in such a pitiless and inhumane manner. No one did, as far as he was concerned.

Did all parents treat their children this way, he often wondered at night as he stared up at the ceiling? Was every child afraid of the adults in their lives? Did

they hate their parents as much as he did? He didn't think so. At least the grownups he saw on television seemed to love their families. But maybe that was just wishful thinking on the part of the writers; maybe there was no such thing as love. He knew he felt no love for his parents, or anyone else for that matter. His parents didn't love their children, and they clearly despised each other. Why else would they beat their kids and flirt with every man or woman they encountered? He was to learn later that both his mother and father had done much more than just flirt with other people.
As Ricky picked up the dented cans and boxes from the floor, he made a decision. This would be the last time he would endure such treatment from his parents. As soon as he got home, he was leaving for good!

"Where the fuck you think you're going?" his mother taunted him. She was standing in the doorway of the small bedroom, lazily puffing on a cigarette.
"None of your damn business," Ricky said calmly. He zipped up the duffel bag and walked past her without looking back.
"You'll be back," she chuckled. "Not that I care if you're here or not."
Ricky ignored her and headed out the back door.

That night, Ricky lay on a makeshift cot under the stairs at the home of one of the cafeteria workers from his school. She had seen firsthand on many

occasions the bruises and welts that usually covered his arms, neck, and face when he went through the line with his food tray. Everyone else had seen them as well, he thought wryly, but Doris was the only person to acknowledge them and show any concern for him. When he told her about the ruthless treatment he and his siblings suffered at the hands of their parents, she had hugged him and told him in private that if things got too bad, he could come and stay with her. Ricky's eyes had welled up at this unexpected bit of kindness. She hugged him again and then gently shooed him away while she returned to her work.

With those words in mind, he had walked across town to the house Doris shared with her husband Fred and their daughter Kelli.

Doris and Fred greeted him kindly, and Ricky experienced an unfamiliar sensation; he felt welcome for the first time in his life, like maybe this could be his chance to be part of one of the television families he had admired. Fred and Doris were so different from his own parents. They spoke with great affection to each other and their daughter, and their house was clean and pleasant. It had nice furniture, and there were curtains on the windows rather than old bed sheets.

For the next few weeks, Doris cooked delicious meals for them and treated Ricky as if he was her own son. Fred gave him chores to perform after school and then supervised his homework while the family watched television together. Fred's favorite

show was 'Gunsmoke', and it soon became Ricky's as well. They watched 'The Mary Tyler Moore Show', 'The Brady Bunch', and others, giving Ricky his first opportunity to actually enjoy television and laugh at the silliness of the characters.

That first night at Fred and Doris's house, Ricky's mind relived his entire childhood at a feverish pace. This wasn't the first time he had run away, he remembered. The first time had been a year or so ago when the family lived in Rhome, Texas.
He and his sister had been playing with an old secondhand skateboard under the carport. The two of them laughed loudly at their clumsiness until their father stormed out through the back door, yelling and cursing at them to be quiet so he could sleep. He grabbed Ricky by the arm and proceeded to give him a brutal beating before finally picking him up and stuffing him in an old metal trashcan beside the house.
"You ain't nothin' but garbage," he sneered at the boy. "That's where you belong."
He turned to his terrified daughter and glared at her, causing her to cower back and run away from him.
"Now I better not hear another goddammed sound from either of ya, or you'll both get a real beatin'." With that, he returned to the house, slamming the door behind him. Ricky managed to extricate himself from the garbage can, painfully rubbing his injured buttocks and bruised legs and arms.

Leaving Justiceville: A Life Behind

That night, Ricky ran away with a friend from school, a boy named Cyrus, whose home life wasn't much better than his. The two fled to the nearby town of Newark, where they both hid out at the home of another friend of Cyrus's. For two weeks, the two remained concealed there until the friend's parents discovered them and drove them back to Rhome. They dropped the boys off at Cyrus's house, where Ricky's father was waiting impatiently for them. Ricky remembered that his father hadn't spoken to him or even looked at him on the drive home. As soon as they got out of the car, his father had spanked him ruthlessly and told him if he ever pulled a stunt like that again, he wouldn't live to regret it.

It was after that beating that Doris had noticed for the first time his bruises and black eyes and swollen face. She took him aside and asked what had happened. Reluctantly, he confided in her the details of his home life. To his relief, she was properly indignant. The two of them talked on several occasions after that.

Many other memories flooded his mind, the earliest ones from about the age of two or three or so. The first one was when he had soiled his diaper and received a beating for it from his annoyed mother. Another was from the age of four, when he and his sister were fighting over a hammer that had been left lying carelessly on the living room floor, both claiming current ownership of it. They had each been tugging on it, trying to take it away from the other

when Ricky's grip on it suddenly slipped, and it flew uncontrollably at his sister's mouth, breaking out two of her front teeth. That had resulted in another beating from his father, even though he tried to explain that it was an accident. He felt badly for injuring his sister, but his father hadn't cared whether he was sorry or not.

Come to think of it, most of the things he had been punished for in his life weren't even his fault. Often times it was his older brothers, Jimmy and Theo, who had misbehaved. He noticed that their parents rarely scolded them, however, and when they did, it was much less severe than what he received. Somehow they managed to always find a way to put the blame on Ricky. The two older boys never accepted responsibility for their actions and would stand by indifferently while their younger brother received a whipping.

On one such occasion, he remembered his grandparents coming for a visit. They didn't come by often, and he only had the vaguest memory of them, just that they were very stern, and his grandfather carried a paddle with him to use on any unruly child. After his grandparents left, the four children were pushed out of the house by their parents. The doors were locked behind them. Fortunately, the weather was fair and warm that day, although it wouldn't have mattered to their parents if it had been pouring down rain with lightning and thunder.

"Let us in," Ricky called through the window. "I have to go to the bathroom."

Leaving Justiceville: A Life Behind

"Get the fuck away from that window and shut up!" his mother yelled back.
"Go piss behind the chicken house," Jimmy told him.
"No, I have to…" Ricky said.
"You are such a fuckin' pest," Jimmy shrugged. He turned to his other brother. "What are they doin' in there?"
Theo was the eldest brother and five years older than Ricky. He grinned mischievously.
"Let's find out."
After a few minutes of working with the lock on the back door, he managed to break his way into the house. The three boys snuck quietly through the kitchen and peered around the doorway into the living room. Their parents were on the couch, obviously engaged in an intimate act. Jimmy and Theo started laughing silently while they watched the two adults. Ricky tugged at his brother's shirt.
"I gotta go to the bathroom," he whispered loudly.
"Shut up," Theo whispered frantically.
But it was too late. His father looked over at them with an angry scowl.
"Goddammit! What the fuck are you doin'?" he yelled. "Get out of here!"
The boys scurried out the back door. Their father stormed out of the house a few minutes later. The boys cowered under his irate glare.
"I oughta beat the shit outa all three of you!"
"It's his fault," Theo pointed at Ricky. "He wouldn't shut up about the bathroom."

Leaving Justiceville: A Life Behind

Edgar grabbed Ricky's arm and dragged him behind the chicken house, yelling and cursing at him the whole time. A few minutes later, Ricky ran tearfully to his room, his back and buttocks stinging and already beginning to bruise from the beating he had just endured.
"I didn't do it!" he had cried as his father hit him repeatedly. "It was Theo that opened the door."
"Don't try to blame your brother for this, you worthless little shit!" the angry man shouted.

A little later his father threw open the door to his bedroom and yanked him roughly off of his small bed. He snatched the blanket and pillow off the cot and dragged the startled child to the side porch.
"From now on, this is where you sleep," his father said coldly. "This will teach you to go where you ain't wanted. Maybe you'll listen to me from now on."
For weeks, Ricky was made to sleep on the side porch, alone and frightened by the unfamiliar noises of the night; dogs barking, owls hooting, the rustling of unknown creatures in the darkness. He huddled under his blanket, trembling with fear, finally falling asleep out of sheer exhaustion.

One night when Edgar and Stella had gone out and left the children home alone, which they often did, Theo pushed Ricky into the bathroom and locked the door.
"Take off your clothes," he instructed the small boy.

Leaving Justiceville: A Life Behind

"Why?"
"Just do it," Theo said with exasperation.
"Am I taking a bath?"
"Uh, yeah," Theo said.
Ricky did as he was told and watched as Theo disrobed as well.
"Lay down on the floor," Theo told him.
Warily, Ricky lay on the cold and dirty linoleum floor. Seconds later, he was trying to fight off the bigger boy as Theo forced his penis into his mouth and pressed the crack of his ass onto Ricky's face. For several minutes, Theo forced himself on Ricky, while the younger boy struggled against him. When Theo finally climaxed, he climbed off his younger brother.
"Put your clothes back on," he said gruffly. "And if you tell anyone about this, I'll make sure you regret it. No one will fuckin' believe you anyway, runt."

Ricky cried himself to sleep that night on his makeshift bed on the side porch of blankets and pillows he had managed to sneak out of the house. The next morning, his brother Jimmy, who was three years older than him, let him into the house to get something to eat.
"What's the matter with you?" he asked curiously.
Ricky hesitated, but finally confided in him what Theo had done to him the evening before.
"You're lyin'," Jimmy said. "Theo's no fag."
"I'm not lying!" Ricky insisted. "What's a fag?"

"It's a guy who fucks other guys instead of girls," his brother told him.
A little later, Ricky was sitting up on the lower half of the bi-level chicken house roof when his father bellowed his name. He scooted down to the edge of the roof and was yanked off of it.
"You fuckin' little brat!" his father yelled angrily. "Tellin' lies about your brother. I'm gonna give you the beatin' of your life, you little faggot!"
"It wasn't a lie!" Ricky retorted. "He really did those things."
"He did not, and you know it!" his father shouted. "He ain't a faggot like you."
Ricky tried to defend himself against the onslaught of hitting and kicking and slapping that his father released on him for the next few minutes. When he was done, Ricky lay curled in a fetal position on the ground.
"You ever lie about your brothers again, and I'll give you a real beating," his father panted. "Now get outa my sight."
Later that night as he lay on the porch, trying to find a less painful position in which to lie, he considered this new word that he had heard several times in less than two days: fag, or faggot. It sounded like a derogatory term, one that was used as an insult, at least the way his brothers and father had said it. Apparently it meant people who were attracted to people of the same sex. People like himself, he thought with a sense of wonder. He had always known he was different from the rest of his family

Leaving Justiceville: A Life Behind

and from his classmates. Up until this moment he hadn't understood what it was that made him unique, but now it was dawning on him that he was attracted to other guys. True, he was still very young, but with his introspective nature, he spent much of his time alone trying to understand who he was. Now he had another piece of the puzzle.

A few other memories came to mind as he lay in his small cot. Hiding in the bushes while playing hide and seek with a few neighbor children, only to run yelling and screaming out of hiding because a huge snake had wrapped itself around his ankle. Romping on the swings and monkey bars at the school playground, playing tag. Hedgeapples, or horse apples as they were commonly known, raising chickens, and the family dog, Charlie. Those were the few good memories he had, other than the snake of course, and wasn't it strange that none of them included his parents or brothers? Shouldn't that be where his happiest memories lay?

He remembered a young Latino boy following him around the playground and into the boys' bathroom. He couldn't think of his name, but he remembered him pulling him into a bathroom stall and kissing him on the lips. When he told his teacher about it, without mentioning who had kissed him, he was sent to the principal's office. His mother was called, he received a spanking, and was made to sleep outside on the porch again. He had learned by now to cover himself on his makeshift bed with pieces of an old cardboard

box as a shield from the elements and frightening noises of the night.

One day Ricky's brother Jimmy pushed him off the roof of the chicken house. To get his revenge, Ricky picked up a small chunk of broken concrete and dropped it on Jimmy's head. Jimmy received no punishment for pushing his brother off the roof, but Ricky was severely castigated.

Leaving Justiceville: A Life Behind

CHAPTER TWO

A new convenient store opened down the street, and Ricky's mother began frequenting it on a regular basis. It was about this same time that Ricky noticed his father was rarely at home. He claimed to be working late, but Ricky was skeptical. The man had few redeeming qualities, and he had never found honesty to be one of them. He had heard him lie to neighbors as if it came naturally to him. Often times he would come home with the smell of cheap perfume clinging to him over the overwhelming stench of body odor and cigarette smoke that was his norm.

One day while his father was "working late", Ricky came home from school to find an old rusty car with missing hubcaps in the driveway. It looked right at home with his mother's old sedan and the other disintegrating vehicles moldering away beside the shabby garage. He stepped up to the back door and turned the knob, only to find it locked. With a resigned sigh he knocked on first the back door, then the front door, and finally the side door that opened onto the porch where he usually spent his long lonely nights.

"Hey, let me in," he called out.

There was no response, so he pressed his ear up to the glass on the living room window. He could hear noises coming from inside, muffled voices, moans, and cries of pleasure. As young as he was, he wasn't

so naïve as to not understand what was happening in the house. His mother had one of her visitors.

This had happened before when he was about four years old. He and his sister had accompanied their mother to a strange house across town. It had been a chilly gray December day, he remembered.

"Now you sit here on the porch and don't move," she said sharply.

"Can't we come in?" Ricky had frowned at her. "It's cold out here."

"No! Quit being such a baby," she said impatiently.

The back door opened, and a large, dark-haired man stepped out onto the sagging porch. He looked around the immediate area warily.

"What the fuck did you bring them kids with you for?" he scowled. "I ain't into that, ya know. Now if the girl was a little older…"

"I had to bring them," she said, unfazed by his disgusting insinuation. "No one at home to watch them; they'd probably burn the place down or somethin'. Besides, the neighbors are getting a little too nosy lately, and they wouldn't hesitate to call the cops on me. All I need is for some asshole to report me and have them come into my house and check things out. Deed's got enough illegal shit there to have us both put away for good."

"Well, keep 'em outside," the man said. "Now, come on. I'm fuckin' horny."

Ricky watched the two of them go into the house and heard the lock click behind them. He and his sister wrapped their thin coats around them tighter and

huddled together out of the sharp wind while they listened through the un-insulated walls to their mother having sex with this stranger. Ricky was to have nightmares about it for months afterward.

This particular visitor of his mother's made several guest appearances to the house over the next several weeks. Each time, the children were locked outside. Ricky preferred to conceal himself away on his side porch hideaway, but Jimmy and Theo would always listen outside the bedroom window while the two adults had sex.
It was shortly after one of her trysts that Ricky's father confronted his mother.
"I knew you was a fuckin' whore!" he shouted. "Tony told me how that Bobby's been comin' around here. You and him are fuckin', ain't ya? I knew that was cum on the sheets, and it sure the fuck ain't mine!"
"Tony's a goddammed liar," she retorted. "I don't even know no one named Bobby."
"You fuckin' bitch!" Deed yelled. "I knew I couldn't trust you. How long's it been goin' on?"
"I ain't havin' no affair," she said. "I can barely stand to have sex with you, let alone anyone else. And don't act so high and mighty. You think I don't know what you been doin' with that cunt in the office?"
"Marie's just a coworker," Deed said defensively. "I ain't never touched her."

"The fuck you ain't. And don't pretend that my sister's baby is her husband's. I know goddamm well it's yours."

Oh, wow, Ricky thought with surprise, his little cousin wasn't his cousin at all; she was his half-sister.

Deed moved to strike her, and Ricky quickly ran from the house to hide in the chicken house. Jimmy and Theo stayed put, apparently enjoying the soap opera drama unfolding in front of them.

"Hit the bitch!" Theo yelled, encouraging his father. "She deserves it!"

"You shut the fuck up!" Deed snapped angrily. "Now git outa here!"

Theo and Jimmy laughed and ran from the room, while the fight continued to rage between their parents. A little later, Ricky peered cautiously in the front door. It was relatively quiet; apparently the fight was over. His two brothers were standing at their parents' bedroom door. One had his ear pressed to the hollow wood while the other was squinting to see through the keyhole.

"They're fuckin'," Jimmy whispered with a grin. "We're watchin' them."

"They'll whip you if they catch you," Ricky warned them. "You'd better get away from there."

"Shh!" Theo hissed with annoyance.

He placed his eye to the keyhole again for a moment. "Shit!" he whispered. "He saw us!"

Leaving Justiceville: A Life Behind

He and Jimmy hastily moved aside and pushed Ricky in front of the door just as their father abruptly pulled it open.
"You little bastard!" he bellowed angrily, grabbing the boy by the arm and shaking him roughly.
"It wasn't me!" Ricky cried. "It was –"
"Don't go blamin' your brothers again," his father yelled. "It's always you pullin' shit and trying to blame everyone else."
With that, he ripped Ricky's shirt off over his head and yanked his dirty jeans off of him. He spent the next ten minutes beating his son's underwear clad ass while cursing and yelling at him. The next thing Ricky knew, he was pushed out the front door wearing only his stained and worn undershorts.
"Now you sit right there and let everyone see what a little pervert you are!" his father seethed.
He slammed and locked the door, while Ricky struggled to push it open. Finally he gave up and curled into a ball as he sobbed his little heart out with tears of anger, frustration, pain, and humiliation.

Late that night, the front door finally opened.
"Get your ass in this house," his mother said coldly.
It had been a long day for Ricky as he lay on his side in a fetal position facing away from the street, trying to make himself as inconspicuous as possible to passersby. He was hungry and thirsty, his belly aching and his lips dry and cracked. His buttocks were tender and sore with purple and black and

yellow bruising all over them from the beating he had received.

The rest of the family was sitting at the battered and rusted kitchen table eating supper.

"That's what you get for spyin'," his father said as he sat down in his chair.

"Yeah, you shouldn'ta gone spying on Mom and Dad," Jimmy taunted him. He took a bite of his fried Spam.

Ricky ignored him and sat down in his usual chair.

"What the hell do you think you're doin'?" his father scowled.

"I'm hungry," Ricky said.

"You ain't gettin' no supper," Deed snorted. "You just sit there and watch the rest of us eat. Maybe one of these days you'll learn not to spy on people."

"It wasn't me," Ricky said.

"There he goes again, Dad," Theo said. "Lyin' again. You watch and he'll try to blame me and Jimmy."

"Get outa here," their mother said to Ricky. "Go sleep on the porch. You sure as hell ain't sleepin' in this house. Just lookin' at you makes me want to wear your ass out."

Not long after that incident, the family moved from the old rock house they were living in to a small white house across the highway, which they rented from a tall, thin man named Mr. Burnham, who was around seventy or so. He lived up the hill in a large brick house that Ricky had often admired. It was a nicely maintained property, and the few times he had

been in the house, he was amazed at how clean and nicely decorated it was, just the opposite of his parents' house.

Ricky suspected the reason they moved was because his parents had failed to pay the mortgage on the dilapidated house in which they lived. He had heard snippets of phone calls and heated conversations with visiting bank officers demanding payment.

"Mrs. Blain, I understand that money is tight," one suit-clad gentleman said irritably on his third visit to the house. He had tried to be friendly and sympathetic, but Ricky could see that his patience was wearing thin with his mother's sullen and sarcastic attitude.

"You wanna see my kids go without food?" Stella said. "Just so you can have your money? Well, my fuckin' kids come first. I ain't gonna deprive them so's you can live on your fancy wines and steaks."

"The bank just wants its money," the man said evenly. "The money you and your husband agreed to repay when you bought this house."

He looked around distastefully at the dirty carpets, streaked walls, stained windows.

"This house ain't worth shit," Stella snorted. "And I didn't fuckin' agree to nothin'. You want your money, you take it up with Deed. This dump was his idea, and it's in his name."

"Then I'll talk to him. Where is he?"

"Aw, who the hell knows," she shrugged indifferently. "Probably at a bar somewhere."

Leaving Justiceville: A Life Behind

Good luck, Ricky thought as he listened to this conversation. He was just a little boy, and even he knew that the banker was never going to see that money.

It was a few days later that Ricky and his sister toted most of their belongings across the street to the white house owned by Mr. Burnham. Jimmy and Theo helped their father move the few mean sticks of furniture over in a borrowed pickup. Ricky accidentally broke a couple of the mismatched and chipped dinner plates while putting them in the rusty metal kitchen cabinet. His mother slapped him across the face and sent him to bed without supper.
This house had three bedrooms, so his sister had her own room, while he continued to share with his older brothers. He spent the evening setting up the double bed that they would all sleep on while the rest of the family ate a couple of frozen pizzas. The thin stained mattress was too heavy for him, but with his burgeoning mathematical mind, he managed to figure out a way to use an old board as a lever to wriggle the mattress up onto the tattered box springs. He arranged the furniture as best he could and placed his few threadbare clothes in the bottom dresser drawer; he knew full well that his brothers would make him take it anyway so that they could have the upper drawers. All of his clothes were hand-me-downs from his brothers or from garage sales. He often wondered what it would be like to wear new clothes that had been bought in a store.

Leaving Justiceville: A Life Behind

Well, that was something that he would never know as long as he was living with his family, he thought grimly as he struggled to put the dirty sheets and blankets on the mattress. He had never owned anything new in his life. Toys, books, clothes; anything his parents grudgingly bought for him was secondhand and usually old and in poor condition. His favorite playthings were his Matchbox cars. They were scratched and broken, but that didn't detract from the pleasure he enjoyed while playing with them. There were so few things in his life that were good, and Ricky was determined to make the most of what little there was.

Mr. Burnham seemed rich to Ricky. He drove a big long Cadillac and lived in a large brick house up on the hill east of the small dwelling his parents were renting from him. Once when he had gone with his mother to Mr. Burnham's home, he had come inside the house after having waited outside for more than an hour. He used the downstairs bathroom and was awestricken by its opulence. Shiny chrome fixtures, gleaming porcelain, a separate tub and shower, ceramic tile floor; everything was spotlessly clean in the oversized room. How did people get this much money, he wondered? How pleasant it must be to live in a clean environment like this.

After using the facilities, he wandered through the first floor, astounded by the lovely furnishings and crystal chandeliers. He looked for his mother and Mr. Burnham but didn't see them anywhere. He came to a

closed door and heard muffled noises coming from behind it. He was familiar enough with his mother's past indiscretions to know exactly what was happening. She and Mr. Burnham were obviously hooking up in the bedroom. Ew, he frowned distastefully. Mr. Burnham was at least seventy years old and not even the slightest bit attractive.
Apparently that didn't matter to his mother; of course, she was no prize either. So far, none of her illicit paramours had been nice looking, at least in his opinion. He knew what she was after, and that was their dicks.
He knocked hesitantly on the door.
"Get away from that fuckin' door!" his mother yelled with annoyance.
He heard Mr. Burnham whisper something.
"Don't worry about it," she whispered back. "He's just a stupid kid; he don't know what we're doin'."
"I'm hungry," Ricky called back.
"I don't give a damn if you're hungry or not," she retorted angrily. "Now shut the fuck up and get outa here!"

That night Ricky heard his parents arguing about Mr. Burnham. His mother walked out of the bedroom and slapped him across the face.
"Did you tell your father about this afternoon?" she demanded furiously. "You goddammed little snitch!"
"No, I didn't say anything," Ricky rubbed his stinging cheek.
"You fuckin' little liar," she said.

Leaving Justiceville: A Life Behind

"I didn't," Ricky insisted.
"Then how did he know about old man Burnham?"
"I don't know," Ricky said.
He never did know how his father had found out about his wife's affair with the landlord, but nothing was ever mentioned about it again. After all, his father was having his own trysts, so he couldn't very well point fingers at her.

It was about this time that his parents acquired a number of animals from somewhere: horses, cows, goats, and chickens. It was the children's responsibility to care for the menagerie, which included feeding and milking and picking up eggs. Jimmy and Theo usually managed to find an excuse to avoid doing their share, so most of the chores were left to Ricky and his sister.
One day, his brothers took turns riding one of the horses while he milked the cows. He looked out of the shed door and saw Jimmy slapping the animal repeatedly on the rump and yanking roughly on the reins.
"Don't hit him!" Ricky yelled.
"You stupid horse!" Jimmy shouted angrily, ignoring his little brother. "I'll fuckin' teach you a lesson!"
As Ricky watched, the agitated horse reared back on its hind legs, throwing Jimmy from the saddle and into a barbed wire fence before galloping away from his tormentor. Ricky jumped up from his milking stool and ran to help his brother, calling for his father all the while. His eyes were as big as saucers as he

stared at his injured sibling. It seemed to him that there was blood everywhere. The more Jimmy struggled to free himself from the sharp barbs of the fence, the further he injured himself. He was crying and screaming with pain and fear.

"Hold still," Ricky told him in a frightened voice. "I'll try to get you out."

His young hands were ineffectual for the most part as he tried to help him. His father shoved him roughly out of the way, sending him reeling on all fours into the dirt.

"Quit makin' it worse," he snapped. "Go fetch me the wire cutters." He turned back to Jimmy. "Hold still," he said soothingly.

"Ricky spooked him," Jimmy lied. "He threw me because Ricky was hittin' him."

Ricky returned with the wire cutters and handed them to his father. He was totally unprepared for the vicious beating he was subjected to for the next few minutes. His father cursed at him while he hit and kicked him.

"I was milking the cow," Ricky cried. "It wasn't my fault."

"You callin' your brother a liar again?" his father roared.

He shoved the boy away once more. Ricky got to his feet and ran for the chicken house, where he climbed up on the lower roof and cried with pain and anger and humiliation. Why did his father always believe Jimmy and Theo's lies, he wondered? He had never told an untruth about anything in his life, but he was

Leaving Justiceville: A Life Behind

always punished anyway, while his brothers were rarely subjected to the mistreatment he endured every day of his life. It was so unfair!

During her stint of dreaded playground duty, one of his teachers at school had told him bluntly that life was unfair, while a cigarette dangled from the corner of her mouth. She was a sullen woman, who had clearly given up on her dreams of a happy existence, and she was more than glad to pass on her depressing mantra to her students. Ricky recognized this, but he sensed in his heart that she was right. After all, nothing in his life was fair. Cruel parents, mean older brothers, terrible living conditions, and brutal beatings on a daily basis for mistakes he had made, or infractions that he hadn't even committed.

Jimmy had to be taken to the hospital and received numerous stitches to close the wounds he had suffered. He cried and moaned while he lay on the old musty smelling sofa in the living room. Ricky watched in disbelief as his parents doted on him, bringing him sweet treats and presents. The whole thing with the horse had been Jimmy's own fault but, as usual, Ricky had been the one punished.

After Jimmy's episode with the horse and the barbed wire fence, the animal became increasingly skittish. Jimmy and Theo teased and taunted him constantly, making him nervous and unruly. Ricky and his sister were riding him one day when the horse suddenly bolted, throwing the two children from his back. Ricky landed on the hard dirt, jarring his teeth and injuring his ankle. He immediately looked around for

his sister and was relieved to find her unhurt. When he told his mother about it, he was punished for being so careless and sent to his room.

Not long after Deed and Stella's argument about Mr. Burnham, the family picked up and moved to a brick house in Rhome, Texas. One of Ricky's most prominent memories from this house was the time his grandfather handed him a wad of chewing tobacco and told him to chew it. Ricky, being a small child, did as he was told and inadvertently swallowed it. He spent the next few hours vomiting off the side of the front porch while his family laughed and mocked him.
It was while they lived in the brick house that Ricky started first grade. His teacher was a young woman named Miss Kinney, who had a significant caffeine addiction; she was never without a white Styrofoam cup of coffee on her desk. She was also somewhat overly eager and enthusiastic, he often thought. His class shared a huge room with the second grade class, separated by a partition in front of which Miss Kinney's desk sat so that she could see both sides. Many of Ricky's classmates came from well-to-do families, very different from his own. At lunch one day, Ricky opened his paper bag and began to eat his biscuit with peanut butter and Karo syrup that he had made himself that morning. The biscuit was several days old and somewhat stale, but it was the best Ricky could come up with.

Leaving Justiceville: A Life Behind

"What's that you're eating?" a classmate named Danny asked him. "It looks gross."
"It's a biscuit with peanut butter and syrup on it," Ricky explained.
He looked enviously over at Danny's lunch box, a domed yellow Walt Disney school bus lunch box with a matching thermos. It was new and shiny and filled with peanut butter and jelly or ham sandwiches on white bread, with flavored potato chips, apple or pear slices with the peeling removed, and chocolate milk. Ricky had never even seen a pear before, much less tasted one. And the only milk he had drunk was what he took from their cows. He would strain it through a dishtowel into a plastic pitcher and then place it in the refrigerator. He and his siblings were allowed to drink it at supper time unless his mother needed it for a recipe. That was rare since she almost never did any actual cooking. Her idea of making a meal was frying Spam slices or heating macaroni and cheese on the stove and then tossing it carelessly onto the table for her children to help themselves. Jimmy and Theo always got the lion's share of the food, which was why Ricky and his sister were underdeveloped for their ages.
"You live in that brick house, don't you?" Danny smirked. "That place is a dump. My dad says your parents are poor and nothing but trailer trash. That makes you trailer trash too."
"I ain't no trailer trash!" Ricky exclaimed indignantly. "We don't live in a trailer."

Leaving Justiceville: A Life Behind

"You don't have to live in a trailer to be trash," Danny laughed at him. "You're so stupid."

After a few months in the first grade, Miss Kinney took Ricky aside.
"Give this note to your parents," she said confidentially and handed him a folded piece of paper.
Ricky did as he was told. His mother read through the note and showed it to her husband.
"Ya see, I told you he was stupid," she said. "He ain't never gonna amount to shit."
"I'm not stupid," Ricky said.
"You're teacher said you are," his dad said. "So ya are. They're gonna separate you from the smart kids and you're gonna go along with it."
From that point on, Ricky was forced to sit at the back of the room with a small group of less advanced students. It was grossly unfair, not to mention humiliating, he thought. He was just as smart as anyone else, probably smarter. So what if he wasn't that good with vocabulary or phonics. Did that really matter? He could communicate as well as anyone else his age, and he was great at math and problem solving. He was even able to help his older brothers with their math homework. As a matter of fact, he was smarter than either of them at just about everything, now that he thought about it. The highest grade either of them had ever received was a 'C-'.

Leaving Justiceville: A Life Behind

One day, he couldn't take the embarrassment of sitting apart from the rest of the class any longer. The work the teacher was having them do was ridiculously basic and demeaning to him. With an annoyed look on his face, he carried the picture puzzle book he was working on up to Miss Kinney's desk.

"This is dumb," he told her, holding up the book for her to see. "I'm not stupid, but this makes me feel that way. This stuff is for babies. I'm just as smart as anyone else, and I shouldn't be treated different from the others."

"Ricky, sit down in your chair," Miss Kinney told him sharply before returning her attention to the papers on her desk. "This isn't up for discussion."

"But I'm smart!" he protested. "I'm as smart as anyone here."

"I'm your teacher, and I think I know what's best for you," she said. "So go back to your seat."

"You don't know me at all!" he said impatiently. "You've said like three words to me since school started."

He met her angry gaze evenly, and the next thing he knew, he was sitting in the principal's office with three angry adults staring down at him, including the principal, the school secretary, and his mother.

"You know better than to sass your teacher," his mother said severely. "I didn't raise you to be a smart ass."

She glanced nervously at the principal.

"You didn't?" Ricky said dryly.

"Of course I didn't," she said impatiently. She looked back up at the scowling man. "I've always taught my kids to be respectful and to behave themselves."
Yeah, right, Ricky thought derisively, you worthless piece of shit! The only things he'd learned from her or his father were how to lie, steal, run out on your bills, be lazy, and commit adultery. His parents had no concept of decency or goodness, and they certainly hadn't taught him anything worthwhile.
If there was good in him, it's because of him, not his parents, he told himself. All on his own, he'd learned responsibility and how to work hard, to be honest and do his best; there were no adults in his life to teach him those things.
"Of course you have," the principal said. "Mary, take Ricky to your office and make him sit there and think about what he's done until I'm ready for him. I want to talk to his mother in private."
"Yes, sir," the secretary said as she ushered the child out of the room.
Ricky wasn't fooled. He saw the lascivious look between his mother and the principal, the same look he had seen between her and Mr. Burnham and any number of other men in town. Good god, he shook his head, were all the men around here so desperate to be with a woman that they would actually hook up with someone like her?
A few minutes later, his mother walked out of the principal's office, straightening her pedal pushers and blouse as she did so. Once again, Ricky thought to himself that anyone with a fat ass like his mother

should never wear tight clothes. Obviously she thought it made her more attractive, but she was sadly mistaken.

"I'll deal with you when we get home," she scowled at him as she strode from the room.

"Ricky, come into my office," the principal said briefly.

Once Ricky was sitting in a straight back wooden chair, the principal sat down next to him. Ricky noticed the framed picture sitting on the principal's desk.

"Is that your family?" he asked.

"That's my wife and kids," the principal said vaguely. "Now you know it's not right to talk back to any adult, don't you?"

"I wasn't talking back to her," Ricky said. "I was just trying to get her to listen to me."

"What were you trying to tell her?"

"That I'm not dumb," Ricky said. "I don't belong with the slow kids."

"I understand," the principal said. He moved closer and put his arm around Ricky's shoulders. "But your teacher is only doing what's best for you."

"But –"

"I'll talk to Miss Kinney for you," the principal said soothingly. "Provided you do something for me."

"What?" Ricky asked warily.

"You're becoming a big boy."

The principal began rubbing his shoulders. His hands moved down Ricky's chest to his groin, which he massaged gently.

"Yeah, I feel something big down here," he whispered in the boy's ear.
The next thing Ricky knew, the principal had opened his own fly and was stroking his half-hard penis while he watched the youth's face.
"Someday it will be as big as this," he grinned. "You wanna touch it?"
Ricky shrank back from him and shook his head.
"Touch it, Ricky," the principal said, his smile fading. "I want you touch it."
Timidly, Ricky reached out and placed his hand on the principal's manhood.
"That's it," the man sighed and closed his eyes.
Ricky had never seen an adult penis before; it was both fearful and fascinating to him. Would his own member become that large one day, he wondered?
A knock came at the door, and the principal quickly shoved him away and straightened his clothes, placing his dick back in his trousers.
"Just a minute," he called to the person on the other side of the door. He turned to Ricky and grabbed him forcefully by the arm. "Don't you ever mention this to anyone! If I find out you've told anyone about this, I'll beat your ass and make school a miserable experience for you. You got that?"
Ricky nodded and then ran for the door. He yanked it open and rushed past the startled secretary.
That night, as he expected, he received a beating with a belt from his father for speaking back to an adult. He was sent to bed without supper, which once again

Leaving Justiceville: A Life Behind

consisted of fried Spam and frozen okra that had been boiled until all the flavor had been cooked out of it.

Leaving Justiceville: A Life Behind

CHAPTER THREE

Ricky had little time for his school work anymore. He had many chores to do, which included caring for the small menagerie of livestock and mowing the grass with an old reel-type push mower that he struggled to push across the sparse and weedy lawn. One blistering hot day, he had finished mowing and was trimming the grass around the house and trees with a pair of old scissors since he had no other tools available to him. The temperature was well over one hundred degrees, and he was sweating profusely. Impatiently, he would wipe the sweat out of his eyes and continue his task. At one point, the heat overwhelmed him, and he suddenly felt nauseated and weak. He crawled to a nearby dying spirea bush and lay down under its cascading branches to cool himself from the relentless rays of the sun. As he lay there with his eyes closed, panting for breath, he felt himself abruptly yanked out of the shade by his ankle.
"What the hell are you doin'?" his father yelled angrily. "You're s'posed to be workin'."
Without another word, he pulled Ricky up by his arm and started beating his ass and shaking him.
"Don't let me ever catch you slackin' off again!" Deed shouted.
Ricky cowered down in an attempt to protect himself from the onslaught. He opened his eyes and saw the neighbor, an older man named Bob, standing in his driveway watching the spectacle. When he saw Ricky

Leaving Justiceville: A Life Behind

looking at him, he turned away and went into his house, closing the door firmly behind him. As Ricky watched, the blinds on the front window next to the front door were closed and the curtain drawn.

Ricky and his sister did their best to keep the house clean since their mother made no effort to do so. Dishes would pile up in the sink until there were no more plates or glasses or silverware with which to eat. Ricky would take it upon himself to wash them, mostly because he despised disorder of any kind. He kept the room he shared with his brothers organized and tidy, hanging up the jeans and shirts the two older boys had tossed carelessly on the floor. He and his sister ran the vacuum and dusted the furniture, but with four other people living in the house who cared nothing about cleanliness, it was a losing battle for the small children.

As a result of the work he was doing at home, his grades suffered dramatically. It wasn't as though he couldn't do the work; he simply didn't have time. And if he was honest with himself, he really wasn't interested in school, although he did enjoy math since it came so easily to him.

Over the next few years, Ricky would get up at five o'clock every morning, milk the cows, feed the chickens and collect the eggs. He would rouse his brothers and then duck when one of them threw a pillow at him before falling back to sleep. He put on whatever clothes he could find that were the least

wrinkled and dirty, make him and his sister toast for breakfast when there was bread in the house, and then by 6:30, the two of them would walk several blocks to ride the bus to school. It didn't matter whether it was windy or cold or storming; the two of them would brave the elements, while their lazy mother continued to sleep.

When Ricky was in the fourth grade, he was invited to church by one of his bus mates, a tall, overweight girl named Jamie. Ricky was intrigued by Jamie because, in spite of being very feminine, she was tough and independent and not afraid of anything. She wore heavy men's combat boots and jeans, unlike the other girls at school, who always wore dresses.

Her father was the minister of the local Church of Christ, and she invited Ricky to attend Sunday morning services. He donned his best tee shirt, which was dingy and torn and had a faded American flag on the front of it. Baggy jeans and worn and scuffed shoes completed his outfit as he hesitantly walked in the front door of the dignified looking church building. Jamie met him and escorted him to the basement, where Sunday school classes for the children were held.

She introduced him to the teacher, an older woman, who looked over her reading glasses and wrinkled her nose at Ricky as she studied his ragged attire.

Leaving Justiceville: A Life Behind

"Okay, children," she said, turning her attention to the small gathering. "Let's open our Bibles to Leviticus and see what God has to tell us."
She went on to read from the book, which Ricky noted was heavily highlighted and bookmarked. Wow, he thought, she really takes this religion stuff very seriously.
To his surprise, the lesson was on the cities of Sodom and Gomorrah and the evils performed there by sinful homosexuals.
"These men were the worst of the worst," she said piously. "So evil that God destroyed them as a warning to other homosexuals to change their ways."
"How did they change?" Ricky raised his hand and asked. "And why were they evil?"
"Why?" she looked puzzled. "Well, because God said so. They were doing things that went against nature."
"So God told them to stop what they were doing?" Ricky asked. "How did he do that?"
"Well," she hesitated. "I think he just expected them to know better. They knew what they were doing was wrong."
"What were they doing?" Ricky persisted.
"They were doing bad things," she frowned. "Things that aren't fit to talk about in church."
"But they're in that Bible of yours, so it sounds like God talked about it. Why can't you talk about it?"
"Ricky, that's enough," she said impatiently. "All you need to know is that God says it's wrong. Now we won't discuss it any further."

The lesson continued, and afterwards the teacher took him aside.

"It isn't right to question me like that," she said sternly. "Don't ever do that again."

"But my teacher at school says that the best way to learn is to ask questions," Ricky said.

"That's fine for school," she said. "But church is no place to be asking questions. You have to accept the teachings in church and not question them."

"Why?"

"Because the Bible isn't to be doubted. It's the word of God, and you just have to accept what it says and never doubt it."

She eyed him up and down for a moment distastefully.

"And the next time you set foot in this church, I expect you to be dressed a little better," she said primly. "God doesn't want to look at you when you're wearing a tee shirt and dirty jeans."

"Why does he care what I wear?" Ricky looked down at himself. "I thought he only cared about what's on the inside, not the outside."

"He cares about everything, and when you come to church looking like that, it offends him. So don't you come back here unless you can dress better and show the respect that God deserves."

With that, she gathered up her Bible and papers. "Now go on upstairs for the worship service," she said. "And you listen to the minister because he's God's messenger, and what he says is fact."

Leaving Justiceville: A Life Behind

Ricky walked upstairs and sat down in a pew near the back. His first instinct was to keep on walking and never come back after having been insulted by the grim Sunday school teacher. He was also annoyed at being told that gay people were evil. In his heart, he knew that his attraction to other boys and men was perfectly natural and nothing to be ashamed of. It was hurtful to him to have other people tell him he was bad just because he liked boys instead of girls. It wasn't as if he had chosen to be this way; it was simply who he was. He was honest and hardworking, kind and good and trustworthy too. He always tried to do the right thing, so why was he being condemned based on words someone wrote in a book thousands of years ago? It was stupid and unfair. Not that anything in his life was fair, he thought wryly. After the service, Jamie sought him out. Today she was wearing a dress and Mary Jane's appropriate for an occasion such as church or a funeral. As far as he was concerned, what he had just sat through was as dreary and dull as a funeral. The preacher had intoned self-righteously how vile and disgusting virtually everyone in the world was, excluding the hundred or so people in this congregation, of course. He read passages from the Bible that supported his assertion that everyone was bound for hell unless they accepted Jesus Christ as their Lord and Savior. Well, that's just nonsense, he thought as he considered the minister's words. Why would God, who was supposed to be all loving, create hell in the first place? Why would he condemn anyone if he

truly loved them? And the whole thing about Jesus being God in human form and dying for our sins was absolutely preposterous as far as he was concerned. If God loved mankind, he would punish them on earth based on their actions and then take them all to heaven to live happily ever after. Why did he need to kill himself and then come back to life after three days? What a load of bullshit!

"So what did you think of the service?" she asked him.

"It was dumb," Ricky shrugged. "A bunch of people telling other people how bad they are and then taking their money. Why do they want everyone to feel bad about themselves?"

"It's not about that," she said.

"Yes, it is," he stated firmly. "It's all about looking down on other people so they feel good about themselves. I mean, look at how they're all looking at me right now."

The two of them gazed around the auditorium where a number of people were frowning disapprovingly at Ricky. They quickly looked away when they saw him staring back at them.

"See?" he said. "They think I'm nothing but trash. They don't want me here."

"Yes, they do," she insisted. "You're just imagining things."

She frowned at the congregants around them. She hated to admit that Ricky was correct; they were judging her friend, and she didn't appreciate it. Still, she didn't want his feelings to be hurt.

Leaving Justiceville: A Life Behind

"They're all Christians," she said. "They don't judge. They love everyone."
"Bullshit," he snorted. "They're all judging me because my clothes aren't as nice as theirs."
"They just don't know you yet," she tried to excuse them. "Once they do, you'll feel part of the group."
"I don't want to be part of this group," he said flatly. "I don't like them, and they don't like me."

Ricky never went back to church. The people there had shown their true colors to him and, as young as he was, he was fully aware of their disdain of him. He received enough bad treatment from his family, and he sure as hell wasn't going to tolerate it from perfect strangers. He had no problems voicing his thoughts to Jamie's dad, who encouraged him to overlook some of his congregation's less than Christian behavior.

He and Jamie remained good friends, in spite of his opinion of her father's church. There were a few occasions when some of the older boys on the bus would pick on him, usually with a high school youth named Tony as their leader. He was a large, mean-looking boy who seemed to take extra pleasure in harassing Ricky. One morning on the bus, he snatched the paper sack containing Ricky's biscuit and Karo syrup sandwich and crumbs of potato chips out of his hand.

"You call this a lunch?" he taunted. "This shit ain't even worth feedin' to my dog."

Leaving Justiceville: A Life Behind

"Give it back!" Ricky shouted, reaching in vain as Tony held the bag aloft.

"What are you gonna do, pipsqueak?" the older boy said. "You want it back, come and get it."

Ricky reached out again for his property, and Tony shoved him to the floor in the bus aisle. Jamie watched this for a moment and finally had enough. Tony was older than her by several years, and he was taller than her, but that didn't intimidate her in the least. She stood up and walked calmly back to where Tony was standing. She helped Ricky up off the floor and guided him back to his seat before turning her attention to his tormentor.

"Give him his lunch back," she said.

"What, are you fightin' his battles for him now, fatso?" Tony sneered at her. "The little sissy boy has a big stupid girl standing up for him."

He and some of the other students laughed and jeered.

"I'm not fighting his battle," she said. "But I am standing up for him. And I'm gonna beat the shit out of you unless you give him back his lunch."

"You're a fuckin' girl," he snorted. "You ain't gonna hit anyone."

Without warning, Jamie balled up her fist and punched him in the stomach. Tony doubled over in pain, and Jamie took both her fists and brought them down hard on his back, sending the boy to his knees. The other students looked on in astonishment.

Leaving Justiceville: A Life Behind

"I am a girl," she said. "The girl that just beat you up and will do it again if you don't give him back his lunch."

"That's not fair!" Tony panted as he got to his feet. "I can't hit a girl."

"Sure you can," Jamie said. "I'm giving you permission to hit me. So go on and try it."

With that, she punched him again in the stomach and then began slapping him about the head and face, while the other children cheered her on. He cowered down and tried to shield himself from her attack. Finally, he held out the bag in front of him.

"Take it!" he shouted. "I was just messin' with him anyway."

Jamie took the bag from him and handed it to a grateful Ricky. She turned back to Tony.

"If I catch you bullying him again, I'll really fuck you up," she told him. She looked around threateningly at Tony's openmouthed friends. "Any of the rest of you want some?"

The other boys quickly found their seats and avoided looking at her for the rest of the bus ride.

Jamie was not afraid of anyone or anything. A few years later, she and her then boyfriend Jay ran away from home in the pickup truck his parents had bought for him, intending to head to Connecticut. His parents notified the police, who set out after the pair. A high speed chase ensued and finally ended when Jamie and Jay rolled the truck in a cotton field. Since the

two were underage and Jamie was the daughter of a minister, no charges were filed against them.

Ricky was to encounter Jamie again many years later. As it turned out, he learned that Jamie and her sister had rented a house together across town when they were in their twenties. Jamie told him about a bizarre incident that took place during that time.

She had met and was intimate one night with a stranger she met at a bar called the Country Castle. Their relationship had gone no further, but the man ended up falling for her sister, and they eventually married.

Jamie and her sister and her sister's new husband shared a house for a while until Jamie moved out. Jamie didn't see her sister for several months, but one night, the girl sought her out, crying hysterically and covered in blood. Jamie questioned her frantically about it. The truth eventually came out. Jamie's brother-in-law was a serial killer, who had murdered at least four people, and probably dozens more. Jamie's sister stayed in the marriage even after she found out what he had done because he threatened to kill her if she left him or told the police. He even forced her to help him on two occasions. He was eventually tried in a court of law and sentenced to life in prison. Jamie's sister was also tried but found not guilty.

Ricky listened to this story with incredulity. He was astonished to find that someone he had known in his youth had endured such an experience. He even

Leaving Justiceville: A Life Behind

remembered hearing about the story on the national news but had no idea that anyone he knew had been involved.

Tony may have stopped bullying Ricky on the bus out of cowardice and fear of Jamie's retribution, but he still managed to bother him at other times when Jamie wasn't around. There were a number of bullies who picked on Ricky, taking their cue from Tony and a few other high school boys. All twelve grades shared one building, making the younger children easy targets for the older ones on the playground or lunch room.

The bullying became particularly problematic in the fifth grade for Ricky. Because of his shyness, size, and lack of skill at sports, he became the prey of several of his classmates. One of them tormented him especially cruelly one morning, and Ricky reached his limit. He stood up from his desk and confronted the boy.
"Stop it!" he shouted angrily. "Leave me alone."
"What's going on?" the teacher frowned. "Ricky, get back in your seat!"
"He keeps poking me with his pencil!" Ricky said, pointing to his harasser.
"I'm just sitting here," the other boy said innocently with a smirk on his face.
"Now that's enough from both of you!" the teacher snapped. "Sit down!"

Leaving Justiceville: A Life Behind

Ricky resumed his seat, and the teacher turned back to the blackboard. The student behind him began pestering him again. Ricky tolerated it for a few minutes and then turned around and shoved the boy's books off his desk. They clattered to the floor, and the instructor turned to glare at him.

"All right, that's it," he said. "Go to the principal's office."

Ricky kicked his desk and then stormed irately from the room. But instead of going to the principal's office as he had been instructed, he left the school building and started walking home. A few minutes later, a late model sedan pulled up beside him.

"Where do you think you're going?" the principal asked him. This was the same man whose penis he had touched a few years before.

"Anywhere but school," Ricky said coldly as he kept walking.

"Get in the car," the principal said.

"No," Ricky said. "I don't want to go back there. The teacher wouldn't listen to me, so why should I sit there and listen to him?"

"I won't make you go back there right now," the older man said. "Just get in the car, and we'll talk about it. I'll listen to anything you want to say, I promise."

Reluctantly, Ricky walked around the car and got in the front seat. He was startled to see the principal's fly was open and his hard manhood was standing straight up out in the open.

Leaving Justiceville: A Life Behind

"Now, if I'm going to listen to you, I want you to do a little something for me," the principal said as he pulled away from the curb. "If you do it, you don't have to go back to school today."

He began stroking his penis with his left hand. With his right hand, he pulled Ricky in and instructed him how to masturbate him while he drove.

"Don't you have a wife to do this?" Ricky asked.

"That bitch doesn't touch me unless I make her," the principal snorted. "I have to slap her around to get her to do anything. That's why I want you to do it."

"I don't want to," Ricky said. It was true that he was fascinated by the sight of the man's impressive appendage, but he knew instinctively that the principal was wrong to encourage this sort of behavior from an innocent child.

"Do it!" the principal scowled. "I'm not gonna tell you again!"

Later, the principal stopped alongside the road on the edge of town and told him to get out.

"Remember," he said. "You can't tell anyone about this. You'll be sorry if you do!"

"Why are you trying to write with your left hand?" Ricky's teacher frowned at him one morning. "What's wrong with your right hand?"

"Nothing," Ricky winced painfully as he tried to hide his right hand under his desk.

"Let me see it," the teacher said sternly.

Reluctantly, Ricky showed him his bruised and tender right hand and wrist.

"What happened?" the teacher asked him.
"I…I don't know," Ricky lied with a shrug. "I can't remember."
The truth was that his injured arm was the result of another beating, a particularly severe one from his father, because he had accidentally spilled one of the milk buckets as he was carrying them to the kitchen that morning.
"These are some very bad bruises," his teacher said. "And you don't remember how you got them?"
"I fell down," Ricky said.
"Did your parents do this to you?" his teacher asked.
"N-no," Ricky lied again.
He glanced up at his teacher for a moment and then looked quickly away.
"Your father did this, didn't he?"
Ricky merely shook his head uncertainly and stared down at his desk.
"Have you told anyone about this?"
Again Ricky shook his head.
"Well," his teacher sighed. "Try to write a little neater. And whatever you did to deserve a beating like this, don't do it again."

And that was the end of it. As usual, his teacher, like all adults, sided with his father. It was obvious to his teachers, the principal, and the neighbors that Ricky and his siblings were being abused, but no one lifted a finger to do anything about it. No one offered to help. From the screams and crying issuing forth on a daily basis from the Blain house to the children going

Leaving Justiceville: A Life Behind

to school with bruises and other injuries, the community had more than enough evidence to have his parents put in jail for child abuse/endangerment. But nobody cared, Ricky thought grimly. Not even when his father was abusing him in the front yard with a neighbor watching from less than thirty feet away. He and his brothers and sister were trash and unworthy of anyone's time or concern.
How could the world be so unkind, so insensitive to another person's suffering, especially that of a child? Instead of helping him, his teachers and principal were abusing him and blaming him, making him a victim all over again. Apparently all adults were just as nasty and loathsome as his parents.

Most days, Ricky would go without lunch unless there happened to be something he could bring from home. His parents gave him no money to buy a hot lunch in the cafeteria, so usually he would go sit in the gymnasium by himself during the lunch hour, while the other students laughed and talked and ate together.
One day, the principal walked into gym and saw him sitting on the bottom bleacher trying in vain to comprehend his geography textbook.
The gym teacher had sent him to the bleachers after one of the older boys hit him in the head with a rubber dodgeball.
"Ricky, get out of the way and go sit down. You're ruining the game for everyone else, so you can just

watch while the rest of us have fun," the man taunted him.

When the class ended, Ricky continued to sit in the big gymnasium alone as usual while the rest of the students went to lunch.

"What are you doing?" the principal scowled. Since their episode in his car, he had been extremely cold and abrupt whenever he encountered Ricky. "Why aren't you in the cafeteria?"

"I don't have any money for lunch," Ricky said, "and there was nothing at home to make."

"Well, that's not my problem," the principal said harshly. "You can't stay here alone, so come with me."

Ricky gathered his books and followed the principal to the cafeteria. Instead of showing him to a table, he guided him into the kitchen.

"Put this kid to work," he told Doris, the head cook. "He can wash dishes or do something else to make himself useful since he's not going to eat anything." With that, he strode from the room, leaving Ricky to stare back at the kitchen staff, all of whom were glaring at him with annoyance. All except Doris, that is.

"Why aren't you eating lunch?" she asked him. "Don't you like the food?"

"I didn't have any money for lunch today," he said.

Doris glanced down at his ragged jeans and tee shirt, and scuffed shoes and nodded knowingly.

Leaving Justiceville: A Life Behind

"Well, I need an impartial food taster, so before I put you to work, you're going to sample some of my cooking and tell me if it's any good."

She scooped up some of her potato and hamburger casserole, green beans, and red Jello with fruit in it onto a divided tray and set it on her desk in the corner. She fetched him a carton of chocolate milk and instructed him to sit down and eat.

Ricky eagerly did as he was told, and within minutes, the food was in his growling belly. This was real food, he thought, nothing like what he was accustomed to at home. An honest to goodness meal with vegetables and everything. Someone had actually taken the time to plan and cook a meal to make it tasty and relatively healthy.

"So how was it?" Doris gave him a motherly smile.

"It was good," Ricky said. "Really good."

"I'm glad you liked it. Now, do you want to help me wash these trays?"

What's this, he frowned? An adult asking him to do something instead of ordering him to do it? That was literally the first time in his life that he could remember any grownup doing such a thing.

"Sure," he said.

The two of them stood at the big industrial stainless steel sink, while Ricky rinsed the trays under the hot sprayer and handed them to Doris.

"Do you like school?" she asked him.

"It's okay," he shrugged. "Except for bullies like Tony and Danny. And geography is hard. So is history."

"I know what you mean," she nodded. "I always had trouble with history when I was in school. Trying to remember all those dates; it made my head swim." And so the two of them chatted while they worked. Ricky felt like Doris really listened to him, something no other adult in his life had ever done. She seemed genuinely interested in what he had to say and didn't correct him or interrupt him like everyone else.
For the rest of the school year, Ricky ate lunch at Doris's desk. She told him that his help as her taste-tester was an invaluable service and that his opinion was important to her. He would then help her with washing trays and silverware or cleaning the lunchroom after the students had gone out to engage in recreation on the playground. He felt a growing attachment to Doris, who was unfailingly kind to him, and it was thanks to her that he had one good meal each day.

One day when Ricky was ten years old, his parents went out for the evening.
"You kids behave yerselves," his father scowled at them. "If I find out otherwise, I'll beat your asses when I get home."
"Where are they going?" Ricky asked Theo as the two adults departed in separate vehicles.
"They said they're goin' to a party," Theo smirked. "But that's a fuckin' lie."
"So what are they doing?"
"They're going to fuck other people, stupid," Theo said. "What else would they be doin'?"

Leaving Justiceville: A Life Behind

"You mean they're having sex? Why do they do that with other people? Why don't they just do it with each other? Isn't that why people get married?"
"Man, you are really dumb," Theo rolled his eyes. "Bein' married don't mean shit to them or anyone else. Dad said he fucks around because Mom's fat and ugly."
"He talks to you about it?" Ricky said incredulously.
"Sure he does," Theo said smugly. "I know all about the women he's fuckin'; there's a bunch of 'em. He brags about it all the fuckin' time."
"Why?"
"Cause fuckin' a bunch of women is something to be proud of," Theo said as if the answer should have been obvious. "Don't you know nuthin' about the bible?"
"Some," Ricky shrugged.
"The bible says men are s'posed to spread their seed around. He's doin' just like the bible says. That's what I'm gonna do too, as soon as I'm old enough."
"Dad plants seeds in women?" Ricky looked confused. "How?"
"His cum, you idiot," Theo said, exasperated.
"What's cum?"
"It's what comes out of the end of your dick during sex," Theo explained. "It's what makes babies."
"The only thing that comes out of my dick is pee," Ricky frowned, still not understanding.
Theo suddenly grabbed him by the arm and pulled him into the bathroom. He closed the door and locked

it before turning to his brother with a leering grin on his face.
"What are you doing?" Ricky asked nervously.
"I'm gonna show you what cum is," Theo said as he began undressing. "Take your clothes off."
Ricky hesitated for a moment. He remembered what had happened once before with his brother when he had removed his clothing. Theo slapped him across the face.
"Do it, goddammit!" he shouted.
"What are you guys doin' in there?" his brother Jimmy called through the door.
"I'm teaching Ricky a lesson," Theo replied. "Keep an eye out for Mom and Dad."
"Okay," Jimmy said unconcernedly.
Theo turned his attention back to his youngest brother. In a matter of moments, Ricky was forced down to his knees in front of Theo and had his erection in his mouth. After a couple of minutes of this, Theo shoved him away.
"Not like that, stupid," he said impatiently. "Let me show you how to do it."
He knelt down and took Ricky's dick into his mouth and began sucking on it. The sensations that coursed through the boy's body had an unexpected effect on him. Before he could stop himself, he began urinating in his brother's mouth. Theo immediately pulled away, coughing and sputtering. He rushed over to the sink and rinsed his mouth with mouthwash for a few minutes.

"I'm sorry," Ricky said. "It just came out before I could stop it."
Theo wiped his mouth and came at his brother. He pinned him down to the cracked linoleum floor and punched and slapped him furiously while Ricky tried in vain to defend himself.
"You little cocksucker faggot," he shouted. "I'll fuckin' teach you to piss in my mouth again!"

CHAPTER FOUR

Stella and Deed bought an old, run down gas station on the edge of town. Ricky wondered how they were able to get a loan with their bad credit history, but later learned that the owner was letting them buy the place on time.

The four Blain children were enlisted to paint and clean the establishment until their parents were satisfied with its appearance. Once it reopened, they were expected to go there immediately after school and work until closing at seven o'clock. Theo and Jimmy patched tires and helped their father with tune-ups. Ricky and his sister helped with lube jobs, pumping gas, and mopping floors, and it was Ricky's job as well to run the cash register. He kept track of invoices, and it didn't take long for him to figure out that his father was cheating many of the customers on their bills.

"Don't worry about it," his father growled at him. "Just do as you're told and keep your fuckin' mouth shut."

There was a room above the gas station that served as an office, but it also contained a small kitchen and a bed in case anyone needed a place to sleep. Ricky soon realized that its true purpose was for his dad to hook up with one of the cheap looking women with whom he was having an affair.

Late one night Stella drove over to the business to pick up her children.

Leaving Justiceville: A Life Behind

"Where's your father?" she frowned as Ricky and his sister climbed into the back seat of the old rusty car.
"I think he's up in the office," Ricky said uneasily.
"Oh yeah?" his mother scowled. "Whose car is that?" She pointed to a newer Mustang with mag wheels on it parked off to the side.
"Is that that bitch Sheila's car?"
"I dunno," Ricky shrugged.
"Yes, you do," his mother turned and reached over the seat to slap him. "Don't you fuckin' lie to me!"
"They're upstairs right now," his sister volunteered.
"That figures," their mother muttered. She thought for a moment. "Ricky, you go back in there and tell your father you're going to stay here full time from now on."
"I have to stay here?" Ricky said. "You mean all the time? What about school? What'll I eat?"
"There's stuff in the vending machines," his mother shrugged. "You can eat that. That cook at school feeds ya, don't she? That's all you need."
"So I'm still going to school?"
"Ya got to go to school, stupid," she said impatiently. "They'll come after us if you don't. But when you're not in school or doing chores at home, you'll be here. That'll keep Sheila away from here."
She thought another few seconds and then got out of the car. She walked to the bottom of the narrow, steep stairway that led up to the office.
"Deed!" she yelled. "Get your fat ass down here!"
"What do ya want?" he asked in a surly voice. "I'm working up here."

Leaving Justiceville: A Life Behind

"Yeah, I know good and well what you're working on," she retorted. "But stop it 'cause Ricky's gonna stay here from now on and keep an eye on you and that cunt Sheila."
Deed came down the stairs a few seconds later, pulling down his stained tee shirt over his hairy belly as best he could.
"I don't want that fuckin' kid here," he told his wife. "He's weird."
"I don't care if he is," she said coldly. "Now go tell that skank to get out of here and you come home. The kid'll look after the station."

With Ricky at the station most of the time now, Sheila offered to care for the cows and chickens and goats. Deed agreed and moved the livestock over to her property since the older boys were unreliable in caring for them.
Deed's illicit relationship with Sheila came to an abrupt end a few months later. After an evening of carousing with Deed at the Country Castle, he dropped her off at her house, and she staggered into the old trailer she called home. She drunkenly picked up a handgun that was lying on the kitchen table and accidentally shot herself. With her aggressive German Shepherd keeping guard over her, the ambulance personnel were unable to help her. They finally called for Deed to come and remove the dog so they could rescue her. The dog knew him well since he had been a guest in Sheila's bedroom on numerous occasions.

Leaving Justiceville: A Life Behind

Over the next several months, Ricky lived at the gas station. In some ways, it was a relief to him to be away from his hateful parents and filthy house. He could keep the office clean and orderly, and he didn't have to listen to the yelling and fighting that took place almost constantly in the Blain household. Sometimes his father would insist that Jimmy go and stay with him at the station, especially if he was concerned about someone breaking in and stealing gas. On those occasions, Ricky soon learned what to expect. He would go to bed with his clothes on, but Jimmy would make him undress and then proceed to sexually molest him. At one point, he spit in his hand and then forced himself into his brother's ass. Ricky begged him to stop and cried out in pain, but his brother was relentless and refused to stop until he had climaxed.

"There," Jimmy panted when he was finished. "Now you don't tell anyone about this, ever. If you do, I'll beat the shit out of you. No one will believe you anyway."

Ricky would nod and curl into a fetal position, crying as quietly as possible.

"Aw, shut up," Jimmy nudged him with his elbow. "Ya fuckin' baby. You know you liked it, faggot. Now be quiet or go downstairs; I'm trying to sleep here."

Jimmy and Theo abused him on a fairly regular basis at the station until his father fell behind in his

payments on the station and the original owner took it back. Deed reluctantly went back to work as a welder on tanker trucks. He had enjoyed owning the gas station because, with his children as his work force, he had had little responsibility and could pursue his sexual affairs more easily.
In one sense, Ricky was actually glad to come home; at least there, his brothers were less prone to abuse him with his parents in the same house. On the other hand, it was back to the beatings and cruelty from his parents.

One afternoon while their parents were out, Ricky walked past the bedroom which he shared with his brothers.
"What are you doing standin' out here?" he asked his brother Jimmy who had his ear pressed to the door.
"Shh," Jimmy hissed. "I can't hear."
Ricky listened for a moment with a frown and then pushed past Jimmy. He thrust the door open to find Theo lying on top of their sister with his pants down. She was screaming and struggling against him, but Theo was relentless. He slapped her across the face and tried to silence her with his hand over her mouth while his other hand tried to force himself into her body.
"Hey!" Ricky shouted. "Get off of her!"
"Shut up!" Jimmy grabbed him and held him back and covered his mouth with his hand.
Theo scowled over at them and yelled at his brothers to get out of the room.

Leaving Justiceville: A Life Behind

"I told you to keep watch!" he said angrily to Jimmy. While his attention was diverted, their sister managed to slide out from under him. She ran from the room in fright. Theo yanked up his pants and ran after her. Ricky tried to block his way, but Theo shoved him aside and set out in pursuit. As Ricky watched from the back door, he saw his sister clear the fence and race across the field to the neighbor's house. Theo chased her for a moment and then gave it up.
Later that evening, Ricky peered cautiously around the doorway as his parents talked gravely in low voices to their neighbors Tom and Mary. The couple had kept his sister safely with them for the afternoon until the Blain's arrived home. They had called the police immediately after she had told them what her brother tried to do, but since the police chief of their small town was a drinking buddy of Deed's, the accusation was ignored and dismissed.
"This is a very serious matter," Mary said. "He tried to rape your daughter."
"That's a fuckin' lie," Deed snorted. "Theo is a good boy. He was just messin' around."
"It was kids being kids," Stella agreed. "You're makin' way too much of this whole thing."
"It doesn't bother you that your daughter has been traumatized?" Tom said incredulously.
"She was brutalized," Mary said. "What if he had succeeded?"
"What about the effects of this attack on her? She'll be dealing with this for the rest of her life."
"She wasn't hurt," Stella rolled her eyes.

"That's not the point!" Tom said. "She very easily could have been if Ricky hadn't walked in when he did."

"Theo and Jimmy need to see someone," Mary added. "A child psychologist or professional counselor."

"They don't need to see no fuckin' doctor," Deed said. "And I don't appreciate you saying that they do."

"So you're not going to do anything about this?" Mary said, not believing her ears. "What if he tries this again?"

"I'll tell him to leave her alone," Deed shrugged. "Otherwise I'll beat his ass."

"What about Jimmy?" Tom demanded. "He acted as an accomplice to his older brother."

"I'll talk to both of them. I'll tell them both that their sister is off limits."

"Off limits?!" Mary looked outraged. "You seriously have to tell your sons not to have sex with their sister?! Are you kidding me with this?"

"Boys will be boys," Deed chuckled dismissively. "They like to experiment. Tom, you musta played around with your sister when you was kids. Maybe even with your brother. That's what I did; it's what boys do."

"They most certainly do not!" Tom said indignantly. "My brothers and sisters and I never –"

"Talking to them isn't enough," Mary said, placing a calming hand on her husband's arm. "You have to do more."

"Then I'll beat their asses, like I said," Deed shrugged.
"And you really think that will take care of things?" Tom said. "Are you seriously this naïve?"
Stella and Deed scowled at one another for a moment and then turned back to their guests with annoyance.
"We ain't naïve, and we can raise our own kids without any fuckin' interference from you!" Stella snapped coldly.
"I think it's time you got the fuck out of our house!" Deed snapped.
"Very well," Tom said. "But if your daughter needs us, you can tell her she's always welcome in our home. The same goes for Ricky."
"What's he got to do with this?"
"He's the one who stopped his brother from…you know," Tom said. "And if Theo tried to molest his sister, he may have done the same thing to Ricky."
"Theo ain't no queer," Stella scowled. "And I ain't gonna say it again; get the hell out of my house!"
After Tom and Mary departed, Ricky's parents grabbed him by the arm and shook him violently.
"This is your fault!" his father shouted at him.
"It wasn't me," Ricky protested. "I just tried to stop him."
"He wasn't doing nuthin'," his mother said.
"He was trying to –"
"You don't know what he was doin'!" his father said huffily. "And it ain't up to you to monitor what your brothers are doin'. You just stay out of it next time."
He called his two older sons into the room.

Leaving Justiceville: A Life Behind

"Now, I don't want nuthin' like this to happen again," he said.
"I was just practicing'," Theo shrugged. "It ain't like I was gonna cum in her."
"It don't matter," Deed said. "I ain't faultin' ya for what you was doin'. Ya just can't get caught next time!"

Ricky walked into the bedroom, where his brothers were waiting for him. For the next couple of hours, the two older boys took turns shouting at him while they beat and kicked and abused their little brother, taking all of their anger out on him. When they were finally done, Ricky cowered in the corner on the floor at the head of the bed, crying in pain and fear. His body was covered in bruises and welts and slap marks from the beating his angry brothers had inflicted on him.
"That'll teach you for tattling on us," Theo sneered down at him.
"Ya little snitch," Jimmy spat. "Next time it'll be even worse for you. You just remember that."
How much more of this could he take, Ricky wondered tearfully? He scrunched down with his arms over his head in case his brothers attacked him again, his whole body aching painfully. This was the one place in the whole world where he was supposed to be safe, and yet he was learning that as dangerous a place as the world was, his own home was far worse.

Leaving Justiceville: A Life Behind

A few days later, Ricky was told to fetch his sister to help him wash the stacks of moldy and malodorous dishes in the sink. He returned from her room without her and told his parents that she was nowhere to be found and that her closet was empty.

Eventually, the family learned that she had run away to stay with a school friend named Anna. When Anna's family brought her back, there was a violent altercation among the entire Blain family in the hot kitchen. Ricky's sister was especially angry.

"He and Jimmy keep trying to molest me, and you won't do nothin' about it!" she cried. "That's why I ran away. It ain't safe for me here with them, especially since you're lettin' 'em do it."

"Dad says it's no big deal," Theo said scornfully. "You're just a big baby. And I know you want us to do it."

"That's right," Jimmy chimed in. "It's your fault, the way you look at us. You may be fighting against it, but we can tell you want it."

"She does not!" Ricky said indignantly.

"Now I told you boys to leave your sister alone," Deed lied. "I know you got lots of hormones swarmin' around your bodies, but there's plenty of girls out there for you to screw; you forget about your sister."

"And you," Stella said to her daughter. "If you don't want 'em botherin' you, keep your door locked."

She slapped the girl across the face.

Leaving Justiceville: A Life Behind

"And the next time you go to one of our neighbors about family business, I'll give you a beatin' you won't ever forget."
In a fit of rage at the injustice of the situation, Ricky's sister picked up a large knife and, with a scream, ran at her mother with it. Ricky struggled to hold her back, while she tried repeatedly to stab her mother. Theo wrestled the weapon away from the girl and tossed it carelessly aside.
She freed herself from Ricky's grasp and ran to her bedroom and locked the door, screaming, "I hate you, I hate you, I hate you!" all the while.
Theo and Jimmy shrugged and went into the living room to watch reruns of 'Dragnet' on television. Stella lit a cigarette and Deed slapped Ricky across the back of the head, yelling at him to get busy with the dishes before he beat his ass.

The school bus dropped Ricky off at Toy's house, the woman who was now keeping the Blains' livestock since Sheila's unfortunate accident with the gun. Her real name was Toyla, but she went by her nickname. It was still his job to feed and milk and collect eggs. He opened the back door of the house as usual and picked up the old metal buckets that sat by the back door. The sound of the door opening startled the two people kissing and running their hands over each other's bodies.
"What are you doin'?" his father shouted at him.

Leaving Justiceville: A Life Behind

Ricky tried to make a hasty retreat, but his father grabbed him by the arm and started spanking him roughly.
"You don't mention this to your mother, you got that?" he said angrily.
"I won't," Ricky cried, trying in vain to shield himself from his father's blows.
"Beat his ass," Toy said. "Make sure he keeps quiet. I don't need Stella coming over here and makin' a scene."
When his father was done with him, he shoved Ricky outside and locked the door. When Ricky was finished with the chores, he sat down on the back step to wait on his dad. Instead of riding in the front of the old pickup truck, his dad made him ride in the back among the empty beer bottles, old tires, and other assorted junk.

"You're goin' to stay with your Grandpa Artie for the weekend," Deed told the three boys one morning.
"Why?" Theo and Jimmy asked at the same time.
"I'm talkin' about Ricky," their father said. "Your sister's stayin' with Anna, and I don't give a shit what you and Jimmy do as long as you don't burn the house down."
"Where are you and Mom goin'?"
"Your mom's goin' to Dallas with some of her girlfriends, and I'll be spendin' time with…well, you know," Deed winked at Theo.
"What's her name this time?" Ricky asked dryly. "Is it still Toy, or did you find someone else?"

Leaving Justiceville: A Life Behind

"You shut the fuck up," Deed scowled, slapping the boy across the face. "That ain't none of your business. And don't you sass me."

The next thing Ricky knew, he was being packed off in his grandfather's sedan and driven to his house, which was about twenty miles away.
"Looks like you're getting fat," his grandfather observed as he eyed his grandson in the backseat. Ricky looked down at himself and frowned self-consciously. It was true that he wasn't as skinny as he had been in his younger days. He was able to get more of his fare share of the food now that he and his sister were a little older and were doing more of the cooking. His mother never cooked anymore. She would sit at the kitchen table with a cigarette hanging from the corner of her mouth while she read one of her dime-store romance novels. Her two youngest children learned how to make a few things other than fried Spam, such as Chef Boyardee spaghetti, grilled cheese sandwiches, hamburgers, and a few other easy items.
"I'm not fat," he told his grandfather.
"You take after your mother," Grandpa Artie said. "Have you seen how big her ass is? That'll be you someday."
Ricky's grandparents' home was an old house with two bedrooms, living/dining room, and one bathroom. It was small and smelled of mothballs, Pine-Sol, and coffee, an unpleasant odor to Ricky's

young nose, but at least it was clean, unlike his parents' house.

Grandpa Artie showed Ricky to a bedroom with a queen size bed. Oh, boy, he thought with wide eyes, a big bed all to himself! What a treat! No having to share with his brothers and their unwashed bodies. As he set his paper bag down on the bed, the bedroom door opened.

"Hey, kid," his Uncle Artie grinned at him. "Pop said you was gonna stay with us for the weekend."

"What are you doing here?" Ricky frowned at him.

"I'm livin' here now," his uncle said. "Didn't they tell you? You and me's gonna be bunkmates."

"Why are you living here?" Ricky asked. "Where's your wife?"

"Aw, that bitch left. Ran off with some trucker while I was in the pen," his uncle explained. "She found out I'd been screwing her best friend."

"But why are you here?" Ricky asked again.

"I ain't been able to find a job since I got out."

"Why'd you go to jail?"

"I borrowed my neighbor's truck without telling him and wrecked it. They said I was drunk, but I wasn't. I'd only had about six beers. That ain't enough to make me shitfaced."

After supper, Ricky, his uncle, and his grandparents sat down in front of the television in the living room to watch 'Hee Haw', his grandparents' favorite show. Uncle Artie proceeded to drink a six-pack of Pabst Blue Ribbon beer.

"Haven't you had enough?" Grandma Vera frowned at her son. "That's your fourth one."
"Leave the boy alone," Grandpa Artie said. "He's a grown man."
"That's none of your business, Mom," Uncle Artie said coldly. "You'd be smart to listen to Dad."
Ricky took off his old jeans and put on a pair of ragged pajama bottoms he had swiped from a neighbor's garage sale at his mother's insistence. He climbed into bed and turned out the light. A few minutes later, his uncle staggered into the room and took off his clothes before flopping down heavily on the mattress. Within a few seconds, he was snoring loudly. Ricky scooted as far away from him as possible to the edge of the bed and tried to go to sleep.
Uncle Artie tossed and turned restlessly for a few hours until he had worked his way over to Ricky's side of the bed. He lay with his arm and leg splayed over the boy. Ricky tried to push him off, but the man was dead weight. Finally he fell asleep, only to wake a little later to feel something strange happening to him. His uncle's tongue was in his mouth as the man French kissed him. He felt something unusual in his groin, and he realized that his uncle's hand was inside his pajamas, masturbating him. Ricky soon felt his uncle's manhood sliding into his anus. Not knowing what to do, Ricky just lay still with tears in his eyes, listening to his uncle breathing heavy and making moaning sounds. A moment later he ejaculated for the first time in his life. There was no

thought in his mind at the time; it was merely the friction of his uncle's hand that caused it. A moment later, his uncle rolled over and resumed his snoring. The next night his uncle called him into the bedroom, but Ricky refused.
"I said, get in here!" Uncle Artie demanded. "It's time for bed."
"I'm going to sleep on the couch," Ricky told him.
"No, you're not," his uncle frowned. "I want you in here with me."
"No!" Ricky said.
"Get in here, you little fuck!" Uncle Artie scowled.
"I don't want to," Ricky said. With that, he lay down on the sofa with a blanket over him.
"Goddammit," Uncle Artie muttered before slamming his bedroom door.
The next morning, the four of them sat down at the kitchen table for breakfast.
"Why'd you sleep on the sofa last night?" his grandmother asked Ricky as she dished out a couple of sausage patties onto his plate.
Every morning she prepared the same breakfast: sausage patties, bacon, toast, and two eggs over which she poured a generous amount of bacon grease.
"Uh…" Ricky hesitated.
"He was keepin' me awake," Uncle Artie answered for him. "I told him to get out."
"You were asleep as soon as your head hit the pillow," Grandpa Artie snorted. "You were dead to

the world after all that beer; I doubt Ricky could do anything to keep you awake."

"Well, if you must know, he got a little handsy, if you know what I mean," Uncle Artie lied. "The kid's a fag, and I didn't want no queer in my bed, even if he is only eleven years old."

"Is that true?" Grandpa Artie scowled at his grandson.

"No!" Ricky exclaimed. "He's the one who –"

"Now don't lie to your grandpa," Uncle Artie said. "I'm sorry to have to tell on you, but you know it's true. That's why I couldn't let you sleep in my room."

"It is not!" Ricky insisted. "You were the one who touched me. I never touched you at all."

"It's a sin to lie," his grandmother scolded him.

"I'm not lying!" Ricky said. He pointed across the table. "He is!"

"Your uncle doesn't lie," she said.

"Yes, he does," Ricky shouted. "He lies and drinks and steals and cheats too."

"Your uncle has made a few mistakes…" Grandpa Artie began.

"Yeah, like jerking off and fucking his nephew in the middle of the night!" Ricky retorted.

Uncle Artie reached across the table and slapped him. "You goddamm little liar!" he yelled.

"Get your clothes on," Grandpa Artie said sternly. "I'm takin' you home. I won't have a liar in this house."

Leaving Justiceville: A Life Behind

That was the same year that his parents bought the local bar that they frequented on a regular basis, the Country Castle. It was located in a rundown building a mile or so from town, set among a gravel parking lot and an overgrown tangle of weeds and trash trees. Typical of him, Deed immediately enlisted his children as the unpaid workforce for this rather seedy establishment. Their duties included washing dishes, cooking pizzas, buffalo wings and poppers, fried pickles and cheese sticks, and so on. They also carried drinks to customers, emptied the trash and ashtrays, swept the floors, and did any other task their father demanded of them.

Ricky's main responsibility was to do the books and work the front door. With his innate talent at mathematics, his father relied on him to keep the business in the black. Ricky was well aware of his parents' foray into the gas station business and what a miserable failure that had been. He knew that if this business was to succeed, it would be up to him to make that happen.

Each afternoon after school, the Blain children made their way to the bar to get it ready for opening. Saturdays and Sundays were also spent there, cleaning and restocking, etc.

One night as Ricky sat on his tall stool at the door, checking ID's, his brother Theo came in with tears in his eyes. He was now sixteen and had begun spending all of his free time away from home. He had quit school and obtained a fake ID that stated he was twenty-one years old.

Leaving Justiceville: A Life Behind

He sat down on a barstool and reached over the bar to help himself to a glass and a bottle of whiskey. He poured some into the glass and downed it in one gulp.
"What's the matter with you?" a bearded bar patron asked him.
"I got married today," Theo said, pouring himself another drink.
Ricky looked up sharply at this.
"You got married?" the man said doubtfully. "Ain't you just a kid?"
"I'm twenty-one," Theo lied, flashing his fake driver's license at him.
"Who'd you marry?"
"Uh…her name is…Sally," Theo said.
"That's a big fat lie. You didn't get married," Ricky scoffed.
"I did too!" Theo snapped. "You shut up and mind your own business."
"Well, if today's your wedding day, what the hell are you doin' here?" the man asked. "Where's your wife?"
"She's dead," Theo shrugged.
This took the man aback for a moment. Ricky just shook his head in disgust.
"You married her today and now she's dead?" the man said incredulously. "How'd she die?"
"We was in a car accident," Theo said. "We rolled my car in a field."
Ricky peered out the front door of the bar and noted his brother's old white '66 Oldsmobile Eighty-eight with the black top parked off to the side. It was rusty

Leaving Justiceville: A Life Behind

and dented and was missing the hubcaps, but otherwise intact. He rolled his eyes and turned back to listen to his brother's story. By this time, a sympathetic crowd had gathered around Theo.

"I can't believe I'm only sixt– I mean, twenty-one and I'm already a widow," Theo said sorrowfully.

"It's widower," Ricky corrected him. "A girl is a widow, a boy is a widower."

"Shut up, smartass!" Theo said. "Can't you see I'm in mournin'?"

"You didn't get married," Ricky said. "You're making this whole thing up."

"I ain't neither. We got married over in Bowie by a preacher," Theo insisted. "We got a burger at Mabel's Diner, drove out to Slack's pond and parked. After that's when we had the accident, and she died."

The other patrons offered words of condolences as Theo continued his story.

"You are such a liar," Ricky snorted.

Theo slammed down his empty glass and grabbed his little brother by the arm. He dragged him out the front door and began beating him with his fists.

"You think you can make me look stupid in front of everyone?" he shouted. "Well, I'll fuckin' teach you!"

Customers were coming in and out of the establishment a few feet from the boys, but no one did anything to stop Theo as he attacked the smaller boy. When Theo had exhausted his anger, he yanked his bruised and bloodied brother back inside and shoved him roughly onto his stool at the front door.

Leaving Justiceville: A Life Behind

"Now, you say one more fuckin' word, and I'll do even worse to you tonight," he threatened icily. "Ya got that?"
Ricky nodded and dried his eyes.

Ricky watched the newspapers for any obituary for a young woman named Sally, but there was nothing. Nothing on the news about a fatal accident, either. As he already knew, his idiot brother had fabricated the whole story, probably for attention.

Leaving Justiceville: A Life Behind

CHAPTER FIVE

The following Friday night, Ricky looked up in surprise as a uniformed police officer walked into the bar with a firm grasp on Theo's arm.
"Ricky, where's your dad?" the officer asked.
"He's over there," Ricky pointed to where his father was drinking and laughing with a rather heavyset woman with bright orange hair. He assumed that wasn't the color for which she was going but had settled for instead.
The policeman pulled Theo roughly over to his dad, who looked up from his conversation with annoyance.
"What'd he do now?" he frowned.
"I caught him looking in the Snyder girls' bedroom window."
"So?"
"I wasn't doin' nothin'," Theo said sullenly.
"There ain't no harm in a young man lookin' at girls," Deed said. "It's the most natural thing in the world."
"He was…" the officer lowered his voice, "he was masturbating."
"No one saw me, except for him," Theo scowled, pointing at the officer. "I wasn't hurtin' no one."
Deed stood up and slapped his son across the back of the head.
"You can't pull your dick out in public like that," he said. "You only do that if you're sure there's no cops around."

"Whatever," Theo shrugged.
"I don't want to see him doing anything like that again," the policeman said sternly. "He needs to keep it in his pants when he's out in public, and no more peeping in people's windows."

Late the next evening, Ricky answered the wall phone at the end of the bar.
"Hello?" he yelled into the phone. He struggled to hear what the caller was saying over the loud twangy country music that was blaring over the bar speakers. "What?"
He listened for a moment.
"Okay, I'll tell him," he shouted and then hung up the receiver.
He nudged his father on the shoulder.
"Why ain't you at the door?" his father said with a frown. "Git back there."
"Jimmy is in jail," Ricky said. "The policeman said you have to go bail him out. They want two hundred dollars."
"Aw, goddammit!" Deed scowled. "Why do they keep pickin' on my boys?"
"He was driving without a license and stole a tank full of gas from the Phillips 66 station," Ricky said dryly. "I don't think they're 'pickin' on him."
Deed smacked him on the back of the head.
"Don't talk back to me," he said. He opened the cash register and pulled out some cash. "Here. Take this down and bail your brother out. Then you get back here."

Leaving Justiceville: A Life Behind

Ricky walked fearfully through the darkness the mile into town and made his way to the police station. He paid the bail, and Jimmy was released within fifteen minutes. Together they walked back to the bar, but once they were outside of town, Jimmy pulled his brother off the dirt road and into an abandoned corncrib. Ricky struggled against him, but his brother held him down firmly as he molested him. After all the times this had happened before, Ricky knew what to expect, but he still fought against him as hard as he could. Jimmy was just too big and strong, however, and he managed to have his way. Apparently his short time in a jail cell had had a stimulating effect on his libido, and he took it out on his brother. Afterwards, Ricky curled into a ball and sobbed while Jimmy dressed and left him there and walked on to the Country Castle.

Theo and Jimmy began spending quite a bit of time as guests of the local police. Their offenses ranged from driving under the influence of alcohol, underage drinking, and petty theft. Theo was arrested on a couple of occasions for fighting and assaulting a few local young girls. Most of Jimmy's offenses involved peeking in windows, public indecency, and stealing items from many of the downtown stores.
Deed always managed to make a deal with his buddy, the chief of police. Ricky observed money changing hands on several occasions, and he assumed his father was bribing his friend to keep his two sons out of prison.

Leaving Justiceville: A Life Behind

He continued to claim to anyone who would listen that his sons were good boys and were merely the innocent victims of a prejudiced and overzealous police force. Theo and Jimmy were never punished, but their father took his anger and frustration with them out on Ricky instead. One night, he beat the child severely and then tossed him into the bar's dumpster out back while Jimmy and Theo jeered and laughed.

It was then that a plan began to form in Ricky's mind. After a lifetime of abuse, torment, neglect, pain and sorrow, he knew it was time to make a change. So what if he was only eleven. Somehow he was going to take charge of his own life and rise above all of this bullshit; above the beatings, the sexual abuse, the suffering, tears, fears, and bruises.

To that end, he began doing a bit of adjusting with the bar's financial records. He knew his father was too ignorant to figure out that he was stealing from him. He pocketed some of the cash from the cover charge patrons paid at the front door as well. He was smart enough to cover his tracks so that no one would ever know what he was doing.

He was fully aware that what he was doing was wrong, and he saw the irony of the situation. His innate moral character felt a sense of guilt over lying and stealing. Even so, desperate times called for desperate measures, and this was a desperate time if there ever was one!

Leaving Justiceville: A Life Behind

About this time, his mother began having an affair with a door to door salesman, who was making the rounds of the town. Ricky and his sister were locked out of the house as they had been on several occasions before. While they waited out on the grassy top of the old storm shelter, their father's rusty pickup pulled in the drive.

"Whose car is that?" he scowled. "And what are you doin' out here?"

"It belongs to some guy," Ricky shrugged.

"They locked us out," his sister chimed in.

Deed tried the knob on the back door and then began pounding on it angrily.

"Open this fuckin' door!" he shouted.

"You'd better get out of here," Ricky's sister whispered to him.

"Why?" Ricky frowned. "I didn't do anything."

"Don't matter, 'cause Dad's gonna be really mad at Mom, and he can't hit her. He always takes it out on you."

She was right, he thought. After every altercation his parents had ever had, he had been the one who ended up suffering for it.

As they watched, their father kicked in the back door, while the salesman ran out the front door, clutching his pants and shoes in his arms. He started his car and spun the tires in the gravel as he sped away as fast as he could go.

Ricky and his sister listened to their parents shout and curse at each other for a while until they had exhausted all the threats and insults they could come

up with. When everything became silent, he knew it was time to hide out of sight for a while, so he ran and hid behind the neighbor's garage.

That evening, Ricky was making spaghetti on top of the stove, while his brothers and sister sat at the table, waiting impatiently for their supper. His father stepped into the room and sniffed the air.

"Are you fixin' spaghetti again?" he frowned. "Goddammit! I'm getting fuckin' sick of spaghetti. Don't you know how to fix somethin' different?"

"This is all we have," Ricky told him with a resigned shrug. "She didn't go to the store again, and she won't do the cooking."

His father unexpectedly began slapping him. Ricky cowered down and covered his head with his arms as best he could. His brothers and sister looked on impassively.

"Don't you talk bad about your mother," he shouted. "You show some respect."

He took Ricky over his knee and spanked him for a few minutes before shaking him by the arm.

"Now you get supper on the table, and keep your fuckin' mouth shut!"

One night Ricky was tending bar since the regular bartender had called in sick. He was more likely too stoned to come in to work, Ricky supposed. In between pouring drinks for customers, he attempted to work on his science homework.

Leaving Justiceville: A Life Behind

"How's it going, Ricky?" the woman with the tall, stiffly sprayed orange hair said as she sat down on a bar stool.

Ricky eyed her curiously. Out of all the older women who came into the bar, this was the one with whom his father was particularly friendly. She was a reasonably attractive woman, he mused, but she wore far too much makeup with brilliant blue eye shadow and frosted pink lipstick. Her attire was usually a low-cut frilly blouse and pink or blue pedal-pushers with gold slipper-like shoes. Not to be unkind, but all the different colors – orange, blue, pink, gold – made him think of a clown.

"It's going fine," he said cautiously.

"I'm Irene," the woman said with a smile. "What's that you're studying?"

"Science," he said briefly.

"Hmm, I see," she said. "That's a hard subject."

"It is for me."

"What's your favorite subject?" she asked.

"Math."

"Yes, your father told me you do the books for the bar," she said. She pulled a cigarette from her sparkly cigarette case and held it between her fingers with their long pink nails. "You must have a gift for numbers."

"Uh huh," he shrugged and resumed wiping out used glasses the way his father had taught him.

She watched him in silence for a few minutes while she nursed her seven and seven.

"You know," she said, "your dad's a nice guy."

Leaving Justiceville: A Life Behind

"No, he's not," Ricky muttered.
"Sure, he is," she said. "I like him."
"Why?" Ricky frowned at her. "He's mean and ugly and stupid."
"Ricky," she said reprovingly. "Don't be a smartass. I'd hate to have to tell your father what you said."
Typical adult, Ricky thought derisively. Always making threats. He knew instinctively not to trust this woman.
"Why do you like him?" Ricky ignored her. "He doesn't have any money, he's bald and has a beer belly. His fingernails are always dirty, and what hair he does have is always greasy."
"You're looking at him as a father," she said. "I see all his good qualities."
"Like what?" he asked skeptically.
"Well, he's honest and kind and funny."
Hmmph, Ricky snorted to himself. That's a bunch of bullshit; his father was none of those things. Either this woman was stupid, or his father was a very good actor. It must be the latter, he decided, since his father had had affairs with any number of women, probably more than he was even aware of.
"You know he's married, right?" Ricky said.
"I know," Irene shrugged. "For now."
"What does that mean?" Ricky frowned.
"Just that he may not be married much longer," she said. "At least to your mother."
"You mean he's going to marry you?" Ricky said, surprised.

Leaving Justiceville: A Life Behind

"Can you keep a secret?" she leaned forward and spoke in a conspiratorial whisper.
"Yeah," he said.
"Your father wants to divorce your mother and marry me," she said.
"He does? He asked you to marry him? What about all the other women he's sleeping with?"
"What other women?" she said.
"Nothing," he said and looked away.
"Anyway," Irene went on, "Whenever he leaves your mother, I want you to come and live with us."
"No thanks," Ricky said.
"Why not?" she frowned. "What, I'm not good enough for your highness? You'd rather stay with that bitch Stella?"
"I don't want to live with any of you," he said. "All adults are nothing but liars and cheaters. All any of you do is abuse kids, so I don't want nothin' to do with any of you."
"Well!" she exclaimed indignantly.
With that, she angrily picked up her drink and cigarette case and walked away. Ricky watched her go for a moment and then shrugged. He was just being honest with her, something he knew from experience that all adults hated. But why shouldn't he tell her how he honestly felt? No adult really cared what he was thinking or feeling anyway.

Deed didn't care about checking ID's on any of his customers. His only concern was selling as much watered down booze as he could. He instructed Ricky

to make a show of checking their birth dates on their driver's licenses, but he also said not to turn anyone away if they were underage. He figured if they got busted for serving alcohol to minors he could just blame Ricky for it. Besides, with the chief of police being a buddy of his, he had no worries about getting in any sort of trouble.

One night, a frequent patron of the bar, a seventeen year old named Randy, came in and sat down on a barstool. His eyes were red and puffy, and he looked like he hadn't bathed in days.

"How ya doin', Ricky?" he asked.

"I'm okay," Ricky said as he poured him his usual shot of bourbon and placed it in front of him. "But you don't look so good."

"No thanks. I don't have any money," Randy said, pushing the drink away. "I can't pay for a drink."

"Why not?"

"I'm…just a little low on cash right now," Randy said.

He looked so forlorn that Ricky couldn't help but take pity on him.

"Go ahead," he placed the shot glass back in front of him. "It's on the house."

"Won't your dad get mad, you givin' away free drinks?" Randy said worriedly.

"He would if he knew about it," Ricky said. "But he doesn't keep track of anything. I'm the one who does the books. What he doesn't know won't hurt him. Or me."

Leaving Justiceville: A Life Behind

"Thanks," Randy said. He wiped his eyes and downed the brown liquid.
Ricky watched him for a moment and then poured him another shot.
"So what's going on?" he asked.
Randy looked back at him for a moment and then shook his head and dried his eyes once again. He came into the bar a few times a week. He and Ricky had gotten to know one another fairly well over the last few months. He was a pleasant young man, always warm and friendly, but also a bit pensive and melancholy. From their frequent talks, they had found that they had much in common. Both had lived with abuse their entire lives but were doing their best to rise above it. Randy lived with his parents and six brothers and sister in a rundown trailer park on the wrong side of the tracks. His father did odd jobs for a living, and his mother worked at the local laundromat. It fell on Randy as the eldest child to care for his siblings, which he did to the best of his ability. All the while he concentrated on his studies and was at the top of his graduating class.
Randy had told Ricky once that his dream was to go to college and become a doctor one day. He knew, sadly, that the chances of that happening were slim to none. He had collaborated with the high school counselor and applied for grants and scholarships and assistance. To his astonishment, he learned that he had earned several grants and a scholarship to the University of Texas in Arlington.
"I got accepted at UTA," Randy said.

Leaving Justiceville: A Life Behind

"Wow," Ricky said. "That's great."
He studied his friend's unhappy face.
"Isn't it?"
"I told my folks," Randy said. "My dad got mad and beat me up."
"Why did he get mad?"
"He said that I was too uppity and thought I was better than the rest of them," Randy said. "He told me if I was gonna think that way, I should just get out and live on my own."
"He kicked you out?" Ricky said incredulously. "Just because you want to be a doctor? That's crazy!"
"He's such a hateful bastard," Randy said. "He doesn't want any of us kids to think we're better than him. He wants us all to be failures like he is."
"So if he kicked you out, where are you living?"
"In my car," Randy said.
Randy's car was an old Chevy Impala that he had acquired by saving his money from a paper route he had run since he was Ricky's age.
"Well," Ricky said thoughtfully, "if you got accepted to college, why don't you go? There's nothing else in this town for a guy as smart as you."
"I don't have any way to get there," Randy said. "It's sixty miles. I got no gas and no way to live until classes begin. I'm trying to find a job so I can earn some money."
"How much do you need?" Ricky asked him.
For weeks now, he had been holding back money from the bar in preparation for his own plans. So far he had saved four hundred dollars.

Leaving Justiceville: A Life Behind

"I don't know," Randy said. "Probably a couple of hundred dollars to get started."
"When does your school start?"
"Next week."
"You can't earn that kind of money in just a week," Ricky frowned.
He looked around the room for a moment and then peered around the door into the dirty kitchen, where his brothers were throwing raw chicken wings at each other. Ricky knew that those wings would still end up being cooked and served to customers, so he made a mental note to avoid those for the next few days.
Actually, he knew that the only food safe to eat here was the food he cooked himself; he certainly wasn't going to trust his brothers or his father with anything he put in his mouth.
When he was certain that no one was looking, Ricky reached into a hidden recess under the bar and pulled out a bundle of cash held together with a rubber-band.
"Here," he said quietly, handing the bills to his friend. "You need this more than me."
"What's this?" Randy asked, confused.
"It's four hundred dollars. It's a way for you to get away from this hellhole and go to Arlington to become a doctor," Ricky said. "Now hide it before anyone sees it."
"Where'd a little kid like you get this kind of money?"
"It doesn't matter," Ricky shrugged.
"Were you saving it for something?"

"Yeah," Ricky replied. "But my plans can wait. Yours can't. So take it and go to Arlington and become a doctor."
"Ricky, I can't take your money," Randy protested.
"Why not?" Ricky said. "How else are you gonna get to college?"
"I don't know, but I can't take this from you. You need it."
"I got time to get some more and you don't," Ricky said. "Surely you're smart enough to figure out this is your way out of here. So take it and go to Arlington tonight."
Randy reached over the bar and gave Ricky a brief embrace.
"Thank you."
Wow, Ricky thought, that's probably the first time in my entire life that anyone has ever hugged me.
"I'll never forget this," Randy whispered emotionally. "You're the only person I've ever known who's done something nice for me."
"You and me are in the same boat," Ricky said. "Ain't nobody gonna help us unless we help each other. I hope you become a famous doctor someday and find cures for all kinds of diseases."
"I will," Randy promised.
He turned and ran from the building and into his car. Ricky never heard from Randy again, but he hoped that he had the future he dreamed of. Now if only he could have as happy a life as he imagined Randy was going to have.

Leaving Justiceville: A Life Behind

For the next few months, Ricky's life continued as usual: working the bar, skimming money off the top, and dealing with bullies at school and beatings and abuse at home. He knew it was wrong to steal but rationalized it easily enough. After all, he and his brothers and sister were free labor for their father. The bastard was too cheap to pay them any wages, so he was only taking what was coming to him.

Theo got caught driving under the influence of alcohol in a neighboring town, where he had gone to buy some drugs and meet an underage girl for sex. This time the chief of police couldn't help him, and he ended up spending an extended amount of time in jail.

He and Jimmy spent most of their time these days sleeping with every girl or woman they could find, Ricky thought disgustedly, just like their dad. The three of them would boast about their sexual conquests while working in the bar's kitchen, and Ricky would listen and roll his eyes. Knowing them for the liars they were, he figured they had exaggerated their sexual exploits by a factor of at least ten. Still, they must be getting it somewhere since they only bothered him occasionally these days.

He heard no more about his father divorcing his mother and marrying Irene, but he did open the men's bathroom door one night to find the two of them engaged in a full sexual encounter.

"Get the fuck out of here!" his father grunted at him. "And don't you fuckin' tell anyone about this!"

Leaving Justiceville: A Life Behind

Later, Ricky received a beating for being such a nosy spy.
"It's creepy that you want to watch your father havin' sex," his father said angrily. "Ya little pervert!"

One night, an older friend of Ricky's, a girl named Pam, sat with him at the door while he checked ID's and collected money for the cover charge. She was fifteen and a one hundred percent tomboy: tough, butch haircut, and flannel shirts. She was already a smoker and loved to play pool. He kind of assumed she was a lesbian, but like his friend Jamie, who had defended him on the school bus, she turned out to be completely straight. She had what was called a hardship driver's license, which meant that she was allowed to drive to school by herself, but nowhere else and not at night. It didn't matter to her because she drove her old green Mustang wherever and whenever she wanted.

It was Pam that introduced Ricky to smoking. The two of them would sit on their stools in the booth at the door, puffing away on their Marlboro's, Lucky Strike's, Pall Mall's, or unfiltered Camel's. Ricky admired Pam's maturity and toughness, and he took up smoking to be more like her. He wanted to be grown up and badass, even though he knew deep down that that wasn't who he really was. Still, it was nice to imagine himself as someone who didn't have to take the abuse he lived with on a daily basis, someone who could stand up to his brothers or his

Leaving Justiceville: A Life Behind

father or the bullies at school and say, "I'm Ricky Blain, and I don't have to take your shit anymore!" Someone must have said something to his father about him smoking, and one night, Deed came in the front door instead of through the back. With a cigarette dangling from his own lips, he proceeded to give Ricky a severe beating and told him he would do worse if he ever caught him smoking again.
It didn't stop Ricky from doing what he wanted, of course. Pretty soon, he was taking cigarettes from the bar's vending machines. Pam always bought her own, but when she didn't have enough to share with Ricky, he would steal them from some of the stores in town.

All the years that he had gone to school with multiple bruises, injured wrists, black eyes, and wearing dirty and torn clothing, no one ever asked about his home situation. He supposed everyone in town knew about the abuse; how could they not know. But clearly no one cared. Child abuse was a touchy subject, especially in Texas, where everyone was taught that the man is the master of his household, and whatever he says or does is fine. As long as a man was white and straight, Ricky was beginning to realize, he had the right to do whatever he wanted to his wife and children, and no one would question it.

School was becoming more troublesome for Ricky. He was constantly bullied and tormented by the older boys, even though he had Jamie and Pam to look out for him. He avoided the playground as much as

possible. Lunchtime was spent with Doris in the cafeteria, washing trays and pots and pans, sweeping the floors, cleaning the lunchroom after the other students had departed.

Another friend came to his defense on occasion. She was a girl named Judy, and the two of them sometimes rode the same school bus together. Judy's life experiences were very similar to his; she had suffered abuse and neglect just like he had. But unlike Ricky, she was tough and unafraid of anyone or anything. Any time that someone offered to give him a hard time when she was around, she would sit beside him looking all meek and mild. Moments later, his would-be tormentor would either end up on the floor, clutching their wounded privates, or take off running for their lives.

The two of them shared lots of conversation and laughter, and it helped Ricky to have a friend who truly understood what he went through every single day of his life.

It was difficult for him to keep up with his studies. Working at the bar, cooking and trying to keep the house reasonably clean, looking after the livestock, mowing the lawn, and attempting to do homework left little time for anything else. He still excelled at math but was having more and more trouble with his other subjects since he rarely studied. It didn't help that English, Science, and Geography held little interest for him; they seemed unimportant to his practical mind. As a result, he was barely passing

most of his classes. When report cards came around, he signed them himself instead of showing them to his parents. Most of his grades were D's, and he knew that would only lead to more beatings.

CHAPTER SIX

The family moved again, this time into a small gray house with only two bedrooms. As before he was forced to share with his brothers, but now his sister was sleeping in the same room with them. In spite of their past record, their parents were unconcerned about their daughter sharing a room with the boys who had tried to molest her; they assumed Ricky would look out for her as he always did. However, it wasn't a problem since Theo and Jimmy rarely slept at home these days. They were fifteen and seventeen, and spent most of their time picking up girls or sleeping it off in one of their cocaine-snorting buddy's bedrooms. Ricky's parents rarely knew where they were and showed no interest in finding out. Ricky figured that whenever his brothers weren't bothering Deed and Stella, his parents didn't care; as long as they were out of the house, they were somebody else's problem.

The final straw came on a hot May day during his eleventh year. By noon the old rusty thermometer on the side of the hardware store said it was one hundred fourteen degrees. People and animals moved slowly and kept to the shade during days like this. Tempers seemed to flare more easily when the weather was so ungodly hot, and Ricky was no exception.
He had spent the morning listening to his mother bitch about his father. He agreed with her one hundred percent when she called him a no-account

loser, who was as ugly as mud and lied and cheated every chance he got. What he didn't say and longed to was that she was no better. He wisely kept that thought to himself.

His mother sat at the filthy kitchen table and fanned herself with an old takeout menu from the Chinese restaurant that had gone out of business ten years ago.

"Come on," she said, with a cigarette dangling from the corner of her mouth, as usual. "There ain't no food in the house, so I gotta go to the grocery store. You can carry the bags and I'll tell you what your dad did the other day."

All through the store Ricky listened to her complain, rolling his eyes wearily as her monologue continued unrelentingly. Deed had done this, he had lied about that, he wasn't worthy of a princess like her, and on and on it went. Finally, Ricky could take no more, and he spoke up.

"If you hate him so much, why don't you divorce him?"

"What?" she looked startled at this suggestion. She stopped pulling cartons of cigarettes from the shelf and turned to frown at him. "Why the hell would I do that?"

"Neither one of you are happy," Ricky shrugged. "You're both cheating on each other."

She slapped him across the top of his head.

"I ain't never cheated on him!" she snapped angrily. "Who told you that?"

Leaving Justiceville: A Life Behind

"Nobody," Ricky said impatiently, moving out of her reach. "I've seen it for myself. Everybody knows what you and him have been doing. If you ask me, you both deserve each other."

With that, his mother grabbed her big purse from the cart and began hitting Ricky over the head with it. He cowered down until she was done, and they resumed their shopping.

It was when he told her that the stockboy wasn't interested in her that she really flew into a rage. She cursed and screamed at him while she beat and kicked him. He scrunched his eyes closed but opened them long enough to see the other people in the grocery aisle, who were standing by and impassively watching this brutal attack. As he expected, no one offered to intervene or to stop the irate woman who was beating an eleven year old child.

After a few minutes of this, Stella stopped her attack, mostly because she was winded from the exertion and less because her anger had dissipated. Through his tears of pain, anger, and humiliation, Ricky saw the other shoppers turn away and resumed perusing the shelves for their next purchase.

How could adults be so pitiless and uncaring, he asked himself for the thousandth time? Why did nobody care about him? Not his parents, his teachers, his siblings, neighbors, the police, no one. This wasn't the way it was supposed to be. Parents were supposed to be kind and loving. Adults were meant to look out for children's welfare and care for them selflessly. Yet none of the grownups in his life did

Leaving Justiceville: A Life Behind

any of that. Actually, come to think of it, most of the children he knew were unkind and selfish, with a few exceptions such as Jamie and Pam and Judy. He dealt with bullies every day at school as well as at home. It was too much, he decided. He needed to get away from these people and this unfriendly town once and for all.

Justiceville, he snorted! What an ironic name. For there was no justice to be found there, only unkindness, unfairness, cruelty, prejudice, poverty, and hatred. He needed to go somewhere were people were good and true and kind, if such a place even existed.

Once his mother had regained her breath, she yanked him up from the floor and shook him furiously.

"Now you go sit in the car and wait there for me," she said coldly. "And next time you sass me I'll really give you a beating!"

The car ride home was silent until they reached their weedy driveway.

"Now you carry these bags in," Stella ordered him as she thumped her cigarette into the tall grass and lit another one. "And don't drop anything."

Ricky ignored her as he ran into the house.

"Hey!" she yelled. "Git back here!"

Ricky ran for the bedroom and began packing his few belongings into a worn and scuffed duffel bag. After he was packed and ready to go, he walked out the front door to, ready to leave for good!

"Where you goin'?" his mother asked him in a surly voice. "Git over here and carry these groceries."
"No!" Ricky yelled at her. "I'm not ever doing anything you say, ever again! I'm getting out of this place!"
"Oh, yeah?" his mother sputtered. "Yeah? Well…good! You little bastard! I never wanted you anyway!"
"Well, you will never have to worry about it ever again!" Ricky shouted. "I hope you rot in hell!"

With those final words, he ran as fast as he could go down the alley behind the dilapidated house until he decided that no one was pursuing him. Not that his fat, lazy mother would be capable of chasing him; she was out of breath just walking from the living room to the kitchen.
He paused to catch his own breath as he contemplated what he had just done. He had run away from home! A sense of panic threatened to overwhelm him while he stood there. He was eleven years old, and he was suddenly on his own!
In a sense, he had always been on his own, he thought. His parents had provided him food and shelter, but nothing more. His home had never been a safe place; he had endured malicious beatings on a daily basis, sexual and mental abuse from his brothers, and the place had been filthy and unhygienic at best.
He had always taken care of himself, cooking meals, making a futile effort to keep the house clean,

Leaving Justiceville: A Life Behind

washing his hand-me-down clothes as best he could in the bathroom sink. The only thing that was going to be different was that he would have to provide his own food. And any shelter he found would be better than the nasty places he had grown up with so far. Shelter, he mused. There was only one place he could go, only one adult who had ever treated him with any consideration at all.

"Honey, what's wrong?" Doris, the school cook, asked him when she saw him standing on her doorstep with his bag in hand and an anxious look on his face.
"I...I ran away from home," he told her.
Tears filled his eyes, and he brushed them away impatiently. The enormity of his situation was beginning to dawn on him, and he couldn't seem to stop his emotions from welling up inside him. He was frightened, worried, and weary of his life. There had to be a better existence than this, he thought. Surely not everyone's life was this awful, was it? Didn't every person on the planet deserve happiness? He had learned in school about the United States Declaration of Independence, that all men were equal and had the right to pursue happiness. 'Life, Liberty and the Pursuit of Happiness' was a direct quote from that historic document. In other words, life was meant to be enjoyed. Well, he was a man, a human being, and thus far he had found nothing about life that was worth enjoying. He knew that he would never find that enjoyment if he stayed under his

parents' roof any longer. His life would be one long misery as long as they or his siblings were involved in any way in his life.

Doris gave him a sympathetic look and pulled him into a motherly embrace.

"Tell me what happened," she said soothingly.

Ricky told her about the beating in the grocery store, his brother's attempt to molest him again, and that he simply couldn't take the horror of it all anymore.

"I'm so sorry you're going through that," she said. "But don't you worry about it anymore. You can stay right here with me."

She held him close once more.

"You will be my little boy from now on," she whispered in his ear.

That evening, Ricky sat at the kitchen table and watched while Doris hummed cheerfully to herself as she cooked the pork chops, scalloped potatoes, fresh green beans with bacon bits, and a Waldorf salad for their supper. It all smelled heavenly, much better than the grilled cheese sandwiches, frozen dinners, or fried Spam to which he was accustomed to eating at home. He looked around the spotless kitchen. It was rather dated with old white metal cabinets and a Formica countertop, but it was clean and uncluttered. The linoleum floor was worn but spotless, and the wooden kitchen table had a bouquet of fresh flowers in the middle of it, right out of Doris's flower garden by the back door.

Leaving Justiceville: A Life Behind

The house was small, about the same size as his parents' house, but the similarities ended there. Whereas his parents' home was filthy and malodorous and uncomfortable, this home was welcoming and tidily maintained. The furniture was older, but it was good quality and thoughtfully arranged. There were curtains at the windows instead of old dirty bed sheets, and the windows themselves were sparkling clean.

Ricky helped Doris's daughter Kelli set the table in the dining room.

"Mom says you're going to be my new brother," she said. Her other siblings were already grown and living their adult lives nearby.

Ricky knew Kelli from school, but the two of them weren't friends. Kelli associated with all the popular girls in their class, and her circle of friends tended to merely tolerate Ricky and his sister, sometimes making fun and laughing at Ricky's old clothes.

"You aren't allowed in my bedroom," she told him sternly. "And you have to help do the dishes. This is my house so you have to do as I say."

Ricky nodded in agreement. After all, what choice did he have?

"And we won't tell anyone at school that you're living here! My home life is separate from school. You got it?"

Dinner was a novel experience for Ricky. Thoughtfully prepared and tasty food on clean plates, ice cold milk to drink, the whole family sitting

Leaving Justiceville: A Life Behind

together, chatting and laughing easily together. There was even dessert, a buttermilk custard pie which Ricky immediately decided was his new favorite treat.

Afterwards, the family gathered in front of the television to watch some lighthearted sitcoms while Doris resumed knitting the sweater she was making for her husband. It was a warm and cheerful atmosphere, and Ricky savored it. He was grateful to be away from his awful family and with these kind people, who were already treating him like one of their own. He watched and listened with interest to see how similar Doris's family was to the sitcom family on the screen. They were happy, loving people who genuinely cared about each other. Other than on television, Ricky had never witnessed people actually loving one another until tonight.

So people like TV characters really did exist, it seemed. Hmm, that was surprising to Ricky. Obviously they were few and far between, he decided, since every one of his acquaintances other than Doris and his few friends – parents, siblings, teachers, the principal, bar patrons – were for the most part angry, unkind, and judgmental. They were also not to be trusted, he knew; it was his experience that all people were liars and users.

At bedtime, Doris provided him with some old pajamas that had belonged to her son. They were faded and somewhat frayed, but they were clean and smelled of cedar from the cabinet in which they had been stored for the past few years.

Leaving Justiceville: A Life Behind

"My son wore these when he was about your age. I didn't have the heart to throw them away or sell them at a garage sale," she told him as she tucked him into his small bed. "I suppose it was just sentimental foolishness, but I somehow always thought I'd need them again someday. It looks like that someday has come along at last."

She patted his hand affectionately.

"Now, we'll have to get you some new clothes," she told him. "Those things you wear are disgraceful."

"They're all I have. I ain't never had new clothes," he said. "Except the ones she made me steal from Myer's."

He was referring to the local downtown five and dime/department store in Justiceville.

"Your parents made you steal?" she said incredulously.

"I mostly took clothes for Theo and Jimmy, and then I got them as hand-me-downs. Dad said they couldn't afford to buy clothes for me, and that hand-me-downs were good enough," Ricky shrugged. "I only took a few things, though. I'd rather wear hand-me-downs or garage sale clothes than steal."

"Well, you get a good night sleep," she said kindly. "We'll talk more in the morning."

For the next two weeks, Ricky got a sense of the life he had always dreamed of. True, he didn't have his own room, but the cot under the stairs was private and secluded. Best of all, he didn't have to share it with anyone else.

Leaving Justiceville: A Life Behind

Fred, Doris's husband, was a pleasant man. He gave Ricky chores to do, such as mowing and raking the grass, and Ricky was only too glad to be of help. For the first time in his life, he was using an honest to goodness power mower that was self-propelled. It seemed effortless compared to the old reel mower that he struggled with every week.

One evening he was helping Fred carry the dinner dishes from the dining room table to the kitchen and his foot caught on a chair. He stumbled and the plates he was carrying slipped from his hands to land on the floor in pieces.

"Ricky!" Fred scolded him. "Be careful."

Ricky instinctively cowered down and covered his head with his arms to shield himself from the onslaught that he knew was coming. After a moment of nothing happening, he dared to look up through his arms. Fred was kneeling down beside him with a worried expression on his face.

"Ricky, it's okay," he said gently. "I didn't mean to scold you, and I'm not going to hit you."

Doris and her daughter looked on with a distressed look on their faces. Doris knelt down and pulled him into a hug.

"Sweetheart," she said. "No one is going to hit you. You're safe here."

Ricky sat back and looked up at the adults warily.

"I'm sorry," he said. "I didn't mean to break anything."

Leaving Justiceville: A Life Behind

"We know," Fred said. "It was an accident. And it's not a big deal. They're just some old plates, so don't worry about it."

Later, Kelli sat down beside his cot under the stairs, where he had just settled himself in for the night.

"Why did you think Dad was going to hit you?" she asked curiously. "He would never do something like that."

Ricky just shrugged in response. He was embarrassed by how he had reacted in front of all of them to breaking the plates. At home, an accident like that would have resulted in a severe beating. But it was humiliating to admit to this girl that his family was so cruel. After all, he did have at least some dignity. Not that he cared what people thought of him, because he already knew that they all looked down on him; he was a Blain, and he was poor. Still, his ego was fragile enough that he was reluctant to let anyone know how horrifically he had been treated all his life.

"Did your parents really hit you?" she asked.

"Sometimes," he mumbled, avoiding her eye.

"I'd heard that they were bad people," Kelli said. "I'm sorry you had to live like that."

"Your parents never hit you?" he asked. "Not ever?"

"No, of course not. That's not how parents are supposed to be."

"They don't lie to you or cheat on each other?"

"No," she looked horrified at the very idea. "They love each other, and they love me and my brothers and sister."

Leaving Justiceville: A Life Behind

For the first time in his life, Ricky was relatively happy. School was still a nightmare for the most part, but it didn't matter anymore because at home he was surrounded by kind, loving people who treated him with respect, like he mattered. No one had ever made him feel worthwhile before. His parents had done their best to stamp out any feelings of self-worth he might have had, but now he felt a tiny flame of self-confidence flicker to life inside him.

One incident of note occurred during his time with Doris and Fred, and it happened at school. Ricky was walking down the hall toward the cafeteria when he came face to face with his sister.

"Hi," he said hesitantly.

"Hmmph," she said coldly, before turning away and continuing on her way.

"Are you okay?" he asked her.

"I'm not supposed to talk to you," she said primly. "Dad said if I saw you, I was to have nothin' to do with you because you're an ungrateful brat who don't deserve to be part of our family."

With that, she turned and walked away without looking back. Ricky swallowed hard at this snub. After defending her and looking out for her after Theo had tried to rape her, covering for her so her parents wouldn't spank her and taking the beating instead, and now to have her treat him so coldly; it was extremely hurtful. She of all people should have been his ally, yet she had sided with his abusers.

Leaving Justiceville: A Life Behind

It was a few weeks later that Doris and Fred sat Ricky down in the living room. He looked up at them apprehensively. The two adults frowned at one another for a moment before Fred finally spoke.
"We've had a talk with your parents, Ricky," he said hesitantly.
"They know I'm here?" he said worriedly.
"Yes, they do," Doris said. "They were very concerned about you."
"No, they weren't," Ricky snorted. "They don't care about me at all, except to do the books at the bar."
"Now, I'm sure that's not true," Doris said. "We had a long talk with them."
"They seemed like very nice people," Fred added.
"They're not nice at all!" Ricky said emphatically. He had a bad feeling about this conversation.
"They're mean and they hit me all the time. They lie and cheat and make me steal."
"Now, Ricky, are you sure about that?" Fred said. "Maybe you misunderstood the situation."
"They said they would never hit you, and that they love you very much," Doris said.
"You've seen the bruises I came to school with every day," Ricky reminded her. "Where do you think they came from if my parents didn't beat me?"
"Maybe you fell down, or banged your arm on something?" she suggested.
"What about the black eyes and the swollen lips?" he said, not believing what he was hearing. "You think I did that to myself?"

"Maybe you and your brothers roughhoused a little too much," Fred said.
Ricky stood up and glared at them.
"You think I'm lying about everything, don't you?" he cried indignantly. "You think I made all of this up!"
"Ricky, it's not that," Doris said. "We understand that sometimes a little boy's imagination can make him remember things differently from how they actually happened."
"Your parents seemed very sincere when they said they love and miss you very much," Fred said. "They want you to come home."
"The only reason they want me to come home is to do all the chores and work at the bar," Ricky told them angrily. "They don't give a shit about me!"
"Now, Ricky," Fred said reprovingly. "There's no need for such language."
"I think you need to give them another chance," Doris said. "They want you to come home, and I think you should go."
"You're kicking me out?" Ricky said.
"No," Fred said. "We're suggesting that you go home and work on your relationship with your parents."
"He threw me into the garbage!" Ricky exclaimed. "And she beat me in the grocery store. I'm not making that up. Lots of people saw her do it!"
"I know," Doris said. "You told us about that. But I think it's possible that maybe you exaggerated the story a little to make it sound worse than it was. Don't you think that's possible?"

Leaving Justiceville: A Life Behind

"I don't make things up, and I don't exaggerate!" Ricky snapped resentfully. "I'm not a liar. They did all the things I told you about, and a lot more besides. And Jimmy and Theo made me –"

He stopped himself just in time from telling them about the constant sexual abuse he had endured for years from his older brothers.

"The point is," Fred said, "we can't keep you here anymore. Legally, your parents have the right to make you come home, and we can't go against the law. I'm afraid none of us have any choice in the matter."

"It isn't that we don't love you," Doris added hastily. "We love having you here. But your parents love you, too, and we can't interfere."

You've got to be kidding me, Ricky thought angrily. How the hell had his parents convinced these nice people that they were anything but cruel, vicious monsters? Everyone in town knew what despicable human beings they were and how unkind they were to their children – well, mostly him, that is. Neighbors and other family members had witnessed many times the slapping, spankings, beatings he had endured his entire life. Were Fred and Doris really that gullible? Or did they just want him out of their house? The more he considered the situation, the more convinced he became that it was the latter. They were like every other adult after all, apparently. Lying to him and using him to get what they wanted from him.

Leaving Justiceville: A Life Behind

He was to learn later that the truth of the matter was that Fred and Doris believed in their heart that they had no right to interfere with a child and his parents. They honestly felt that Ricky was better off at home with his parents, and not with some well-intentioned people who should have minded their own business. At the time, however, he assumed that he had been right all along; no adult was to be trusted, not even the ones who seemed nice like Fred and Doris.
This was a lesson he would remember the rest of his life.

He ran from the house and hurried across town to his friend Jamie's house.
"I'll ask Dad if you can stay here," she offered. "Wait here."
She walked into her father's study and returned less than a minute later.
"He said no," she told him regretfully. "He says you belong at home with your parents no matter what, and that he can't interfere."
"He's a minister," Ricky said. "Isn't it his job to help people?"
"Yes."
"Just not poor kids who get beat up by their parents every damn day," he said sarcastically.
"I guess not," she agreed. "Isn't there anyone else you can call?"
Ricky thought for a moment.

Leaving Justiceville: A Life Behind

"Well, there's Bea and Jesse, over in Yorkville," he said. "They come into the bar, and they're always nice to me."
"Would they let you live with them?" she said doubtfully.
"I don't know," he shrugged. "But I can't think of anyone else. And I sure as hell ain't going home."
The two looked in a phone book until they found the listing, and Ricky called them. To his surprise, they agreed to come and get him.

"So you're really going back home?" Kelli asked him as he gathered his few belongings.
"I have to," he shrugged. "No one believes me when I tell them how mean my family is, and I haven't even told them half the shit they've done to me."
"I believe you," she said. "I don't think you should go back there. Not after all they did."
He looked around to make sure no one could overhear them.
"I'm not really going back there," he confided in a low voice.
"You're not? Where are you going?"
"I don't know yet," he said. "Just somewhere."
He wasn't naïve enough to think that he could trust Kelli, even though she had become something of an ally over the past few weeks. By now he had learned to trust no one, and to take nobody into his confidence.

Leaving Justiceville: A Life Behind

At that moment, Doris came into the room and walked over to where the two young people were talking.
"So you're all packed?" she said.
"Yes," he said coolly, avoiding her eye.
"Are your parents coming to get you?" she asked. "Or do you want me to take you home?"
"No," he said. "I can get there on my own. I don't need any help from anyone."
"I'm sorry it didn't work out," Doris said. "I would have loved having you stay here for good."
"Yeah," Ricky snorted. "If you say so."
"Ricky, listen to me," she said. "I wanted you to stay, but legally we couldn't keep you here. You belong to your parents, and we have no right to keep you from your rightful home. Besides, they love you and miss you. I hope you can see that."
"I don't see that at all," Ricky said. "But you don't want me here, so I'll just go back home and let them beat me."
"Ricky, they won't beat you," Doris said. "They love you. I could see it in their eyes when Fred and I were talking to them."
Ricky picked up his duffel bag and turned away. Doris stopped him and gave him a hug.
"I'll see you at school," she said. "Just give your parents a chance. Let them love you."
"Bye," he said impassively. He stood woodenly as she hugged him.
"Bye, Ricky," Kelli said. "I hope it all works out for you."

Leaving Justiceville: A Life Behind

Ricky returned to Jamie's house, where Bea and Jesse were waiting for him in their pickup. They were an older couple who lived in a trailer with their children. Jesse worked in a factory, and Bea was currently unemployed. Ricky soon learned that she had a somewhat volatile temper and would quit whatever job she had at the drop of a hat.
He explained his situation to them, and they were properly sympathetic.
"Well," Bea sighed, "I guess we can't let you go back there."
"Are you sure about all of this?" Jesse asked with a doubtful tone to his voice. "It don't sound like Deed to be mean to his kids."
"It's true," Jamie said with annoyance. "I've seen it for myself. The neighbors all talk about it. Everyone in town knows the Blain's are abusive to their kids, especially Ricky."
"Theo and Jimmy seem to get along okay with their dad," Jesse said. "I seen them laughing and bragging about all the fuckin' they do."
"Yeah, and Theo's in prison for doin' drugs and DUI," she said dryly. "And Jimmy ain't no better. They're both worthless pieces of shit. Ricky's the one who gets beat up all the damn time."
"I believe it," Bea said. "Ricky's not a liar."
"I don't know…" Jesse said slowly.
"Well, I do, and he's coming home with us," she said firmly. "So let's go."

Leaving Justiceville: A Life Behind

Bea and Jesse lived in a nice older trailer park. Their trailer had a large lot and a garden in the back. Bea set up a cot in the dining room for him.

"Now, we can drive you to school," she said. "Or maybe one of your friends could drive you."

The only friend at that time with a car was Jamie's friend Jay, the one who she would soon be involved with in a high speed police chase. He had been given a hardship driver's license due to his home situation, and Jamie arranged for him to drive the few miles to Yorkville and take Ricky to school.

Bea and Jesse's two daughters were less than pleased at having Ricky in their home, and they were quite vocal in letting their parents know it, usually right in front of Ricky. The two of them refused to speak to him, making his stay there most uncomfortable.

Jesse liked to drink beer, usually Old Milwaukee's Best or Pabst Blue Ribbon. On the weekends, he and Ricky would chop wood or work in the garden, and Jesse would share his beer with the boy.

During the week, Ricky would attend school and then ride with Jay back to Yorkville. One Saturday night, Jay drove over and asked to spend the night with Ricky on his dining room cot. Once everyone was asleep, Jay began fondling Ricky. The two boys jacked each other for a while until Jay asked to suck his dick. Ricky immediately became uncomfortable as he remembered all the times he had been forced into sexual activities by his brothers. He told Jay no, and Jay dropped the subject then and there. Nothing was ever mentioned about it again.

Leaving Justiceville: A Life Behind

CHAPTER SEVEN

Jay spent several nights with Ricky in Bea and Jesse's trailer.
"How did you get a driver's license?" Ricky asked him as the two lay in bed.
"Because my folks are rich," Jay said. "My dad knows people, and they got me a license so my mom doesn't have to drive me around. She's too busy with her clubs and charities and shit to bother with me. And Dad's always working, so I'm on my own a lot."
"Like me," Ricky said. "But if you're rich, why do you want to stay here with me in a trailer?"
"Because I like you," Jay shrugged. "We're friends, and I don't have that many friends."
"You have Jamie," Ricky reminded him.
"Yeah, she's cool," Jay said. "But I like you special. We got a lot in common."
"We do?"
"You know what I'm talking about," Jay said. "We like the same things. One thing in particular."
He reached down and grasped Ricky's genitals in his hand.
"We both like this," he said.
"How did you know I liked…?"
"I just knew," Jay said. "So you and me are buds. That okay with you?"
"Sure," Ricky said. "I ain't got no other friends, 'cept Jamie and Pam and Judy. There ain't no one else I like."
He thought for a moment.

Leaving Justiceville: A Life Behind

"Judy was cool," he mused. "She used to stand up for me on the bus. Her family was almost as bad as mine. We'd sneak behind the teeter-totters and smoke."
"How'd she stand up for you?"
"There was this one kid who used to bully me," Ricky said. "He called me queer once and Judy said that at least I didn't suck dick. He said he didn't, either, and she said that she knew about some guy sucking him off once. He never bothered me again after that."
On another night that Jay stayed over, the two boys stole a pack of cigarettes from Bea, a six-pack of beer from Jesse, and set out around midnight to explore the small town. They smoked and drank as they walked along the back alleys.
"Hey, isn't that Bea's car?" Jay pointed at an old car parked beside a beat up trailer that sat just off the alleyway.
"Yeah," Ricky nodded. "What's she doin' there?"
Bea and Jesse had had an argument earlier that evening, which is one reason that the two boys had decided to leave the trailer for a while. They stepped closer to the trailer and looked in the wide living room window. Bea and some stranger were clearly in the middle of sex.
The two youths made a hasty retreat and resumed their trek through town while they discussed what they had seen. The next day, Jesse took them aside.
"Bea didn't come home last night," he said confidentially.
"Yeah, we know," Ricky said.

Leaving Justiceville: A Life Behind

Something in his tone made Jesse look at him sharply.
"You know something, don't you?" he said.
"No, I don't know nothin'," Ricky lied, avoiding eye contact with Jesse.
"Where is she?"
"We saw her at a trailer behind the junk store last night," Jay volunteered. "She was with some guy."
"Jay!" Ricky shook his head at his friend.
"Come on," Jesse took Ricky by the arm. "Show me where she was."
"I gotta go home," Jay said uneasily. "I'll see you later, Ricky."

Bea came home later after an unpleasant confrontation between Jesse, Bea, and her illicit lover. There was shouting and cursing and fists flying through the air, while Ricky tried to be as inconspicuous as possible.
Later, when Jesse and Bea were continuing their fight in their bedroom, Bea stormed out of the room.
"Where's my fuckin' cigarettes?" she demanded. "I need a fuckin' cigarette!"
She opened the drawer in the dining room sideboard to find an empty carton. Jay and Ricky had swiped the last pack the night before.
"Did you take my cigarettes?" she scowled at Ricky. "You little bastard. I oughta beat your ass for ratting me out and stealin' my smokes!"

Leaving Justiceville: A Life Behind

She continued to rail at the boy for a few minutes until a coughing fit overwhelmed her. Once she had her breath back, she had a few more words for him. "This whole thing is your fault. You pack your shit and get outa here!" she said icily. "I want you outa my house this minute! You hear me?"
Ricky quickly gathered his few belongings and ran from the trailer.

Ricky walked along the dusty road between Justiceville and Yorkville. Cars and trucks passed him, leaving him in billows of dust in their wake. None of them slowed or stopped to offer any assistance, not that Ricky expected them to. That's because none of them care, Ricky thought grimly. People were selfish and unkind; that's just who the human race was.
Well, it was time to stop trying to rely on anyone else. If he was going to succeed at life, it was going to be up to him. And dammit, he was going to succeed, he told himself!
To do that, he thought, he would need money, and to get money, he would need a job. But he was only twelve years old, he mused; who was going to hire a twelve year old?
He had celebrated his birthday a few days ago by singing 'Happy Birthday' to himself while he lay in his cot under the stairs at Doris's house. No one else knew or cared that it was his birthday, so there had been no gifts or party or any acknowledgement of the

Leaving Justiceville: A Life Behind

important event. Well, he sighed, it was important only to him, so he would sing to himself.

But back to the problem of finding a job. He would never find work in Justiceville. Everyone there knew he was only twelve years old. No, he needed to go to another town where no one knew him, maybe some place like Belwood, a town twenty miles away. That's it, he decided. First thing in the morning he would go to Belwood and find a job. Maybe in a fast-food restaurant or a department store. He didn't care what it was at this point. He just needed money so he could buy food and find a place to live.

So he had a plan for the future, but what about tonight? Where was he going to sleep? He continued walking until he reached the edge of Justiceville. He decided it was safer if he remained unobserved by the town's citizens, so he made his way inconspicuously down alleys and backstreets toward the center of town. Maybe he could walk out to the Country Castle and sneak in to sleep in one of the storage closets. At least that would get him out of the cool night air. Texas days were oppressively hot and humid, but often times the nights were downright chilly.

As he was considering his options, a voice called to him. It was a friend from school, a girl named Carla.

"Ricky, what are you doing?" she asked curiously. She was sitting on the swing set behind her parents' house.

"Just walkin'," he said vaguely.

"I heard your parents kicked you out," she said.

Leaving Justiceville: A Life Behind

"They didn't kick me out!" Ricky said indignantly. "I left because she beat me up in the grocery store and he threw me into a garbage can. She said she never wanted me and called me a bastard! I couldn't stand the abuse anymore."

"I know," she said understandingly. "They're really awful. I hate them."

"I hate them too," he agreed. "That's why I am never goin' back there."

"Where will you go?"

"I don't know," he said. "I guess I could stay out under the bridge on Old Church Road."

"You can't do that," she frowned. "There'd be snakes and scorpions out there. It wouldn't be safe."

"I don't have much choice," he said.

"I'd let you stay here, but Mom and Dad wouldn't allow it," she said. "He's friends with your dad, and he'd tell him where you are and make you go home."

"I won't go home," Ricky reiterated. "It's never been my home. I'd be safer out with the snakes and scorpions!"

She thought for a moment and then turned to look at the garden shed at the edge of the alley.

"I know," she snapped her fingers. "You can stay in the shed."

The two of them walked over to the small building and looked inside. In the center of the single room was an ancient and rather decrepit pool table along with other assorted furniture, mowers, and garden tools. An old twin-size mattress stood on its side along the far wall.

"See," she said. "We can put the mattress on the pool table, and that will be your bed."
"Okay," Ricky said with a sense of relief. "Thanks."

That night Ricky lay on his makeshift bed, glad to be in any sort of shelter. The door opened suddenly and he jumped up in alarm.
"It's just me," Carla grinned at him. "I brought you some leftovers and a pillow and blanket. And this too."
Triumphantly, she held up an old milkhouse heater attached to a fifty foot orange extension cord that she had plugged into an outlet on the back of the house.
"This will keep you warm if it gets too cold," she said.
"Won't your dad see the cord?"
"He never comes out to the backyard," she said. "No one will ever know you're here."

Ricky was grateful for the heater that night as the temperature dropped down into the forties. The old shed was drafty, and he could see sky through holes in the roof, but it was still a place to stay while he figured out his next move. He devoured the scraps of food that Carla had brought to him within minutes. He hadn't realized just how hungry he was until he smelled the fried chicken and biscuits.

"What about school?" Carla asked him the next morning. "Aren't you going to go?"

"Nah," Ricky shook his head. "I'm done with school. I've got to find a job to support myself, so there won't be time to go to school."
"How are you going to find a job?" she asked.
"You're only twelve. No one will hire you."
"I'll lie about my age," he shrugged. "I'll get a job, buy me a car, and live on my own."
"But you're only twelve," she repeated. "You have to be an adult to live on your own."
"I've been on my own all my life," he said wryly.
"The only difference was that the people I lived with beat me. From now on there won't be anyone to hit me or force me to do sex things."
"Sex things?" she wrinkled her nose. "What are sex things?"
"What Theo and Jimmy made me do," he said.
"Is that why you like guys?" she asked.
"No," he said. "I've liked guys for as long as I can remember. It has nothing to do with them. If anything, the stuff they did to me would have made me like girls."
"So you didn't like doing sex stuff with them? Maybe you do like girls after all."
"No, I like guys," he said. "I just didn't like being forced to do it, or doing it with my brothers. They were gross."
Carla looked at her watch and sighed.
"I guess I should go," she said reluctantly. "I don't want to be late for first period."
"Or you could skip school," he suggested. "We could go down to the creek and skip rocks."

Leaving Justiceville: A Life Behind

"That would be fun," she said. She thought for a moment and then smiled. "Okay! Let's do it."

The two young people slipped unobtrusively out to the edge of town to the bridge that Ricky had considered as a hiding place. They spent the morning wading in the stream and then returned to Carla's house. Both of her parents were at work, so she and Ricky went into the kitchen to fix themselves some lunch. Before he knew it, she had gotten out their new deep fryer and the two of them began cooking just about everything edible in sight: pickles, potatoes, mushrooms, chicken, onions, and more. It was a pleasure to Ricky to be unsupervised by adults for a change, and to do something without the anticipation of the dreaded repercussions. There were no unkind parents or teachers or other grownups to scold or thrash or berate him. Carla was proving to be a true friend, and she was fun to be around. She also knew about his sexual preference and didn't judge him for it. He knew better than to reveal a secret of that nature to anyone, but Carla had figured it out for herself. Thankfully, she was living up to her promise never to tell anyone about it.

That night Ricky was awakened by the sound of thunder and flashes of lightning. The wind was whipping around the corners of the small shed, making him fear the building was going to be swept away. The roof leaked like a sieve, and no matter how he readjusted his position on the thin mattress,

the rain still managed to find him. Finally, he took his blanket and pillow and crawled under the ruined pool table to keep dry.

The next day, Ricky borrowed Carla's bicycle after she and her parents left for work and school. It was twenty miles to Belwood, a long trek for a young boy to pedal. He stopped to rest a few times whenever he could find a bit of shade in the flat, mostly barren landscape. When he reached the town a few hours later, he made his way to a newly built up business district on the edge of town. There were a number of popular fast-food restaurants clustered together, and Ricky stopped at the nearest one, a small establishment called Taco Rio.

"So your name is Ricky. I'm Sean. You're kinda young, ain't ya?" the young manager drawled with a toothpick dangling between his lips.

"I'm sixteen," Ricky told him.

"You're kinda small for sixteen," Sean frowned.

"My parents are midgets," Ricky said, not missing a beat.

"Oh," the young man nodded. He seemed to accept this without question. "You live around here?"

"Just around the corner," Ricky told him.

"You got a car?"

"No, just a bicycle," Ricky said. "That's why I need this job, so I can earn money for a car."

"You know how to cook? Can you make tacos?"

"Oh, sure," Ricky said. "I made them all the time at my parents' bar."

Leaving Justiceville: A Life Behind

"I see," Sean said thoughtfully. He studied Ricky's ingenuous face and then smiled. "All right, we'll try you out for a few weeks. If you do a good job, we'll make the job permanent."

He discussed the particulars of the job with Ricky and then sent him on his way. Ricky left the building elatedly. His first real job, a job that was going to be the beginning of his future! He could see it now; Taco Rio for now, and then soon the president of some big company. He would have a boyfriend and a fancy house and a Cadillac. Maybe two Cadillacs, one for him and one for his boyfriend!

It was all beginning, he thought happily: his future with no more hateful parents or cruel brothers or indifferent sister. The only adult he would have to answer to now was his new boss.

When Ricky reached Carla's house a few hours later, he was greeted by Carla's scowling parents.

"I'm sorry, Ricky," Carla said regretfully. "Dad found the extension cord."

"What do you think you're doing, hiding out in our shed like a…a fugitive!" Carla's dad said angrily. "You could get us in a lot of trouble. I've already told your dad where you are. He's on his way here now to get you."

"No!" Ricky cried. "I won't go back there."

"Ricky, I know the stories you been telling around town about Deed and Stella. And I know they aren't true. You're trying to make them out to be bad people, but it's not so. Deed's a decent guy."

Leaving Justiceville: A Life Behind

"No, he's not!" Ricky said. "And if you think he is, then you're just stupid."

"Come on," Carla grabbed him by the arm and pulled him hurriedly toward the shed. "Let's pack up your stuff."

Once they were out of earshot of her father, she released his arm.

"Are you out of your mind, talking to my dad like that?" she hissed. "He's always gonna stand up for your dad since they're friends. You can't talk to adults like that."

"I was just telling the truth," Ricky shrugged. "It's not my fault if grownups don't like to hear it."

He gathered his few belongings together in his duffel bag.

"It doesn't matter anymore," he said. "I gotta get outa here."

"Listen, I have another idea," she said. "I talked to my older sister Brenda. She and a friend of hers have a place over by Skylark Lake. She said you can stay there for a while."

"Really?" Ricky said. "That's closer to Belwood. I got a job there today."

"Great," Carla said. "Then this will work out perfect for you. I'll tell her to pick you up at the old bridge."

They heard a car door slam in the driveway next to the house.

"Ricky, you get yer fuckin' ass in this car!" Deed shouted. "I've had enough of this shit! I'm gonna give you a whipping like you've never had before."

Leaving Justiceville: A Life Behind

"Quick," Carla whispered. "Go before he comes back here."

Ricky slipped out of the shed and ran as fast as he could toward the agreed upon rendezvous point, the ancient bridge over Skylark Creek. An hour later, an old rusted '59 DeSoto Firedome sedan stopped on the wooden bridge, and Ricky climbed into the back seat. Carla's sister Brenda drove them to Skylark Lake and a somewhat decrepit trailer located on the shore. The place smelled of stale cigarette smoke and marijuana and mildew, Ricky noted. The carpet was worn and the furniture threadbare. Still, it was reasonably clean; at least it was better than the old shed in her parents' backyard.

"There's only the two bedrooms for me and my roommate," Brenda told him. "But you can sleep on the couch."

"How far is it to Belwood from here?" Ricky asked her.

"About five miles or so," she said. "Why?"

"That's where I got a job," he told her.

"Well, you'll have to walk there," she said. "And don't eat any of our food. My roommate and I put labels on everything, so anything that has a name on it is off limits. You'll have to get your own if you want to eat."

She looked at him appraisingly for a moment.

"You know, I dated your brother Theo for a while, before he went to prison," she said. "I hope you're not like him."

Leaving Justiceville: A Life Behind

"I'm nothing like him!" Ricky said emphatically. "I'm not anything like any of my family."
"Well, that's good," she said. "Because he's a creep."
"Yes, he definitely is," Ricky agreed.

Ricky set out at six o'clock the next morning for Belwood. He estimated it would take a couple of hours to walk the five miles to work, and he didn't want to risk being late for his first day.
By the time he reached Taco Rio, the temperature was already ninety degrees, and he was sweating. His clothes hadn't been washed in many days, and he was beginning to smell.
"Tomorrow I want you to bathe and wear clean clothes," Sean told him sternly. "Don't come to work like this."

Ricky's first day was long and trying. He listened closely to his boss and the other workers while they taught him to do the job for which he had been hired, namely that of cook. He concentrated on the work, ignoring a few jabs from his coworkers about his small size. Some of them were sullen and lazy, apparently already succumbing to the realization that, with their lack of ambition, this was as good as their lives were ever going to be.
Not me, Ricky thought determinedly. I'm going to make something of myself, to be proud of who and what I am. I will never be the victim that fate is determined to make of me; I'm going to win, not fate!

Leaving Justiceville: A Life Behind

For the next few weeks, Ricky worked long hours at the restaurant. He would arrive early each morning before anyone else was there and wash up in the mop sink. He would work straight through until closing. At night, after he was certain that everyone else had left, he would strip down and hand wash his clothes in the same sink that he had bathed in that morning. Once they were as clean as he could get them, he would don the damp attire again and let them dry on him as he walked back to Skylark Lake.

Because there was no food for him to eat at Brenda's trailer, and he had no money to buy his own food, he ate food from the restaurant. Since he was the cook, it wasn't too difficult to sneak a few bites here and there throughout the day. It wasn't a particularly healthy diet, but it at least filled his belly.

One night, after a particularly long and difficult day, Ricky tiredly made his way the five long miles to the trailer. In his weariness, his footsteps became slower and more labored. Before he was halfway there, his legs gave out on him, and he dropped to the ground, exhausted. He sat there for a few minutes and looked around. After a while, he got to his feet and limped over to a nearby corrugated metal culvert that spanned the road and opened into the fairly deep ditch. He crawled inside the currently dry thirty foot long tube and curled up into a fetal position. I'll just rest here for a few minutes, he told himself.

The next morning, Ricky awoke with a start to the sound of an extremely loud diesel engine somewhere

overhead. In fright he scrambled hurriedly out of the culvert and ran several feet away before he turned to look back. An enormous green and yellow sprayer was just pulling into the adjoining cotton field. Dammit, he thought as he rubbed the tiredness from his eyes, he hadn't meant to sleep in a ditch all night. These long double shifts were kind of kicking his butt. But he was just going to have to cope with it, he knew, if he wanted to make something of himself. He needed the money so he could buy a car, get his own place, and start living like a normal human being. With a sigh, he started walking back toward Belwood. He couldn't be late for work.

Ricky lay on the sofa in the living room of Brenda's small trailer. He was startled when the front door banged open, and Brenda stumbled into the room. She wasn't alone, however. There was a heavy set bearded man with her, who smelled of strong body odor and liquor. The two of them were giggling as she led him past the sofa and into her bedroom. Ricky kept his eyes scrunched shut until they had passed by, but then he had to listen to the sounds of the pair having sex. Ew, he grimaced, that's gross! There was groaning and moaning and yelling and shouts of 'oh god!' He covered his ears as best he could, but nothing he did was able to drown out the sounds coming from the next room.

The next morning, he avoided looking at Brenda when she came out of her room wearing an old loosely tied chenille bathrobe.

Leaving Justiceville: A Life Behind

"Sorry if we kept you awake last night," she smirked as she grabbed a couple of beers from the small refrigerator. "He was such an animal."
"He smelled like one," Ricky said dryly.
"What's that supposed to mean?" she frowned.
"Just that he has B.O. really bad," Ricky said.
"So what? You're judging me?"
"No," he said.
"Yes, you are," she scowled. "You're judging me for sleeping with a guy I just met at your dad's bar."
"I don't care what you do," Ricky said honestly. "You should sleep with whoever you want."
"Oh, so you think I'm a whore?" she snapped. "You know, I oughta tell your folks where you are and make them come and get you. You got no right to judge me, you little pansy."

Ricky was standing at the fryer in the back of Taco Rio when Sean came up to him and told him he had a visitor. He stepped out the back where Brenda greeted him by the dumpsters.
"Here," she said in a surly voice. She threw his duffel bag at his feet. "Here's your shit. You need to find someplace else to live, 'cause you ain't livin' with me anymore."
"Why not?" Ricky asked her.
"'Cause you're a fuckin' liar," she said. "You told Carla your folks beat you and all that shit, and it's a damn lie!"
"It isn't a lie," Ricky insisted. "Just ask Jimmy or Theo. They'll tell you the truth."

Leaving Justiceville: A Life Behind

"Jimmy and Theo couldn't tell the truth if their lives depended on it," she snorted. "At least most of the time. But I asked Jimmy if it was true, and he said you're nothing but a cocksuckin' liar. Your folks never laid a hand on you."
"Yes, they did, dammit! I'm telling the truth!"
"You're just like Theo," she sneered. "A worthless piece of shit. I knew I shouldn't have gotten involved with him, or you neither."
With that pronouncement, she flounced back to her old car and drove away. Ricky's shoulders sagged, and he sighed despondently. Dammit, he was back to being homeless again. At least he had his job and in a few months would be able to get his own place. But what to do until then?

That night was especially cold. Ricky shivered as he walked along the dark, quiet streets of Belwood. As he passed through the parking lot of a nearby apartment complex, he noted steam coming off the heated outdoor swimming pool. That looked inviting to him with the chilly air around him. He walked over to the area and found a small nook between the pool heater and the building. It was warmer there out of the breeze and with the heat source right next to him. He gathered a few towels he found on some patio furniture and fashioned himself a little bed as best he could. With a resigned sigh, he settled down and tried to go to sleep. After all, he had to be back up first thing in the morning.

Leaving Justiceville: A Life Behind

None of this was getting any easier, he told himself. Tears filled his eyes, but he was determined not to cry. He was a survivor, not a victim, and he wasn't going to be beaten down by the constant setbacks that the world was hurling at him. Still, it was a lot for a twelve year old boy to deal with, with no home, no one to care about him, long hours of hard work, unfriendly coworkers, hunger…sometimes it was just too much, and he felt like quitting everything. Maybe life wasn't going to get any better than this. Maybe he should just give up and let himself die from hunger or exposure. At least then his suffering would be over.

After feeling sorry for himself for a while, Ricky dried his eyes and shook his head. No, he told himself sternly, he wasn't a quitter; that's not who he was. He'd made it through life thus far and endured constant beatings, mental cruelty, and sexual abuse. He had survived that, and he would survive this. If he just kept focused, he knew he would one day have the life he had always dreamed of. A happy childhood was something he had never known, but there was no use crying over that now. The important thing now was to stay strong and continue working toward his goal.

Leaving Justiceville: A Life Behind

CHAPTER EIGHT

Ricky continued to sleep in his hiding place at the apartment complex for the next few weeks. He worked his long hours at work and ate what food he could steal while he prepared the customers' orders. One day, a coworker happened to mention that her brother had a one bedroom apartment in Grey Mound, a small town a few miles east of Belwood. He was looking for a roommate, she said, so Ricky told her he was interested. She called her brother and a deal was soon struck. That night, she drove him to Grey Mound, where her brother showed Ricky the cot he could sleep on behind the couch. Ricky paid him a week's rent and immediately fell asleep on his small bed.

The next several days seemed to run along smoothly enough, Ricky thought. He spent sixteen hours a day at work, coming home to the apartment long enough to sleep and take a shower. There was a washing machine and a dryer for him to use, but there was an extra charge for that, he soon learned.

A couple of other coworkers who lived in Grey Mound would pick him up in the mornings and drive him home at night. Now that he didn't have to walk all those miles to work and had a place to bathe and wash his clothes, he didn't have to go in so early and stay so late.

His coworker's brother turned out to be, in Ricky's words, a real dick. He had seemed pleasant enough when he moved in, but within a few weeks, he

Leaving Justiceville: A Life Behind

revealed his true character. As with the washer and dryer, there was an additional fee to use the shower or refrigerator. After all, his host informed him, all he was paying for was a place to sleep; everything else was extra. He was expected to provide his own linens, dishes, soap, laundry detergent, and so on unless he wanted to pay him for those things. By the time the first week was up, Ricky had paid him nearly double for the privilege of staying there.

Each morning, Ricky would make up his bed neatly, making sure that everything he had touched or used was spotless and in its proper place. Even so, he would come home at night to find his cot folded up and stowed in a closet, with a handwritten note listing each and every infraction he had committed the day before. Ricky crumpled up the notes and was tempted to throw them in the trashcan in the kitchen, but knew that that would only add an extra charge to his ever growing rent.

One night Ricky closed the window over his cot to keep out the chilly night air. The next day he was instructed to pay another five dollars for 'using the window' without permission.

Okay, he thought with annoyance, that just about does it. At this rate, it's going to take every bit of money I'm making just to live with this guy. So after the fourth week, he gathered his things and told the guy to fuck off. His coworker, the young man's sister, berated him for being such an unpleasant tenant for her poor brother, who was only trying to do

him a favor out of the goodness of his heart. She refused to speak to him after that.

As it turned out, one of Theo's ex-girlfriends, a young woman of twenty-two named Rhonda, who he had slept with and briefly married when he was seventeen, lived in the apartment complex where Ricky had been sleeping by the swimming pool heater. He ran into her one day at the restaurant.
"So I hear Theo's in jail," she snapped her gum at him. "Serves the bastard right."
Ricky merely nodded in agreement.
"How'd a little guy like you get a job here?" she asked him. "You ain't old enough to have a job."
"Shh," he hissed at her. "They think I'm sixteen."
"Oh, I get it," Rhonda nodded knowingly. "I heard you ran away from home. How'd you get all the way over here?"
Ricky gave her a brief explanation of how he had come to live in Belwood.
"So where ya stayin'?" she asked curiously. "You got your own place?"
"No, not yet," Ricky admitted. "But I'm working on it."
"Good for you," she said. "But ain't your folks trying to make you come back home?"
"No," he shook his head. "They don't give a shit about me. The only reason they'd even want me back there is to do the books for the Country Castle. I'm just an unpaid slave to them."

Leaving Justiceville: A Life Behind

"Yeah, Deed's a real piece of work, that's for sure," Rhonda agreed. "Well, if you need a place to stay, I got an extra room in my apartment. You could stay there for a few weeks. But only until I get engaged."
"You're getting engaged?"
"Well, maybe," she shrugged. "If I meet the right guy. Anyone'd be better than that sonofabitch brother of yours. Ya know, I slept with him and Jimmy at the same time once, and they was both more interested in each other than they was me, if you know what I mean. I don't know why I ever married the bastard. I guess I would've married Jimmy if he'd been a little older, but that wouldn'ta been no better."

Ricky carried his few belongings from his hiding place to Rhonda's apartment the next day. She had no furniture in her spare room, but he didn't care. Even a carpeted floor was better than sleeping out in the weather. She let him use some blankets and a pillow, and even allowed him to eat her food and smoke a few of her cigarettes.

He was just beginning to settle in and feel comfortable when he came home late one night a few weeks later to find Rhonda waiting up for him.
"Kid," she said. "I got some great news. I'm gettin' married."
"You are?"
"Yeah, to this guy I met at the bar the other night," she said.
"You just met him?" Ricky said incredulously. "And you're already engaged?"

"Well, he ain't got no job or place to live," she explained. "So I told him he could move in here if he promised to make an honest woman of me."
"So why do you want to marry him if he's got no job?"
"Oh, you should see his dick," she said. "It's really nice."
"You can't marry a guy because he has a nice dick."
"Why not?" she said with a puzzled frown. "I wouldn't wanna marry someone with a bad one. I mean, what's the fuckin' point of that?"
"On TV they get married because they love someone," Ricky pointed out.
"I love his dick," she said. "That should count."
"I guess," Ricky said doubtfully.
"Anyway," she said cheerfully, "he's movin' in today, so you'll have to get out."

Ricky resignedly moved his few belongings back to his hiding place beside the pool heater. He was getting tired of sleeping on people's sofas or floors for a few nights and then being kicked out because it was too inconvenient for them. If only he had some family he could stay with, someone he could count on like other people did.
As he lay in his hidden nook, he tried to think of someone in his family who might help him out. Not his parents or grandparents, of course; they were the cause of all of his problems in the first place. But what about uncles or aunts? No, most of them were just as bad as his immediate family.

Leaving Justiceville: A Life Behind

An image of a face popped into his head suddenly. His uncle's ex-wife, June. She lived somewhere around here. She had never been overtly cruel to him, but then again, he didn't really know her well. Maybe she would help him.
The next day, he looked in the phonebook at the restaurant and found his ex-aunt's name.
"Aunt June?" he said hesitantly into the wall phone.
"Who's this?" came the surly reply.
"It's Ricky," he said. "You know, Deed's youngest son?"
"Oh yeah," she said thoughtfully. "Ricky. What do you want?"
"I was wondering…I mean, I kind of need a place to stay," he said tentatively. "I was wondering if you maybe had an extra room I could stay in."
"Well…I suppose it would be all right," she drawled slowly. "As long as you don't cause me no trouble."
"I won't, I promise."
"Why aren't you livin' at home?" she asked. "Is it because of them?"
"He threw me in the trash," Ricky said simply.
"He's a sonofabitch," she said. "Course, so's his brother. That's why I divorced the bastard."

Aunt June lived across town, so Ricky made his way there after work that evening. It was an old apartment building in a less than reputable part of town, and she lived on the second floor up a dark set of stairs. The apartment reeked of cigarette smoke and was cluttered with stacks of magazines and old

newspapers and dozens of porcelain cat figurines. She cleared a spot on the sofa for him in which to sleep and told him to keep the noise down so she could watch her favorite television show.

Ricky faced the back of the sofa as he attempted to sleep while his aunt watched 'The Tonight Show' and laughed loudly at the antics of Johnny Carson. Okay, Ricky thought, it's not ideal, but it's only temporary, and I've lived with far worse than this. I can handle this situation for a while, at least long enough to save up enough money to get my own place.

The third night of staying with his ex-aunt, Ricky worked until closing at eleven o'clock. He made his way wearily through the dark streets of Belwood and climbed the stairs to the apartment. He turned the doorknob only to find the door locked. He pressed his ear to the door and could hear noises coming from inside the apartment. With a sigh, he knocked a few times, but there was no response. He tapped on the door repeatedly with still no answer. After fifteen futile minutes, he finally slumped down against the door and closed his eyes.

It was a chilly night, and there was a strong breeze funneling up the staircase to where he was huddled, trying to stay warm. Finally, he moved over and found a spot out of the wind under the stairs that led up to the third floor. He curled into a fetal position to conserve his body heat.

Leaving Justiceville: A Life Behind

After about three hours of shivering and attempting to sleep, he got up and knocked on the door again. This time he was persistent and knocked repeatedly for several minutes. A naughty idea occurred to him, and he decided he couldn't resist.

"That's my husband you have in there!" he yelled in an angry voice.

A moment later, the door burst open, and a half dressed delivery man that Ricky had seen around the complex ran frantically from the apartment clutching his boots and shirt. He sprinted down the stairs. Ricky couldn't help but grin as he watched the fleeing man disappear into the night.

He turned back to see his ex-aunt's scowling face staring at him from the doorway. She was wearing an old and rather threadbare pink bathrobe with tiny yellow flowers across the breast.

"You little brat!" she snarled. "Look what you just did. He'll never come back now after you scared the shit out of him."

"I'm sorry," Ricky said apologetically. "I didn't mean any harm. I was just cold."

"Well, you're gonna have to just be cold from now on," she said. "'Cause you ain't stayin' here anymore after that little stunt. So git your shit together and git outta here!"

"But –"

"Deed and Stella was right about you," she said. "You're nothin' but a troublemaker!"

Leaving Justiceville: A Life Behind

With a resigned sigh, Ricky gathered up his things and made his way back to his hiding place at the other apartment building across town.

A week later, Ricky overheard one of his coworkers at Taco Rio, a girl named Paula, tell a customer about an old car her father had for sale. He took her aside.
"How much is he asking for it?" he asked her in a low voice.
"Five hundred fifty dollars, I think," she shrugged. "Why? You interested in it?"
"Yeah," Ricky nodded. "Would he sell it to me?"
"If you got the money," she said. "You got five hundred fifty dollars?"
"No," he admitted. "But I got a hundred."
"Hmm," she said. "I guess I can ask him about it."

The next day, Ricky worked only a single shift and then rode home with Paula to her parents' split-level house on a cul-de-sac in a nice neighborhood. In the short sloping driveway sat a 1960 Volkswagen. It was painted red, but had faded to almost an orange color. Someone had converted it into a Baja Bug at some point in its history. The car was dented and rusted, with bald tires and a cracked windshield, but to Ricky it looked like the nicest, newest Cadillac on the road today. The back seat had been removed and the entire interior covered with orange and black shag carpeting.

Leaving Justiceville: A Life Behind

"So what do you think of it?" Paula's dad asked him after showing him the engine, trunk, and other features of the small automobile.

"It's great!" Ricky replied, his eyes shining as he gazed at the car. He hesitated a moment. "I, uh, only have one hundred dollars."

"I see," the man said. "How old are you, Ricky?"

"Sixteen," Ricky lied.

"And you have a driver's license?" Paula's father said doubtfully.

"Sure," Ricky said.

He wasn't happy about lying to this nice man, but he knew he had no choice. Lying was a necessary evil for his survival.

"Well, I suppose I could let you make a couple of payments since you're a friend of Paula's."

"Really?" Ricky said hopefully.

"You really want the car?" Paula's dad asked him.

"Yessir," Ricky nodded eagerly. "I promise I'll pay you the rest as soon as I can."

"Okay, then I think we have a deal."

He reached out and shook Ricky's hand with Ricky grinning delightedly from ear to ear.

A little later, after a brief teaching session on how to drive a stick shift, Ricky drove away in his new car. He lurched and ground the gears at first, but eventually he got the hang of the clutch and the manual transmission.

Wow, he thought happily, my very own car! No more sleeping on other people's sofas or beside a

swimming pool heater or in a culvert. This vehicle was not only his means of transportation, it was his home, someplace to call his own. It was a place he could keep his belongings safe without having to constantly move them to whatever spot he was staying in for the night.

That first night, he parked the car as unobtrusively as possible in the Albertson's Grocery Store parking lot next to a couple of semi-trucks with sleeper cabs that were stopped for the night. With a new sense of pride and contentment that he had never before experienced in his young life, Ricky climbed into the back of the small car and lay down on the carpet. He gazed around the miniscule cabin and smiled for the first time in months. This was his, and his alone, and no one could take it away from him.

It was his safe space, he thought with a sense of wonder, the first safe space he had ever had in his life. With a sigh, he closed his eyes and soon fell into a peaceful, worry-free sleep.

Ricky continued to work as many hours as possible at Taco Rio. With a pay rate of a dollar sixty-five an hour, he needed every cent he could make to pay for his new car, gasoline, and food. He bought groceries for the first time, mostly just bread and peanut butter and jelly, cookies, crackers, and other supplies that didn't require refrigeration. Most of his meals still came from the restaurant, such as burritos, tacos, and so on, but at least this gave him something to eat at night after work.

Leaving Justiceville: A Life Behind

Some nights he would park his car in various store parking lots, and other times he would spend the night in one of the half dozen apartment complexes in town. Sometimes, when it wasn't convenient to wash up in the mop sink at work, he would wait until late at night and then bathe in the heated swimming pool. Occasionally someone would yell from their apartment window and tell him to get the hell out of there, but usually he could wash up without any problems.

On a few occasions, Ricky would drive across town late at night to the house where his mother's parents lived. He didn't know them well, except to understand that they were no kinder than his mother. He would pull into the alleyway behind their small bungalow and park in front of the ramshackle garage that leaned slightly to the right. If the police ever bothered him here, he could tell them that the people who lived here were his grandparents. If his grandparents discovered him, he could simply drive away and not come back. It wasn't as if he feared damaging his relationship with them.

This was the life, he told himself with satisfaction. He was finally truly independent, a man of means who was going to make something of himself. He was earning his own way and relying on nobody for nothing. Not that he had ever had anyone to rely on in his past anyway, but now there was no one to bitch at him or abuse him. His coworkers treated him with respect for the most part. They knew he was a hard worker, dependable and honest, and he never missed

any of his shifts. He tended to be very serious at work while he concentrated on his duties and rarely joined in the joking and teasing that the other young people enjoyed.

His hard work and attention to detail had not gone unnoticed by his manager, much to his surprise. One day he called him in to his tiny office. Ricky sat down nervously in the straight back chair in front of the old metal desk.

"Ricky," Sean said. "I've been watching you."

"You have?" Ricky gulped nervously. Uh oh, he thought worriedly. This could be bad if he's discovered that I'm staying after closing and using the mop sink as a bathtub.

"You're only sixteen, but you're one of my best workers," the young manager told him with a smile. "You never miss a shift, and you're always willing to work extra to make sure the restaurant runs smoothly. I want you to know that I appreciate that."

"I'm just doing my job," Ricky shrugged.

"No, you're doing more than that," Sean said. "Most people are just here for the money. They don't have any education and they don't want to work. But you're different. You're going to make something of yourself."

"Thanks," Ricky said diffidently.

He wasn't accustomed to receiving praise or adulation for anything he did. The one exception to that was one of his math teachers, a woman named Miss Carlisle, who used to tell him that he was gifted when it came to numbers.

Leaving Justiceville: A Life Behind

"So I want to promote you," Sean said. "How would you like to be a shift manager? It's twenty cents more an hour."
Wow, Ricky thought with awe. That would take his pay up to a dollar eighty-five per hour! He instantly figured the numbers in his head and realized that with the approximately eighty hours a week that he worked, he would be bringing home an additional sixteen dollars or so per week. That would be helpful in paying Paula's father the money he owed him for his car and begin saving for an apartment of his own.
"Me?" he said with wide eyes. "A shift manager? That'd be great!"
"Okay, starting tomorrow, you're my newest shift manager. Congratulations!"

Work went well for Ricky as the new day shift manager. There was still a night shift manager, a rather high-strung young woman named Jane who startled easily. Ricky took his responsibility as a new manager very seriously. He was uncomfortable at first giving his coworkers orders, but since he had been one of them for so long, they knew and trusted him. He worked right alongside them instead of sitting in the office like some shift managers had in the past. Over time, he learned how to delegate some of the tasks but continued to do more than his fair share. It was all a matter of doing what was best for the business, the customers, and in the long run, himself and his coworkers.

Leaving Justiceville: A Life Behind

One day Ricky was working the drive-thru window when a familiar voice came over the intercom.
"Yeah," the customer drawled. "Give me one of them burrito meals with a Coke and a couple of tacos too."
Oh god, Ricky thought with a sense of dread. It's my mother! His stomach clenched painfully at the very sound of her whining, nasal, uneducated voice. What do I do, he wondered? Should he let her see him or ask someone else to wait on the bitch? He looked around, but all of the other employees were hard at work waiting on their customers. Dammit! She would surely make him come home once she knew where he was, and that was something he simply couldn't do.
"Will that be all?" he asked her via the two-way radio. He struggled to keep his voice steady.
"If I wanted somethin' else I would have fuckin' asked for it, you stupid kid," his mother snapped at him.
He heard her rev the engine of her vehicle and then squeal her tires as she drove on around the building. A moment later, he peered around the wall of the drive-thru at her. His sister was sitting in the passenger seat in the tall pickup truck she was driving. Well, that was something different, he mused. It looked relatively new, but was already covered with dirt and mud. Steeling himself, he walked over to the window and slid it open.
"That'll be five dollars and twenty-seven cents," he told her.

Leaving Justiceville: A Life Behind

"Well, look who the fuck it is," she said as she chomped her gum. "How the hell did you get clear over here to Belwood and find a job?"

"That's five dollars and twenty-seven cents," he repeated, avoiding eye contact with the odious woman.

She handed him six dollars.

"I figured you was dead," she sneered.

"I'm not dead," he said.

"Well, it don't matter either way," she said cruelly. "I'm glad to be rid of you."

"That makes two of us," he muttered.

"What the fuck did you just say?" she scowled.

"Here's your change," he said. He handed her the seventy-three cents and her Coke.

"Ya like my new truck?" she said. "I just got it. Now that there's just your sister to feed and clothe, I can finally have somethin' nice."

"It doesn't look very nice," he said honestly. "It looks filthy."

He looked past her and took note of the fast food cartons and other junk that littered the seat and floorboard.

"You'll have it trashed in no time, just like you do everything else."

"Why you goddammed –"

"Here's your food, ma'am," Ricky said as he noticed his manager approaching out of the corner of his eye. "Thank you and have a nice day."

"You fuckin' little bastard," his mother said. "I oughta –"

Leaving Justiceville: A Life Behind

"Is there a problem here?" Sean frowned.
"No, sir," Ricky said. "Just thanking this nice woman for her business."
"I heard you," Sean said. "And I also heard how she talked to you. Ma'am, if you can't treat my employees with respect, then you are not welcome here."
"You can't talk to me like that," Stella shouted furiously. "I'm his fuckin' mother!"
"Is that true, Ricky?" Sean asked him.
"I have no idea who she is," Ricky shrugged. "She sure isn't *my* mother."
"Well, you ain't no kid of mine, neither!" his mother yelled before slamming the truck in gear and squealing away.

Ricky waited for repercussions from the incident with his mother, but he soon relaxed. He had expected her to force him to come home or tell his boss how old he really was, but nothing happened. He knew he shouldn't care about the unkind things she had said to him. After all, they were no different from the words she had spoken to him all of his life. Even so, her nastiness still hurt him. A mother was supposed to love her children unconditionally, he thought. It was her responsibility to care for and protect them, to instruct them and keep them healthy and clean. Stella Blain had done none of that for him or any of her other children. She was too lazy to even take care of herself, he thought wryly. He knew that's who she was and that she would never change, so why did it

still cause him so much pain when she treated him so coldly?
It didn't define who he was, he decided firmly. He was a good person, honest and nice and reliable. He didn't steal or lie, except for when it came to his survival. In short, he was a worthwhile human being, who was determined to make something of himself and be an asset to society. Not that society deserved it, he mused. What had society ever done for him? Nothing that he could think of, that was for damned sure. When he was suffering beatings and abuse at the hands of his parents and brothers, where was society to help him? It had turned a blind eye to the horrible things that were happening to him right in front of its nose. It didn't care, so why should he care about making society better? He knew why, he thought resignedly. It was because of the symbiotic relationship that existed between a society and its citizens. The worse off the people were, the worse things were for society as a whole.
Ricky was too young to articulate these ideas into cogent thoughts, but he understood their importance nonetheless.

One evening as Ricky was getting ready to close the restaurant, there was a terrible thunderstorm, with torrential rain and driving winds. The wind speed was so strong that the rain seemed to be falling sideways, Ricky thought. It was rather scary for him; it felt at times as though the whole building might be swept away.

Leaving Justiceville: A Life Behind

Jane, the night shift manager, had left early with complaints of one of her nervous headaches. Before she departed, she instructed Ricky and another employee to clean up and do the prep work for the next day. While they worked, Ricky noticed the lights flashing erratically out in the dining room. When he went to investigate, he suddenly realized that he was standing in three inches of water. To his amazement, there was a wave of water spreading across the room like a river. He looked out the nearest window that overlooked the parking lot and was astonished to see that it was no longer a parking lot, but a vast ocean as far as the eye could see!

A sense of panic filled him as he tried to think what he should do. He couldn't stop the rain or the wind or the flooding, but he had to do something. Call Jane, he decided with a sense of relief. She would know what to do. After all, this was her shift.

He waded back to the phone and called Jane, anxiously explaining the situation to her.

"Well, what do you expect me to do?" she said.

"You need to help me stop the water from coming in!" he said. "We can't handle all of this ourselves."

"I am not coming in there!" Jane said impatiently. "You'll have to deal with it on your own."

"But I don't know what to –"

"Then lock it up and go home!" she snapped. "Taco Rio doesn't allow any overtime anyway. So clock out and leave it for tomorrow."

"I can't just –"

Leaving Justiceville: A Life Behind

But Jane had already slammed down the phone in Ricky's ear. He hung up the receiver and looked around. Oh god, what was he going to do? The water was already reaching back to the office, so he instructed the other employee to help him put everything moveable up off the floor. They constructed a barricade of sorts out of trashcans and towels to help stem the flow of water into the office and the back line. After making sure the breakers to the front lights and major appliances were turned off, he shut out the remaining lights and locked the back door behind him.

The next morning, Sean was waiting for him. He was wet and disheveled and was wearing tall rubber boots.
"I'm very disappointed in you, Ricky," he said angrily. "Jane called me last night to tell me about the flooding, and that she told you to wait for her. But by the time she and I got here, you were long gone. We have spent the whole night trying to clean up this mess. No thanks to you!"
"But Jane told me to go home," Ricky said, surprised. "She said she had a headache and wasn't going to come in, and she told me to lock it up and go home."
"That's not true, and you know it," Sean said. "She said she told you to stay and help clean things up so we could open today, but what did you do? You high-tailed it out of here as fast as you could go."
"That's not true!" Ricky insisted. "I was going to stay and try to deal with it all, but she said not to."

Leaving Justiceville: A Life Behind

"Jane is not a liar, but apparently you are," Sean said coldly. "I obviously can't trust you like I thought I could. Now take this mop and start cleaning up the dining room."

Ricky worked hard all that day helping clean up the mess left by the storm. The business remained closed due to the flooding except for the drive-thru. Sean didn't speak to Ricky at all. The normally friendly man was exceptionally quiet and somber, even when Ricky or other employees tried to engage him in conversation.

Just before Ricky was to leave for the day, Sean handed him a piece of paper.

"I'm transferring you to the Watauga store starting tomorrow," he said briefly. "You'll be working there from now on."

Watauga was a small town located about ten miles away.

"Why?" Ricky frowned.

"Because they need the help," Sean told him. "So make sure you have all of your belongings together. You won't be coming back here anymore."

"But I only left last night because Jane said to," Ricky said. "Please, you have to believe me. I didn't want to leave, but she told me to, I swear."

"It doesn't matter," Ricky said impatiently. "You've been transferred to the Watauga store, and that's the end of it."

Ricky drove to Watauga that night and searched for an inconspicuous place to park his car/home. He

finally settled on a strip mall where a number of other cars were parked overnight.

The next day, he started his new job at the Taco Rio. His new coworkers eyed him curiously.

"You ain't no sixteen years old," one young man snorted. "You can't be more than eleven."

"I am too sixteen!" Ricky lied defiantly.

"How'd you get a car if you ain't sixteen?" another employee asked him.

"I am sixteen!"

"Let me see your driver's license," the youth demanded.

"Now, let Ricky alone," his new manager, a friendly older man with thinning gray hair, scolded the group surrounding Ricky. "He's one of us now, so you treat him good."

"Yeah, you guys," a young woman named Amy said firmly. She was a shift manager and therefore Ricky's boss. "Leave Ricky alone. You bother him, and you'll answer to me."

CHAPTER NINE

For the next few weeks, everything went along smoothly enough for Ricky. Since he was a hard worker and was glad to help his coworkers out whenever they needed it, they treated him well, especially Amy. She had a wicked sense of humor, and no topic was off limits to her. Ricky found himself laughing more with her than he ever had in his life. He even confided in her about his past, although he was wise enough not to tell her his real age.

One evening he and Amy were scheduled to close the store by themselves. With his experience at the other store, he needed very little instruction. He and Amy talked and laughed easily while they worked.

"You know, I think they pay girls less than boys here," she said confidentially.

"That's not fair," Ricky frowned. "Everyone should be paid the same. Unless they have more experience or have been here longer. But girls shouldn't be paid less than a guy if they're doing the same job."

"I agree," Amy said. "And even that bitch Teri gets more money than me, and I've been here longer."

Teri was another shift manager that few employees liked because of her chilly disposition and tendency to gossip.

"That's not fair," Ricky reiterated indignantly. "You should talk to the boss about that."

"I can't if I don't have proof," she said.

"Why don't you ask Teri?"

Leaving Justiceville: A Life Behind

"She would never tell me."

The two of them continued their tasks until the work was finished. As Amy started to close the office door, she noticed that the metal filing cabinet next to the desk was unlocked.

"Hey, look," she said to Ricky. "The cabinet's unlocked."

"So?"

"So go look at her file for me and tell me how much she makes."

"Am I allowed to do that?" Ricky asked doubtfully.

"Sure," she said. "Why not?"

"I didn't think we were supposed to look at stuff like that."

"I'm a manager," Amy reminded him. "And I'm giving you permission to look."

Ricky considered this for a moment.

"I wouldn't ask if it wasn't important," she said pleadingly.

"Why don't you go look?"

"Because it would be unethical for me to look at another shift manager's file," she said. "But it's okay for you to look if I give you permission."

Well, Ricky thought, that sounded reasonable. He couldn't get in trouble if a manager was telling him to do something. He was just following her orders, after all. And Amy was trustworthy, at least as trustworthy as anybody he had known so far. She wouldn't betray him or put him in harm's way, he was sure.

She told him which drawer held the personnel files and waited outside the office while he examined them. He finally found the one in question and opened it hesitantly.

"Here it is," he told her.

"How much does she make?" Amy asked eagerly, still never entering the office.

"A dollar ninety-five an hour," he told her.

"That bitch!" Amy exclaimed angrily. "That's ten cents more an hour than I make!"

She started pacing up and down the floor.

"I knew it! She's probably sleeping with the manager," she seethed. "That's why he always shows her preferential treatment. She gets whatever she wants, and now I know why."

"You don't know that he's sleeping with her," Ricky said. "Maybe she has more experience than you."

"Yeah, and I can tell you what she's experienced in!" Amy snapped. "Fucking the boss! Dammit, I'd quit if I didn't absolutely have to have this job."

Ricky replaced the file and closed the cabinet up. The two of them left the store, Ricky to sleep in his car and Amy to her apartment and live-in boyfriend.

The next morning, Amy was in the manager's office when Ricky came in to start his shift. He set to work getting the various machines and food ready for the busy day ahead of them. Amy came out of the office and avoided looking at him. She had a grave expression on her face.

Leaving Justiceville: A Life Behind

"What's wrong?" he asked her. "Did you talk to him about Teri making more than you?"

Before she could reply, the boss called sternly to Ricky to come into his office.

"Ricky, someone went through the filing cabinet last night. Amy says that she caught you in here last night looking at personal files of your coworkers," the man said. "Is that true?"

Ricky sighed resignedly. Here we go again, he thought with annoyance. Once again, he was going to be blamed for something that someone else had done. And of course, the boss was going to believe everyone but him. It was becoming the story of his life.

"Not exactly, sir," he said.

"What does that mean?" his boss frowned.

"I did look at one file," he said.

"Looking at other employee's files is strictly forbidden. Didn't you know that?"

"No, sir," Ricky said. "But I had permission."

"Who gave you permission?"

"Amy did."

The manager went to the door and called to Amy. She looked worried, her face drawn and pale.

"Ricky says you gave him permission to look at the other employee's files," he said to her. "Is that true?"

"No," Amy shook her head. "I told him that's not allowed."

"So you say you didn't give him permission, and he says you did," the manager said grimly. "One of you is lying."

Leaving Justiceville: A Life Behind

He sat back in his chair and folded his arms.
"We're going to sit here until you tell me the truth," he said sternly.
Amy glanced at Ricky and then quickly looked away. She was trembling, he noted. For some inexplicable reason, he felt a twinge of sympathy for her. It was true that she was throwing him under the bus, but he thought he understood what was happening. She knew she was in the wrong and would end up losing her job because of it, a job that she desperately needed. He sighed and took a deep breath, summoning his courage.
"It was me," he said tentatively. "Amy had nothing to do with it."
"Are you sure?" the manager asked him. He looked between the two of them suspiciously. "That doesn't sound like something you'd do on your own, Ricky."
"I wanted to see how much some of the others made," Ricky said.
"The only file that was disturbed was Teri's," the boss said wryly. "Why would you care what she makes an hour? She's a shift manager."
"I…I just wanted to know," Ricky replied hesitantly.
"Uh, huh," the manager said. His tone indicated he didn't believe him. He sighed. "Very well. Is that the story that you're both sticking to?"
Amy looked at Ricky who nodded ever so slightly back at her. She turned to her boss and nodded.
"Okay, then," the manager said. "My hands are tied in this situation. Ricky, I'm afraid I'm going to have

Leaving Justiceville: A Life Behind

to let you go. Pick up your things while I make out your check."
Ricky waited for Amy to step forward and admit her guilt, but she never did. He didn't really expect her to, but he had been hopeful nonetheless.

That night, Ricky lay in the back of his car and stared up at the roof with tears of anger and discouragement in his eyes. No matter what he did or how hard he tried, something or someone was always there to beat him down. One step forward and three steps back, and he was getting sick of it. He was determined to succeed, but still, a guy could only take so much. Now he was out of a job. And yet, he told himself consolingly, he was better off now than he had been six months ago. He was away from the abuse of his family and teachers, he owned his own car that was bought and paid for, and it may not have been an ideal place to live, but at least it was his and private and reasonably comfortable. So in spite of his setbacks, he was still making progress, if he looked at the long term picture.

A knock on his window startled him and he looked up in alarm. It was Amy. Warily he sat up, dried his eyes, and rolled down the window a few inches.
"What do you want?" he asked her sullenly.
"Can I talk to you?" she asked.
"I guess," he said.
"I'm really sorry about all of this," she said. "I never meant for this to happen."

Leaving Justiceville: A Life Behind

"You ratted me out and didn't think I'd get fired?" he said skeptically. "You knew what you were doing was wrong, but you did it anyway. You lied and you let me take the blame. I thought we were friends."
"We are friends," she said. She took a moment to peer around the interior of the small shabby car. "You really do live in your car, don't you?"
"I told you I do," he said. "I don't lie."
"I know, and I'm grateful to you for saving my job for me," she said earnestly. "I just want you to understand why I did what I did. I can't afford to lose this job."
"I can't either!"
"I know. So I talked to a guy from our church. He manages the Taco Bell in Bedford, and he says you can have a job there."
"Why would he hire me like that?" Ricky said doubtfully. "He doesn't even know me."
"I told him all about you and what a good worker you are," she said. "And I told him it was my fault that you got fired."
"Really?"
"You can start tomorrow," she said. "Do you know how to get to Bedford?"
The two discussed how to get to the small town that was located about ten miles away.
"Good luck with everything," she said.

The next morning, Ricky drove his Baja Bug to Bedford, where he met his new boss, a middle aged man named Jim.

Leaving Justiceville: A Life Behind

"Amy tells me you live in your car," Jim said. "Why's that?"
"I'm trying to save money for a place of my own," Ricky said.
The truth was that Ricky couldn't rent an apartment because of his age. Unlike his employers, apartment owners actually checked on things like age, credit history, and social security numbers. He'd learned that lesson the hard way after a potential landlord threatened to notify the authorities.
"I see," Jim said. "Well, we can't have that. I talked to a friend of mine that lives here in town, and he said you can stay with him and his family until you find a place of your own. He and his family are godly people; they'll be a good influence on you."
Ricky frowned at that. He didn't need anyone to be a good influence on him, and why did this man think that he did? All the 'godly' people he had ever known had been the worst examples a child could have! Most of them were no better than his parents as far as he was concerned.
"You can go to church with them," Jim went on. "A young man like yourself needs to be in church every Sunday."
Ricky nodded noncommittally.
"I'm okay staying in my car," he told his new boss. "It's very comfortable."
"Now, no employee of mine is going to live in a car," Jim said firmly. "I'll take you over there after work today. Now, let me show you what you'll be doing."

Leaving Justiceville: A Life Behind

Jim introduced Ricky to the Taylor family that evening at suppertime. There were Mr. and Mrs. Taylor and their three teenage children. Ricky shook each of their hands uncomfortably and then sat down at the dining room table with them. It was a nice home, spotlessly clean, but with no knickknacks or pictures on the white walls except for a cross hanging in every room. The furniture was plain and utilitarian. Mr. Taylor made them all hold hands while he said grace, a long and pious prayer in which he thanked God for their food and for the young heathen He had brought into their midst for them to save from the fiery pit of hell.

Seriously, Ricky thought? They don't even know me but have decided I'm an evil sinner. I thought Christians weren't supposed to judge people. Not that I've ever actually seen true Christianity in practice, of course, but in theory at least, Christians were supposed to be kind and loving and nonjudgmental.

Mrs. Taylor showed Ricky the sofa where he could sleep and then knelt down beside him to teach him how to say his nightly prayers. As he listened to her pray, he felt vaguely embarrassed for her. Did she really believe in this nonsense, he wondered, or was she merely continuing a tradition handed down to her from her parents and grandparents?

As for himself, he had found no reason to believe in any god or religion. They were all made up things designed to make people feel guilty and to take their money. If there was a god, he reasoned, why would he allow Ricky's parents and brothers and principal

to abuse him in such a horrific manner? Why hadn't he stopped it when he saw what was happening? Or if he really did exist, then he obviously didn't care. What about poverty and sickness and starvation? Why wasn't he fixing those things if he really cared? No, there was no reason to believe in a god. He'd do better to rely on himself if he wanted to get anywhere in his life.

After a few weeks of living with the Taylors, Ricky had just about reached the limit of his patience. There were constant prayers and Bible studies and church services, and they all seemed directed at him, pointing out just how evil and vile he was in the sight of God.

Still, it was a comfortable sofa to sleep on, and Mrs. Taylor was an excellent cook. Ricky wasn't accustomed to eating healthy, tasty meals, so he savored each morsel of delectable food. The other children in the family were well behaved, although not necessarily friendly with Ricky.

The job was going quite smoothly, he thought with satisfaction. His coworkers were generally friendly to him, and Jim seemed to be a manager with whom he could work well. All in all, his life felt like it was finally on track. He was enjoying his job, making decent money, saving it back for the future, and for once, he was eating a balanced diet. The Taylor family treated him well, as a whole. Their children more or less ignored him, which was fine with him. He had no desire to know these overly-sanctimonious

Leaving Justiceville: A Life Behind

young people who carried their Bibles with them all the time.

One day, the oldest son, a tall, homely boy named Caleb, walked into the restaurant carrying Ricky's duffel bag. He slammed it down on the counter, and Ricky looked up at him with surprise.
"There!" he said coldly. "Here's your shit! Now you stay away from my parents, and you get out of their house for good!"
"What?" he said, bewildered by his language and his tone. "What'd I do?"
"You're taking advantage of them!" he snapped. "And I'm putting a stop to it. So don't you come back there."
With that, he flounced out of the building without a backward glance. Ricky slowly picked up his duffel bag and turned to carry it dejectedly to the back of the restaurant. Jim was standing nearby with his arms folded and a scowl on his face.
"What did you do to make the Taylor's kick you out?" he demanded.
"I didn't do anything," Ricky insisted. "At least, nothing that I can think of. I don't know what he's talking about."
"Well, you must have done something, and it must have been pretty bad," Jim shook his head. "The Taylor's are the nicest people in the world. There's no one with more Christian love than them."
That was debatable, Ricky thought derisively. It was true that the Taylor's had given him a place to sleep

at night and provided him with free food once a day, but it had all come with a price. He had been forced to attend church services with them three times a week, listen to their long and pious prayers, attend the interminable Bible studies, and so on.

And instead of love, the only feeling he sensed from the family was judgment. Mrs. Taylor rarely missed an opportunity to tell him how grateful he should be that they had taken him in, and how much of an imposition his being there had been on them, especially her.

Ricky was to learn much later that a few weeks after being thrown out of the Taylor's house, Mr. Taylor had been arrested for embezzlement from the construction company where he served as chief financial officer. He also found out that the man was sentenced to twenty years for his crimes.

And so Ricky moved back into his car. Sometimes he would park it overnight at a local supermarket, and other times, he would drive to nearby Fort Worth where his father's parents lived. He would park along the street in front of their house. He didn't really know them since they had stopped speaking to their son after he stiffed them for three thousand dollars. Deed, of course, claimed they gave him the money as a gift. But it didn't matter to Ricky anyway because he had no intention of letting them know he was there.

Jim had apparently decided to judge Ricky too, because he stopped talking to him except for work

related issues for the next few weeks. He even went so far as to place Ricky on the opposite shift from himself. Ricky merely sighed resignedly and did his work well and without complaint.

One day Jim called him into the office and instructed him to sit down.

"Ricky, I just want to say I'm sorry about the past few weeks," Jim said. "I had no idea."

"Excuse me?" Ricky said with a puzzled frown.

"I didn't know," Jim said regretfully. "I hope you can forgive me."

"Uh, sure," Ricky said hesitantly.

"So I want you back on my shifts starting tomorrow," Jim told him with a fatherly smile. "And the past is water under the bridge. We'll just forget about everything. Sound good to you?"

"Yeah," Ricky said uncertainly. "That sounds good to me."

His relationship with Jim returned to the same comfortable manager/employee relationship that they had enjoyed before the whole Taylor debacle. However, for the rest of his days, Ricky would always wonder what it was that Jim didn't know or what he was sorry about.

One evening after work, Ricky was driving the Baja Bug to Fort Worth to sleep in front of his grandparents' house. He got on the expressway and pressed the accelerator, only to have the engine cough and sputter for a few seconds before it resumed its normal operation. He checked the gauges

Leaving Justiceville: A Life Behind

on the dashboard, but the only one that meant anything to him was the gas gauge. The steering seemed a little off to him as well, but he had no idea why. The car began slowing as he pressed harder on the gas, and it actually veered sharply to the left even as he steered to the right. Nervously, he guided it off onto the shoulder, where the engine gasped and popped one last time before it died with a loud bang and clouds of billowing gray smoke.

With a sigh, he got out and walked back to examine the exposed engine. It smelled strongly of gasoline, and as he watched, the whole engine compartment was suddenly enveloped in yellow and orange flames. In horror, he quickly extracted his stash of cash and other few belongings out of the vehicle before it was completely engulfed in fire.

Dammit, he thought! Now what the hell am I going to do? There went my transportation and my home in one fell swoop! I'm back to where I started, he thought ruefully. As always, life was doing its best to defeat him and make him quit trying. His young eyes filled with tears of hopelessness as he stood and watched everything he owned being destroyed.

After a few minutes of feeling sorry for himself, he dried his eyes and straightened his shoulders with determination.

Nice try, he thumbed his nose at the fates! You thought you could beat me down, but all you're doing is making my resolve even stronger. I will not give up, and you will not win!

Leaving Justiceville: A Life Behind

He picked up his things and started to walk along the highway. He was surprised, or perhaps he wasn't, that no one had stopped to help him. The cars continued to whiz by him as if their drivers hadn't noticed a burning automobile sitting on the shoulder of the road. That's because people don't care, he reminded himself. They were disgusting, selfish, loathsome creatures with no love or empathy in their hearts for anyone but themselves!

After walking for a few miles, he held out his thumb in an attempt to hitchhike a ride. It took a few hours and a number of rides to get back to town. He had the last driver drop him off at the Taco Bell. As he stood in the parking lot, trying to decide what to do next, he noticed the roofline of a nearby apartment complex. Well, that would probably be his best bet, at least for tonight.

Once again he settled himself in a secluded nook next to a metal grate that stayed warm from the steam that issued from it twenty-four hours a day. He missed his little car, rusty and beat up as it was, because it was the best – the only – home he had ever had. Living with his family could never be considered home, not with the beatings and other horrors he endured on a daily basis. At the most it was a shelter from the elements, but a home, definitely not.

He knew from experience that no landlord was going to rent to him, even if they believed him to be sixteen. His only option was to buy another car. Tomorrow he would have to walk to one of the used car lots in town and see what he could find.

Leaving Justiceville: A Life Behind

Ricky told Jim about his car being destroyed the next day, and he was properly sympathetic. A fellow employee overheard their conversation and mentioned that his father had an older car that he was wanting to sell. He offered to take Ricky home with him after their shift and let him look at it if he was interested. Ricky eagerly accepted, and the two drove across town. Before they left the restaurant, Jim took Ricky into his office.
"I'm sorry this happened," he said sincerely. "I'll tell you what I'm gonna do. To help you pay for a new car, I'm making you a shift manager starting tomorrow. That'll take you all the way up to $2.30 an hour. How does that sound?"
Ricky just stared at him, not believing his ears for a moment. Jim grinned at him and shook his hand. "Now, get out of here and go buy that car!"

Ricky's eyes opened wide and his jaw dropped as he gazed at the car sitting in the driveway of his friend's parents' pleasant split-level house. He stared in awe at the creamy white 1964 ½ Mustang coupe. Holy shit, he thought! That's a car he had wistfully yearned after whenever he saw one drive by his parents' house or sit in the parking lot of the Country Castle. He had never dreamed that one day he might own one!
A deal was soon struck for two thousand dollars. Ricky gave the man what cash he had and then signed a paper stating he would pay the remainder

out over the next six months. With a sense of elation that he had rarely experienced in his lifetime, Ricky shook the man's hand and then drove away in his new used car. Wow, he thought, it feels like a million dollars to drive a rich person's car! He would learn later that the car had been in an accident and was made up of mostly Bondo. It also had a rebuilt title, making it worth considerably less than what he had paid for it. But for now, he felt like the king of the world as he carefully drove it to the supermarket parking lot, where he had parked his Baja Bug on many occasions.

Just as Ricky was settling down to sleep for the night on the backseat of the car – an actual backseat with padding and everything! – he was startled by a knock on the passenger window. He looked up in alarm to see a uniformed police officer glaring down at him. "What the hell do you think you're doing?" the officer demanded.
Ricky sat up and awkwardly climbed out of the car. "I was just parking here for a while," Ricky said tentatively, avoiding the man's cold eye.
"You can't sleep in a car," the officer snapped. "Let me see your license and registration."
Ricky reluctantly handed him his fake driver's license and the registration form that showed the car belonging to his friend's father. The policeman examined the license for a moment and then handed it back to Ricky, apparently satisfied.

Leaving Justiceville: A Life Behind

"Who does this car belong to?" the officer demanded. "It's not yours."

"It is…it is mine," Ricky stammered nervously. "I just bought it. I, uh, haven't had time to take it to get the name changed over yet."

"Oh, yeah, I'll just bet," the man said skeptically. "I'm just gonna call this guy, and we'll see whether you're telling the truth or not. You just stay right where you are."

He climbed back into his Chevy Impala police car and picked up the microphone to the two-way radio. Ricky couldn't hear what was being said, but he watched the officer carefully. He also looked around discreetly, trying to figure out which way would be the best route of escape if he needed it.

After a few agonizing minutes, the officer alit from the car and walked back over to him. He grudgingly handed the registration paper back to Ricky.

"All right," he said gruffly. "I guess you were telling the truth. But I don't want to see you sleeping in your car here again. You go home and sleep there like a normal person."

"Yes, sir," Ricky said respectfully.

"You gotta home?" the officer's eyes narrowed. "You ain't living in this car, are you?"

"My parents live in Belwood," Ricky shrugged. "I was just resting before driving home all that way."

"Belwood ain't that far," the officer frowned. "You go on and get home now. Don't let me catch you here again. You got that?"

"Yes, sir."

Leaving Justiceville: A Life Behind

"Then go on," the policeman said.

Ricky was trembling as he climbed back into his car and drove away. Holy hell, that had been a close call! Everything in his life could have fallen apart if the officer had bothered to check out his phony driver's license. He would have been sent back to his parents and been forced to start all over again. He couldn't risk letting that happen. There was no way in hell that he would ever go back there! Maybe things weren't going that well for him, but at least his life was better now than it had been.

So now he needed to decide what he was going to do. The police would be watching for his car from now on, he realized, so he couldn't stay here in town. He considered the situation for a while, and then started the car and put it in gear. There was only one place that he could think of that was secluded enough to keep him safe from police and other prying eyes.

Leaving Justiceville: A Life Behind

CHAPTER TEN

Grapevine Lake was a reservoir located about ten miles from town, and about twenty miles northeast of Fort Worth. He had been there once with some coworkers, who insisted he come with them for a picnic outing. They said that since all he did was work, it was time he let loose and have some fun for a change, to be a normal sixteen year old. It was there that he had taken his first sip of vodka and gone skinny-dipping with the older boys. It had been a fun time for Ricky, and he had attempted to relax and enjoy himself. With his tortured past, however, he found that it didn't come naturally to him to have a good time.

He drove his car to the same secluded cove he and his coworkers had been to before. There was an overgrown path that led back into a small grove of pecan and bur oak trees. The copse of trees and bushes and tall grass was just dense enough to hide his car from view. He would be safe here, he thought with a sense of relief. No one would ever know he was here.

It was actually kind of nice, he thought as he lay down to sleep in the back seat. Quiet and peaceful, the sound of the lake water lapping against the nearby shore, the breeze rustling the trees. There were probably wild animals out there, he frowned, but as long as he stayed in the car, he was safe. Besides, he'd rather face a coyote than a police officer who had the authority to send him back to his parents.

Leaving Justiceville: A Life Behind

Things went along fairly uneventfully for Ricky over the next few years. He kept to himself as much as possible to avoid attracting the wrong kind of attention from his boss or coworkers. He continued to stay in his lakeside hiding place. It was by far the most secure place he had found thus far. Each morning he would take his soap and towel and washcloth to a spot hidden from view by a grouping of boulders and bathe. It was a chilly, uncomfortable bath, but he overcame that by telling himself it was invigorating. Might as well look at the bright side, he decided.

One day, a new coworker, a young woman named Sherry, told her boyfriend Brandon that Ricky was homeless and sleeping in his car at night.

"Is that true?" Brandon asked him with a disapproving look on his face.

"Uh, no," Ricky lied uneasily. "I found an apartment."

Just what I need, he thought. Another person to interfere with my life and my future.

"Then why is your stuff still in your car?" Sherry asked him.

"I don't know," Ricky shrugged. "I just haven't moved everything in yet, I guess."

"I don't think you really have a place," Sherry said.

"Why don't you come and stay with me?" Brandon offered. "You can pay my folks a little rent and share a room with me and my brother."

"No, thanks," Ricky shook his head. "Like I said, I've already got a place of my own."

Leaving Justiceville: A Life Behind

The last thing he wanted now was to stay with anyone else. It never worked out, and he ended up being the one getting hurt when they kicked him out. He wasn't going to go through that again.

At closing that night, Ricky climbed into his car and drove away. He noticed a set of headlights come on behind him and then follow him as he headed toward Grapevine Lake. Instantly, he became alert as he realized that someone, probably Sherry and Brandon, were following him. For the next few minutes, he led them on a circuitous route through town, just to see for sure if he truly was being pursued. The car stayed right with him, so he decided at last that he was going to have to lose them.

He turned onto a four lane divided highway that ran past the edge of town and revved the engine. His speed increased until he was driving at seventy miles an hour, the fastest he'd ever driven in his life. The car shook and shimmied alarmingly, but it held together.

There was a turn off coming up on the left that led onto a side road and a gas station, and Ricky made a decision. He would have to time it just right, he knew. He floored the accelerator and increased his speed even more. At the last moment he hit the brakes and turned the steering wheel sharply to the left. The car skidded and spun around until he was facing the opposite direction on the other side of the median. He instantly hit the gas again and headed down the side road. He looked in his rearview mirror and saw Brandon's car screech to a stop a hundred

feet past the turn off. It began to back up, and Ricky turned his lights off and pulled behind the gas station next to a pair of semis. As he watched, Brandon and Sherry headed down the side road as fast as they could go. With a sense of relief, he pulled back onto the divided highway and drove to Grapevine Lake.

It was Ricky's sixteenth birthday. He worked a double shift as he often did. Just like all of his birthdays so far, there was no cake, no celebration, no one singing 'Happy Birthday'. There were no gifts and no one wishing him well.

Ricky was accustomed to his birthdays being just another day, and he wasn't expecting anything from anyone. Yet for some reason, the fact that his sixteenth birthday was being ignored by the entire world was hurtful to him. This was supposed to be a special occasion, one that comes along only once in a lifetime. He should be surrounded by loving family and affectionate friends and inundated with fierce hugs and kisses and thoughtful presents.

But there was nothing, he thought morosely. No one cared about him. As it turned out, the only person to wish him a happy birthday was the smiling lady at the DMV, where he went after work to get a real driver's license. That was his gift to himself, he decided: a genuine driver's license that no one could take away from him.

That night as he parked in the grove at the lake, he ate some peanut butter crackers and potato chips for supper and downed them with a warm Dr. Pepper. As

Leaving Justiceville: A Life Behind

a special treat, he had bought himself a couple of Hostess cupcakes for dessert.

Very quietly he sang 'Happy Birthday' to himself and then pretended to blow out the nonexistent candles on the cupcakes. A tear rolled down his cheek, and he brushed it aside impatiently. He was angry with himself for allowing such a ridiculous display of emotion over something that didn't really matter.

But maybe it did matter, he told himself. He was a human being, after all, and he had feelings, even if he kept them buried deep down inside. He was worthwhile, and he deserved to be happy.

But he was lonely, so lonely. Most of the time, he was content, as long as he focused on work and didn't think about it too much. But tonight he couldn't stop thinking about his life, such as it was. He wanted someone to love him, someone he could love and count on, but he knew that would most likely never happen. He would have to spend the rest of his life alone, working a dead end job, no friends, no future, no nothing except his car and few articles of clothing.

What was the point of living like that, he wondered sadly? A lifetime of loneliness and drudgery, making just enough money to survive, never having nice things or someone with whom to share them.

He cried himself to sleep, feeling lower than he ever had before. He realized he was being self-indulgent, but dammit, when were things going to get better? He was beginning to believe that his life would never be

more than this. Hiding out in his car surrounded by all of his few worldly possessions, no friends or family to care for him. It was all becoming just too discouraging.

For the first time in his life, Ricky entertained the thought of ending it all. If this was as good as life was going to get, what was the point in going on? Why not just take matters into his own hands and put a stop to all the pain and loneliness he had endured since he was born?

As he was contemplating these dark ideas, a light flashed in through the window followed by a sharp knock on the glass. He jumped in alarm.

"Come out of there!" a male voice said angrily. Hesitantly, Ricky unlocked the door and climbed out of the car to come face to face with a scowling man in a Grapevine Lake security uniform.

"What the hell are you doing?" the man demanded.

"Nothing," Ricky said, shielding his eyes from the flashlight that the officer was shining in his face. "I'm not hurting anything."

"Well, maybe you are, and maybe you ain't," the security man said. "But I'm the security for the lake, so I'm the law around here." His chest puffed out with self-importance. "What I say goes. You got that, punk?"

He shone his light into the car.

"Why's all your stuff in here?" He turned back to Ricky suspiciously. "Are you living in this car?"

"No," Ricky said, avoiding his eye. "I was just taking a nap."

Leaving Justiceville: A Life Behind

"Well, you go on and take a nap somewhere else. You get away from the lake."
"Why?" Ricky said defiantly. "I've got a right to be here. This is public property."
"You ain't got no right to be here after dark like this," the man said angrily. "Now you go on and get outa here!"
Ricky started to get back into the car, but the officer held him roughly by his arm.
"I'll be watching for you from now on," he said. "Don't you come back here."
"I can come back here anytime I want!" Ricky retorted angrily. "You got no right to keep me away from public property."
The man shook him harshly and slapped him a couple of times across the face. An anger such as Ricky had known only a few times in his life filled him, and he decided, foolishly, to fight back against this cocky son of a bitch. He wrenched his arm free and began hitting and kicking the bigger man with all of his strength. The two struggled against each other until Ricky stopped to catch his breath. The older man staggered a bit, and Ricky saw his chance. He gathered his strength and, bending down, he ran at the security guard and hit him squarely in the gut with his shoulder. He knocked him backwards and the man went rolling head over heels down the short hill and into the lake. Ricky caught himself and watched the man fall off the two foot embankment and into the shallow water. Seizing his opportunity, Ricky ran for his car and sped away, spinning his

tires in the grass and gravel, leaving the angry man sputtering and coughing while he emptied the lake water from his hat.

Brandon, Sherry's boyfriend, continued to insist that Ricky come and stay with his family. They lived in Lake Worth, Texas, a moderately sized town that was a suburb of Dallas/Fort Worth. It was about forty-five minutes from town. Brandon's father was a commercial pilot, and he and his wife owned some sort of successful business in town. They lived in a small but elegant home in an upper class neighborhood.
Ricky was puzzled at his persistence, and one day he asked him about it.
"I just don't want to see a nice guy like you living in your car," Brandon said. "Besides, I think you and my younger brother would get along just fine. I'm going to be leaving soon, and he'll be there all alone with my folks. He'll be lost without me there, and you could help fill the gap for him."
A few months later, Ricky reluctantly agreed to stay with Brandon and his family, if only to stop the constant nagging. His boss, Jim, suggested that Ricky go to work in the Lake Worth Taco Bell so he didn't have to make that long drive twice a day, especially after working his typical double shifts. He told Ricky he would take care of the transfer and that he could start there the next day.

Leaving Justiceville: A Life Behind

"But I don't want to change stores," Ricky protested. "I want to stay here. Maybe I'll just tell Brandon I can't come there because the drive is too far."
"Now, Ricky, Brandon's father is a wealthy man with a lot of important connections," Jim told him. "I think this could be a good thing for you. You don't want to work at Taco Bell for the rest of your life, do you?"
"No, sir," Ricky admitted hesitantly.
"Well, Brandon's dad might be able to help with your future," Jim said firmly. "So I want you to do this."

Ricky was introduced to Mr. and Mrs. Evans, a middle-aged couple who were wearing matching tennis outfits with sweaters tied around their necks.
"It's nice to meet you," Mrs. Evans said, shaking his hand politely.
Ricky couldn't help but notice how she eyed him somewhat disapprovingly up and down.
"We're delighted you're going to be staying with us," Mr. Evans said, glancing briefly at his wife.
"Brandon and Brent will get you settled in. We're off to the club, so we'll see you later."
Brandon showed Ricky to the bedroom he shared with his brother. Ricky looked with surprise at the mattress lying on the floor between the matching twin beds. Brandon noticed this and chuckled apologetically.
"Sorry," he said. "Mother insisted that we keep the guest room for actual guests."
He thought about how that must sound and amended his words. "I mean, she and Dad entertain a lot, and

we have family that comes for visits frequently, so she thought you would be satisfied with a mattress on the floor, you know, since you've been sleeping in your car and all."

He thought again.

"I'm sorry, that didn't come out right," he said with a grin. "It's just that we figured anywhere would be better than your car. Am I right?"

"Uh, yes, that's right," Ricky frowned.

"At least you'll be sleeping on an actual bed," Brandon said. "Well, at least it's a mattress."

His younger brother Brent came into the room and eyed Ricky haughtily for a moment before speaking.

"So this is him?" he said to Brandon.

"Brent, this is Ricky," Brandon said. "He worked with Sherry for a while, and she speaks very highly of him."

"Hi," Ricky said warily.

"So you're originally from Justiceville?" Brent said disdainfully. "That place is nothing but a dump. All the people there are trash."

"I suppose," Ricky shrugged. "That's why I left."

Okay, this guy was a real snob, as were apparently the rest of the family.

"Brent, you can't say things like that," Brandon frowned. "There might be nice people there. Just because they're all poor doesn't mean that they're all trash; some of them might be okay."

Leaving Justiceville: A Life Behind

That night, Ricky lay on the mattress between the twin beds. It was just him and Brent for now, since Brandon was out on a date with Sherry.
"Are you really twenty?" Brent asked him. "You don't look that old."
"Who said I'm twenty?"
"Sherry looked at your file at work and figured out that you must be about twenty by now since you were sixteen when you started working."
"Uh, yeah, that's right," Ricky lied. Actually he was soon going to be seventeen, but he saw no reason for this insolent young man to know that.
"Then why are you staying here? Why not get your own place?"
"I, uh, was going to," Ricky thought quickly. "But Brandon kept insisting that I come here. He thought you and I would be good friends."
"He did?" Brent sounded surprised. "I wonder why. Do you play tennis or racquet ball?"
"No," Ricky admitted. "But I could learn, if you want to teach me."
"I have plenty of friends, you know," Brent said abruptly. "I don't need my brother to find friends for me."
"I know," Ricky said. "I think he was just trying to help me out."
"Oh," Brent sounded slightly appeased. "Well, tomorrow I'll take you to the club and we'll see if you're any good at tennis."

Leaving Justiceville: A Life Behind

Ricky accompanied Brent to the country club the next day. He had only his regular clothes to wear, so Brent took him into the pro store there and bought him some tennis clothes. Ricky knew it had nothing to do with being nice but more to do with Brent being embarrassed by his appearance.

The two played tennis for a few hours, and Ricky quickly took to the game. He was unused to sports or competing against someone since he had never had the opportunity for such activities in his life. But he found that he was actually having fun. Brent even complimented him on his game, and the two talked companionably while they played and then ate lunch in the club dining room.

"Just put it on Dad's account," Brent signed the check and handed it back to the waiter.

Ricky couldn't help but be impressed by such largesse, as well as the opulent surroundings of the country club. Very classy, he thought. I've seen places like this on television, but I didn't think they existed in real life.

The next several months went by, and Ricky found himself beginning to like the Evans family. Oh, sure, they were definitely snobs, a bit racist and anti-Semitic, but otherwise they were decent people, and they treated him with respect and consideration. Mr. and Mrs. Evans were rarely home unless they were entertaining, and Brandon spent most of his time with Sherry, so it was just Brent and Ricky most of the time. Ricky was beginning to see why Brandon

Leaving Justiceville: A Life Behind

wanted him here for Brent. Otherwise, the younger brother would have been home mostly by himself. In spite of Brent's assertion that he had lots of friends, Ricky had yet to encounter any of them. Also, Mrs. Evans had insisted that the guest room be kept available for guests, but there had not been a single visitor since he had been here. He suspected she just didn't want a dirty young Taco Bell employee soiling her fancy house any more than absolutely necessary. Ricky had to admit that it was nice living in a pleasant home for a change, with clean sheets and towels and good food. It still didn't feel like home to him, of course, but it was comfortable, and he felt like he and Brent were becoming friends. The two of them talked frequently, mostly at night when the light was out and they were in their beds, or rather when Brent was in his bed and Ricky was on his mattress. Brent was kind of screwed up, Ricky decided. He was spoiled and entitled, and he definitely thought he was better than anybody else, but he was probably no more messed up than everyone else. Everyone had issues, Ricky was beginning to realize, some more so than others.

Mr. Evans was putting a lot of pressure on Brent to make straight A's at school so that he would be accepted at an Ivy League university somewhere out east. Brent struggled with his studies, especially math, and Ricky was glad to help him out. He didn't know enough about geography or history to be of much assistance, but the math classes that Brent was taking were like child's play to Ricky. It was thanks

to Ricky that Brent's midterm report card contained all A's, a fact which pleased Mr. Evans to no end. Naturally, Brent took all the credit for his success without mentioning Ricky's help, but Ricky didn't care. He wasn't helping him because he expected anything out of it.

Brandon and Sherry became engaged and planned to marry at Christmas time. They had a big fancy wedding all arranged at the impressive Episcopal church in Hurst. All the elite citizens of Hurst and the surrounding communities were invited, with an elegant reception to be held at the country club afterwards. Brent was to serve as best man to his brother. Ricky watched him being fitted for his tuxedo.
"Wow, that looks really nice," he said admiringly. "You look handsome."
Brent was a good-looking young man, he thought. Not really his type, but still quite attractive. The two had spent a lot of time playing tennis and racquet ball at the club, and Ricky had admired his physique more than once in the locker room. He usually kept his back toward Brent in case he got an erection, which he seemed to have little control over. He certainly didn't want him to know that he was gay. Brent had made more than one derisive comment over the last year about gay people, or 'queers', as he called them. Ricky had held his tongue, of course, and made himself bite back any sort of retort. Usually he would merely change the subject to some innocuous topic.

Leaving Justiceville: A Life Behind

Brent looked up at him sharply.
"What'd you say?" he said suspiciously.
"Just that you look nice," Ricky said, surprised at his friend's reaction. "I've never seen you in a tuxedo before. I've never seen anyone in a tuxedo before."
"You don't give other guys compliments like that, Ricky," Brent frowned. "Unless you're queer."
"I'm not queer," Ricky said, avoiding his eye.
"You don't go out with girls," Brent said thoughtfully. "In fact, I've never seen you with a girl since you've been living here."
"I work all the time," Ricky said. "When would I have time to hang around with a girl? Besides, I've never seen you with one, either."
"Are you trying to call me a fag?" Brent clenched his fists in anger, his eyes narrowed.
"No, of course not," Ricky said hastily. "But just because I don't date doesn't mean I'm gay, just like it doesn't mean you're gay, either."
"I'm focusing all my attention on school," Brent insisted. "You have no idea the pressure I'm under from Dad to get into a good college."
"I know," Ricky said. "I understand the situation. I'm not accusing you of anything."
"You'd better not be," Brent said. "Because I'm straight, always have been, always will be."

From that time until the wedding, which was held a few weeks later, Ricky noticed a difference in Brent. He was more aloof and standoffish, and often times

Leaving Justiceville: A Life Behind

Ricky would glance in his direction only to find Brent scowling at him.
He didn't need to worry, Ricky thought wryly, because he wasn't the least bit interested in him. Brent was attractive, but he was too spoiled and self-centered to even consider as a potential boyfriend. Even as young and naïve as Ricky was, he sensed that there was more to Brent's protestations regarding his sexuality than met the eye; he seemed much too anxious to assert his heterosexuality. Whenever he spoke to Ricky now, which was less and less often these days, he talked about different girls at his school. He mentioned how pretty they were and that if he wasn't concentrating so hard on his studies, he would definitely be having sex with all of them.

The night of the wedding arrived, and Ricky was expected to help the country club staff set up chairs and tables for the reception. He suspected it was because of Brent that he hadn't been invited to the wedding. Either that or Mr. and Mrs. Evans were embarrassed by his shabby clothes and appearance. It was one thing for them to take in a pitiful charity case, but it was another to invite that charity case to an important social event for all their society friends to see.
When it came time for the reception, Ricky worked in the kitchen to help prepare the food, or behind the bar, assisting the bartender in making drinks, pouring champagne and wine, and cleaning glasses.

Leaving Justiceville: A Life Behind

He watched the guests as they danced and laughed and drank. They were all dressed so elegantly in suits and party dresses, with perfect hair and makeup and smiles. None of them made eye contact with him, he noticed. It was as if he wasn't there, even when he personally handed someone a champagne flute or a napkin. He understood that his appearance wasn't as grand as that of the snobbish partiers, and that it made them happier to consider him invisible or as an inferior being unworthy of their attention.

Once he had been relieved of his duties, Ricky spent the rest of the evening out on the patio, looking in at the revelers with envy. What must it be like to be able to afford to dress nicely, drive these expensive automobiles in the parking lot, to laugh and socialize so gaily with their many friends? All of these people were so different from all the people he had known all of his life, in that they were well dressed and classy. Even so, they were similar to his parents and teachers and ministers in the way they looked down on him and treated him as if he didn't matter.

But he did matter, dammit! He was as good as anyone else, regardless of how he dressed or what he did for a living. All of his life, it had been drilled into him that he was a worthless piece of garbage, but he knew in his heart that that wasn't true. No one was better than anyone else. Everyone had the potential to make something of themselves, even his abhorrent and vindictive parents, his abusive brothers, or anyone else. Unfortunately, most of them made no

effort to make something of themselves; they were far too lazy.

But not him! He was going to be someone. In fact, he already was someone, even if he wasn't rich or refined like these folks. But someday, he promised himself, someday…

Immediately after the reception, Mr. and Mrs. Evans loaded up their Cadillac to drive Brandon's grandparents back to Florida. Ricky caught a ride back to the Evans home with one of the busboys from the country club. The Evans's had taken him to the country club earlier that afternoon so he could help prepare for the reception.

Brent was nowhere to be found. He had ignored Ricky all evening except to glare at him occasionally while he danced with some of the teenage girls in attendance. Sometimes he and his partner would purposely dance near the bar to catch Ricky's attention. Yep, Ricky thought, Brent was trying to prove something to him, ostensibly that he was attracted to women. It seemed odd to him that Brent would work so hard to demonstrate it to him, but perhaps he was attempting to convince himself he was straight as well. He needn't have wasted his time; it didn't matter to Ricky one way or another if Brent was straight or gay.

The young man who gave Ricky a ride dropped him off and drove away. Ricky walked into the house and stopped, startled to see Brent and another young man waiting for him in the living room. Their stance was

wide, their arms crossed, and they each wore a determined look on their faces.

"Hey," Ricky said uncertainly, eying the two carefully. "Something wrong?"

"I'll say something's wrong!" Brent snapped. "You've been here long enough, and it's time for you to get the hell out of here."

"What'd I do?" Ricky frowned.

"You're tearing Brent's family apart, that's what you did!" the other youth said coldly. "So you're leaving here tonight."

"I haven't hurt anyone," Ricky protested.

"You're a fag," Brent said. "I've seen how you look at me, how you watch me. You want to have sex with me, and I can't have you around here."

"I don't want to have sex with you," Ricky said. "And I'm not gay."

"You've disrupted the Evans's long enough," the other boy said. "Brent wants you out of here, so you're going to go."

"Who are you?" Ricky frowned at him.

"I'm a friend of Brent's," the youth said. He stepped forward menacingly. "And I'm the quarterback on the football team."

"So?" Ricky shrugged, not impressed.

"So what I say goes," the young man said. "I'm here to make sure you don't give Brent any trouble or try to fuck him."

"Are you kidding me?" Ricky said incredulously. "I'm not going to try anything with him. I'm not gay.

Leaving Justiceville: A Life Behind

I've lived here for months now and never done anything to him."
"He says you're a queer, and we don't want no queers anywhere around us."
"Well, I hate to tell you this, but there's 'queers' everywhere. You're around them everyday whether you know it or not," Ricky retorted "That just shows how stupid you are."
With those words, the other two boys were suddenly upon him with their fists. The football player alone easily outweighed Ricky, and it was no contest with two against one. The two youths tossed a bloody and beaten Ricky out on the front lawn. Brent threw his duffel bag out the door after him.
"And stay out, fag!" he shouted before slamming the front door.

Ricky slept in his car parked behind a stack of wood at the lumberyard, nursing his wounds and bloody nose. He moved his sore jaw carefully and rubbed his bruised belly. He had fought back against his attackers, but their assault on him had been brutal and unfair.
Of course, that wasn't anything new to Ricky. He had been forced to defend himself from unfair attacks all of his life. He was always outweighed and outmatched in those battles against his brothers and parents and bullies at school.
He had supposed that those days were behind him now that he was almost an adult, but apparently he had been wrong. Clearly there were always going to

Leaving Justiceville: A Life Behind

be bullies, people who were determined to beat him down, and battles to be fought.

On Monday morning, Ricky kept to himself as much as possible, speaking to the other employees only when necessary.
"What happened to you?" a co-manager named Dianna asked him during a lull in business. The two of them were working the cash registers. "You've got a black eye and you haven't said two words all day."
"Nothing happened," Ricky shrugged. "I...I ran into a door."
"Then how'd you get those bruises?" she pointed at his arms and jaw.
"I don't know," Ricky said vaguely, avoiding eye contact with her.
"Hmm," she studied him thoughtfully. "Did you get into a fight at Sherry's wedding?"
"I didn't go to the wedding," he said. "I wasn't invited."
"Did Brent do that to you?" she asked. "That bastard!"
"It wasn't just him," Ricky said in a low voice, looking around to make sure no one could overhear. "He had some football player guy there when he kicked me out of their house."
"The two of them beat you up?" she said indignantly. "Just wait until I tell Sherry!"
"No, you can't tell anyone," he said.
"But why did they beat you up and kick you out?"

"They said I was causing problems for their family," Ricky shrugged.
"You weren't causing any problems," Dianna scowled. She hesitated a moment. "Is it because you're gay?"
"I'm not gay!" he hissed at her. "And you can't ever tell anyone that!"
"It's okay, Ricky," she said reassuringly. "I'm not going to tell anyone. And it's fine with me if you're gay."
Her face lit up as an idea occurred to her.
"Hey, why don't you come live with us?" she asked. "We're looking for a roommate. There's this wonderful apartment I'm just dying to rent. It's two bedrooms, but there's a loft that could be a third bedroom. You could have that."
"You want me to come live with you and your brother?" he said doubtfully. "Thanks, but I think I'll just stay in my car."
"You can't live in that car," she said.
"Sure, I can," he shrugged. "I've lived in my cars for years and gotten along just fine."
"But there's no bathroom or shower or kitchen," she said. "No where to wash your clothes."
"So? I clean up here, eat my meals here, and rinse my clothes out in the mop sink at night. It's no big deal. I'm used to it."
"Well, at least come and meet Dennis," she suggested. "You and he would get along well."
"I don't know…" Ricky said uneasily.

Leaving Justiceville: A Life Behind

He knew exactly how this whole scenario would play out. He would move in with this brother and sister, and everything would be fine at first. But eventually something would happen – either he or they would do something the other disapproved of, and he would be asked to leave. Why even put himself in that situation again? It was always the same story. He was better off depending on himself and no one else, as he had done pretty much most of his life.
"You're coming home with me tonight," Dianna said firmly. "You can at least sleep on the couch until you decide to move in with us."

"Dennis, this is Ricky," Dianna introduced them.
"How old are you, Ricky?" Dennis shook his hand and held on to it.
He was a tall man, approximately twenty-four years old, with light brown hair and glasses. Very attractive, Ricky thought.
"I'm, uh, twenty," Ricky lied.
"Isn't he adorable?" Dianna gushed to her brother.
"Dianna," Ricky frowned, his face turning red.
No one had ever said those words about him, and he found the compliment embarrassing.
"He's blushing," Dennis grinned at her. "And yes, he's very cute."
"You see, I knew you'd hit it off," Dianna said, pleased.

Ricky slept on the sofa that night and again the next few nights. Dianna and Dennis seemed very friendly,

and the three of them got along well. Ricky noticed Dennis staring at him frequently, and he found the attention a bit disconcerting. After all, the only sexual attention that had ever been paid to him had come from his brothers and uncle, his principal, and a few other adults in his life. None of it had been welcomed, and in the case of his brothers and uncle, they had actually used his body for their own selfish and incestuous pleasure. In every instance, he had been taken advantage of by people he should have been able to trust, which obviously he couldn't. As a result, he had a distrust of men in general.

However, Dennis was different, he decided. He wasn't forcing anything, and it seemed as though his desire to be with Ricky was because he liked him and was truly attracted to him. Of course, it could also be that he was a horny twenty-four year old who just wanted to get off with anyone that was willing. After all, that's the way all men were, weren't they?

One evening, Dennis took Ricky into Fort Worth to a triple-x rated drive-in theater. Ricky was unfamiliar with pornography of any kind and was startled when he looked up at the huge outdoor screen to see nude men and women, obviously being intimate with one another.

"What do you think?" Dennis grinned at him. "You ever seen an adult movie before?"

"No," Ricky said, his eyes wide.

"Well, just sit back and enjoy it," Dennis said.

He leaned back in the seat and spread his legs wide. Ricky observed this for a moment and then

awkwardly did the same thing. He stared up at the movie and was so engrossed in what the figures on the screen were doing that he barely noticed when Dennis's hand drifted over and settled on his thigh, next to his crotch.

He looked down and gulped. This is awkward, he thought. What the hell am I supposed to do now? He cleared his throat and continued to focus his attention upward as he tried to calm his breathing and stop himself from trembling. Dennis's hand remained there until the movie ended and it was time to go.

Leaving Justiceville: A Life Behind

CHAPTER ELEVEN

Dennis would sit next to Ricky on the sofa while they and his sister ate a pizza and watched television. He would lean up against him and rub his arm or leg whenever Dianna's attention was focused elsewhere, which was most of the time, since she was usually on the phone with her boyfriend. Ricky had to admit that he enjoyed the physical contact with this nice looking man.
On the third day of staying with Dianna and Dennis, the two approached him with determined looks on their faces.
"Are you ready to move in with us?" Dianna asked him.
"Well…I'm not sure…" Ricky hesitated.
"You have to," she said. "I already rented that apartment."
"Why did you do that?" Ricky frowned. "I didn't tell you my decision yet."
"Someone else wanted it, and I couldn't let it get away," she explained. "So it's all settled. The three of us are moving in together."

The next weekend, Ricky and Dennis moved furniture and boxes across town to the new apartment, while Dianna packed up their belongings. He bought himself a sleeping bag and arranged it and his few other belongings up in the small loft that overlooked the living room.

Leaving Justiceville: A Life Behind

To help pay the rent, Ricky took a second full time daytime job at Church's Fried Chicken while he continued to work forty hours a week at Taco Bell. It was exhausting work, but that didn't bother him; he was used to hard labor and long hours. At least he was living in a real apartment with friends who he felt he could trust. It was nice to be around people who were indifferent to his sexuality, something that was still fairly new to Ricky. The two of them could watch a movie and argue over which actor was better looking.

Dennis and Dianna treated him as an equal, another aspect of this situation to which Ricky was unaccustomed. They all shared in the cleaning and cooking, and Ricky didn't have to ask permission to drink a Coke or eat a cookie. He felt like a real adult, and it seemed as if his future was looking a bit brighter.

One night, Dianna had a date with her on again-off again beau. Ricky and Dennis sat down on the couch with a bowl of popcorn to watch some of the popular sitcoms on television. Since Dianna wasn't there, Dennis sat down right up against Ricky. Ricky shivered and tingled with pleasure at the touch of this older man. At one point, Dennis stretched and yawned and leisurely placed an arm around Ricky's shoulders.

"Is this okay?" he said tentatively.

"Uh, um, sure," Ricky said nervously, trying in vain to sound nonchalant. "It's fine."

"Good," Dennis said. He reached over with his other hand and rubbed Ricky's arm. "You're a good-looking guy, you know that?"
"No," Ricky said honestly. "You and Dianna are the first people to ever tell me that."
"Seriously?" Dennis frowned. "That's hard to believe, because you are totally adorable."
"I don't think so," Ricky said. "But you…you're really good-looking. Way better looking than me."
"Now, that's not true at all," Dennis shook his head. "I think you're totally hot."
"You do?" Ricky gulped.
"You know, we're both guys, we're both over eighteen," Dennis said. "If we're attracted to each other, there's no reason we can't…be together if we want to."
"I guess so," Ricky said hesitantly. "But I thought you were straight."
"I am," Dennis shrugged. He stood up and pulled Ricky up to stand next to him. A moment later, he bent his head down and gave Ricky a gentle kiss. "Come on. Let's go into my bedroom."
"What about Dianna?" Ricky said worriedly.
"What about her?" Dennis said. "She's not here, and she doesn't need to know who I sleep with."
"But we're all friends," Ricky said.
"So? You and I can be extra special friends."
He led Ricky to his room and closed the door. He quickly stripped out of his clothes and stood before Ricky naked. Soon the two of them were lying on the bed making passionate love to one another. When

Leaving Justiceville: A Life Behind

Dennis lay on top of him and entered him slowly and carefully, Ricky closed his eyes and forced away the memory of being raped by his brothers and others. It took some effort, but he was finally able to push them aside and allow himself to enjoy the incredible sensations his body was experiencing. When they were done, Dennis rolled onto his back, panting and sweaty.
"You'd better go back to the loft," he said. "I've got to get some sleep. Early day tomorrow, you know." Something in his tone made Ricky suddenly feel cheap and rather dirty. He had enjoyed his intimacy with Dennis and thought for the first time in his life that sex could actually be a wonderful, beautiful thing. But it seemed now that Dennis had merely used his body like all the other times in his life, and was casting him aside once he had gotten off.
"Uh, sure," Ricky said. He got up and gathered his things together.
"There's no need to tell Dianna about this," Dennis told him as he opened the door. "I don't want anyone to know what we did."
Ricky's face turned red with humiliation, and he nodded silently before closing the door behind him.

The months passed, with Ricky working eighty hours a week between his two jobs. Even so, he found it difficult to make ends meet. Dennis had a very good paying job at Bell Helicopter, a factory not far from home, and he paid most of his sister's rent and share of the bills. She was still working at Taco Bell, and

most of her income went to clothes or buying gifts for her boyfriend.

Dennis invited Ricky into his room at every opportunity, but only when Dianna was out. He continued to insist that no one know that the two of them had engaged in sex. Not that Ricky was going to tell anyone anyway. Who would he tell? Not Dianna, obviously, or his bosses or coworkers, and he had no other friends with whom to talk. It was a secret he was perfectly content keeping to himself. He enjoyed the physical connection he had with Dennis. Because they were friends, and it was a mutual attraction for a change, he found that there was an emotional aspect to it that he had never before experienced, this bonding with another man.

When they were done with their tryst, Dennis would invariably tell him to go back to his room, citing an early morning the next day. Ricky tried not to take it personally, but it still felt like a rejection to him. Dennis was all affectionate and passionate while they were being intimate, but as soon as it was over, he seemed to shut down emotionally.

One morning, Ricky showered and prepared for work. As he was dressing, he noticed that his wallet was not in his pants pocket. He searched his loft room in vain for a few minutes and then descended the steep staircase to the living room. Dianna was standing at the kitchen sink.

"There's your wallet," she pointed to the small wooden kitchen table.

Leaving Justiceville: A Life Behind

"Oh, good," Ricky said, putting the small case into the back pocket of his work pants. "Where was it?"
"I found it in Dennis's room," she frowned. "How'd it get in there?"
Dennis came into the room at that moment and put two pieces of toast in the toaster.
"What are you guys talking about?" he asked.
"I was asking Ricky how his wallet came to be in your room," Dianna said.
"His wallet was in my room?" he frowned as well. He avoided Ricky's eye for a moment and then turned to him. "What was your wallet doing in my room?"
He gave him a meaningful look so that his sister couldn't see.
"I, uh…I did laundry last night," Ricky said hesitantly, thinking fast. "Maybe I dropped it there when I hung Dennis's shirts in his closet."
"What, are you doing his laundry now?" Diana said. Her gaze moved back and forth between the two of them suspiciously.
"Well, no, er, I must have washed them by mistake," Ricky said.
"I don't want you in my room," Dennis scowled at him, looking at his sister out of the corner of his eye. "You just stay out of there." He turned to his sister distrustfully. "And what were you doing in my room?"
"I went in to give you back the money that I borrowed," she said. "I put the cash on your dresser."

"Oh," he said, his expression clearing. "Well, I'm imposing a new rule. From now on, no one goes into my room, ever."

Dianna studied him and Ricky thoughtfully for a moment and then nodded agreeably.

"Sure," Ricky shrugged indifferently. "From now on, we stay out of each other's rooms."

Okay, he decided, that's enough. He wasn't going to be Dennis's dirty little secret any more. Of course, he realized, he shouldn't be having sex with a twenty-four year old man while he was only seventeen, but that was beside the point. For all intents and purposes, he was twenty years old; he'd been a grown up most of his life. For some reason, Dennis was ashamed of what they were doing, or ashamed of him, or had some sort of issue with the situation. Clearly he didn't want anyone, especially his sister, to know he was gay. But that still didn't explain why he insisted that Ricky leave his bed after their times together.

That night, Dennis invited Ricky into his room as soon as his sister left for her date.

"No thanks," Ricky said. "I'm just going to go up in my room to read."

"Come on," Dennis grinned enticingly. "Don't you want to…you know?"

"No, I don't think so," Ricky said.

"Why not?" Dennis's smile faded.

"Because I've got too much self-respect to let you use me to get off with. Find yourself someone else. Besides, I'm not allowed in your room, remember?"

Leaving Justiceville: A Life Behind

"Is this because of what I said this morning?" Dennis said. "I didn't mean that I didn't want to have sex with you."
"No, I know you want to have sex with me as long as it's a secret," Ricky said dryly.
"What you and I do together is no one's business but ours."
"Yeah, but you're ashamed of it," Ricky said.
"You're ashamed of me. So I'm not interested anymore."
"I'm not ashamed," Dennis said. "I'm not ashamed of anything!"
"If you're not ashamed, why won't you let me spend the night with you?" Ricky demanded. "Why do you kick me out of your bed as soon as we're done fucking?"
"You want to stay in my room all night?" Dennis shrugged. "Okay, you can stay."
"I can?" Ricky frowned.
"If that's what you want," Dennis said.
"I don't want it if you don't want it," Ricky said.
"Oh, for the love of god, do you want to spend the night with me or not?" Dennis snapped.
Ricky thought for a moment and then nodded. He knew it probably wasn't the smart thing to do, but Dennis was nice looking and good at sex, and Ricky was horny. He followed Dennis into his room and took off his clothes.

When Dennis and Ricky finished making love, Ricky rolled over on his side to cuddle with Dennis. Just as

he was snuggling his head on the older man's shoulder, Dennis abruptly turned on his side away from him.
"I'm tired," he said briefly. "Good night."
Ricky lay staring up at the dark ceiling for a while, feeling unhappy and rejected. After a few minutes of contemplation, he sat up on the side of the bed. He looked behind him, but Dennis didn't move. With a sigh, he gathered up his clothes and quietly left the room.

"I thought you wanted to spend the night with me?" Dennis said the next morning as he poured himself a cup of coffee.
"I thought I did," Ricky said.
"Then why'd you make such a big deal about it? Why did you get up and go back to your own room?"
"It doesn't matter," Ricky told him. He picked up his car keys. "I'm late for work."

Dennis and Ricky didn't speak for a few weeks. That was partly due to the long hours Ricky was working, usually seven days a week. He would come home and go straight up to his loft bedroom and fall asleep within seconds. Sometimes he was so tired, he didn't even bother to undress.

"I've missed you," Dennis whispered to him one night.
Ricky had arrived at home and fallen onto his mattress on the floor, utterly exhausted after an

eighteen hour work day. Dennis had climbed the stairs to his loft and crawled onto the bed beside him.
"Mmm," Ricky nodded slightly in acknowledgement.
"I'm horny," Dennis said softly. "Aren't you horny?"
Ricky began snoring. He awoke with a start a few minutes later as he felt Dennis's manhood being forced inside him. His pants and underwear were down, and Dennis was on top of him.
"What are you doing?" Ricky said angrily.
"Just go back to sleep," Dennis said soothingly. "This will only take a few minutes."
"No," Ricky protested. "I'm too tired for sex."
"Then go to sleep. I don't need you awake for this."
Ricky tried to push him off of himself, but Dennis was insistent. Finally, Ricky lay still and allowed him to do what he wanted. And so for the next twenty minutes, Dennis fucked him as Ricky's mind returned to those horrific forced sexual encounters from his past. As soon as Dennis was done, he climbed off of Ricky with a satisfied grin. Ricky curled into a ball and hugged his blanket as he tried to calm himself.

He avoided Dennis as much as possible from that point on, although the man did manage to lure him into his bedroom a couple of times. Ricky's libido was sometimes stronger than his common sense, unfortunately. But at least on these occasions, Dennis was gentle and affectionate while they made love.

One night, Ricky arrived home around midnight. He stepped into the dark apartment and made his way quietly to the loft staircase. He jumped in alarm as the light suddenly clicked on, and he saw Dennis sitting on the third step, waiting for him.

"Where the hell have you been?" he yelled angrily. His words were slurred, and it was obvious that he was quite drunk.

"I was at work," Ricky said.

"Oh, yeah?" Dennis tried to stand up, but he fell back onto the step on which he was sitting. "I don't fuckin' believe you!"

"You're drunk," Ricky frowned.

"And you're a fuckin' liar!" Dennis snapped. "You got somebody else, don't you?"

"No, I don't."

"Yeah, you do," Dennis said accusingly. "You're goddammed fuckin' some other guy! Who is he?"

"There is no guy," Ricky said patiently. "I have to work two jobs just to pay my rent. I didn't finish school or go to college like you. I don't make the kind of money you do."

"Liar!" Dennis shouted. "You're fuckin' around on me, aren't you?"

"I'm not fucking around on you," Ricky said, becoming annoyed. "Besides, we're not a couple, we're barely even friends. So if I want to sleep with other guys, I have every right to do so."

"The fuck you do!" Dennis managed to stagger to his feet and he lunged for Ricky. Ricky dodged him easily.

Leaving Justiceville: A Life Behind

"You belong to me, goddammit!" he muttered angrily. "If I find out you've been fuckin' around on me, I'll by god kill you!"

Ricky's face turned pale at these words.

"I'll kill the guy too," Dennis threatened. "You aren't going to make a fool out of me, you little bastard."

"Dennis, we are not a couple," Ricky said firmly. "We're just fuck-buddies. That's all."

Dennis tried to run at him again, just as the front door opened and Dianna stepped into the living room. She frowned at the scene being played out in front of her.

"What's going on?" she asked.

Dennis landed on his knees as Ricky stepped easily out of his way.

"This little fucker has been lying to me," Dennis panted.

"I have not," Ricky said. "I just got home from work and he was waiting for me. He accused me of fucking around with other guys. I tried to tell him I was at work, but he won't believe me."

"Have you two been having sex?" she said, her eyes wide. "What about Elaine?"

"Who's Elaine?"

"Elaine's his girlfriend," Dianna said.

"His girlfriend?" Ricky said incredulously. "You have a fucking girlfriend?"

"He's the one who came on to me," Dennis said, pointing at Ricky. "I tried to tell him no."

"That's a goddammed lie!" Ricky said indignantly. "He's the one who started all of this. I never would have slept with him if I'd known he had a girlfriend."

"Dennis, you said you weren't going to drink anymore," Dianna said, turning to her brother. "You can't keep doing this to Elaine."
"I didn't do anything to Elaine," Dennis protested. "Ricky forced himself on me, I swear!"
"Ricky, I think you'd better go," Dianna said. "This obviously isn't working out. So just go."
"This isn't my fault," Ricky insisted. "He's drunk, he's the one who wanted me, and he's the one who threatened to kill me if he ever caught me with another guy."
"Dennis?" she turned to her brother questioningly.
"The kid's a goddammed liar," Dennis said.
"That's enough," Ricky said. "I'm fuckin' out of here!"
With that, he climbed the stairs, snatched up his few clothes and personal belongings and stuffed them into his worn out duffel bag, the same one he'd had since he left home years ago. He pulled the apartment key off of his key ring and handed it to Dianna.
"What about your mattress?" she frowned.
"Keep it," he said flatly. "Let Dennis and Elaine fuck on it if they want!"
He glared at Dennis one last time and then left the apartment for the last time.

An acquaintance from his previous job at Taco Rio came into the restaurant one day while Ricky was working the front line. The two got to talking, and when Ricky mentioned that he was once again living in his car, she told him there was an empty apartment

Leaving Justiceville: A Life Behind

in her building. She'd be glad to put in a good word for him, she said.

The building she lived in turned out to be an old two story house in a less than respectable part of town. The apartment in question was actually just one room with a kitchenette and a miniscule bathroom. It was unfurnished, so Ricky borrowed a van from his manager and bought a used queen size bed, a lamp, a table, and an old recliner from a second-hand store. The landlord was a middle-aged woman, who lived on the first floor with her husband and fifteen year old daughter. She reminded Ricky of his mother in appearance, although she seemed pleasant enough, unlike his despicable parent.

It was nice living by himself, Ricky decided. For the first time he was truly on his own. Of course, he had always been on his own more or less, but now he was living as an adult with no one to answer to except his bosses. No parents, no roommates; he was his own man. And it felt damn good!

The rent was reasonable, and his landlord insisted that he pay cash. That was fine with Ricky since he had no checking account. Each month he would put the money in an envelope and slip it through the mail slot on the front door as she had instructed.

A few months passed, and one day Ricky's landlady opened the front door abruptly as he was pushing his rent through the mail slot. He jumped back, startled.

"Can you do me a favor?" she drawled as she puffed on the cigarette hanging from the corner of her mouth.

"I guess so," Ricky said warily.

"I need you to take this gas bill payment in for me," she said. "They're gonna shut the gas off tomorrow if they don't get this by today."

"Where do I take it?" he asked with a frown.

"It's downtown Fort Worth," she said. "The address is on the envelope."

"I've never driven in downtown Fort Worth," he said worriedly. "I don't know how to get there."

"Aw, you got that pretty little Mustang," she looked enviously past him at the driveway at the shiny car parked on the street. "I always wanted me one of those cars."

"It's kind of old," he said. "But it gets me around."

"Hey, Lourdine!" she hollered at her daughter suddenly over her shoulder. "Come here!"

A teenage girl came to the doorway and smiled bashfully at Ricky. She was rail thin, with freckles and stringy brown hair.

"Lourdine'll go with you," the landlady said. "She knows the way. It's after five so there won't be no traffic."

Ricky and Lourdine set out in the Mustang toward downtown Fort Worth. It was intimidating to Ricky to drive in a big city. All those lanes on the highways, heavy traffic, tall buildings and one way streets; it was all rather scary for a young man who was inexperienced with city ways.

Leaving Justiceville: A Life Behind

The two talked and laughed all the way into town. As it turned out, Lourdine didn't really know how to get to the Lone Star Gas Company, so it took them almost an extra hour to find the address and slip the payment in the drop box.

When they returned home, Lourdine's parents were involved in a loud argument on the front porch of the old house.

"Where the hell have you been?" the landlord's husband demanded angrily of his daughter.

"We couldn't find the address," his daughter explained.

"Here you are out at all hours of the night with a strange boy," he scowled. "Who knows what he could have done to you!"

"He didn't do anything to me," Lourdine said.

"I don't believe that for a second," her father said. "I know how boys are. He ain't no different from the rest of them."

"I didn't touch your daughter," Ricky said indignantly. "I would never do anything like that."

"You fuckin' liar! You better by-god have not touched her or I'll beat the shit out of both of you!" the irate man said.

"We just drove there and back. That's all," Lourdine said.

"It don't take that long to drive into the city and back," the landlord said. "I know what you were doing!"

Leaving Justiceville: A Life Behind

"We weren't doing anything. I told you we couldn't find the place. Anyway, Ma's the one who made me go," Lourdine said.

"Your ma should have taken the payment down there herself," her father snapped. "I told her to do it this morning."

"That's not my fault!" Lourdine cried. "I was just doing like she told me to do."

Her parents began arguing back and forth for the next few minutes until Ricky tried to back away from them. His landlord noticed this out of the corner of his eye. He stopped berating his wife for a moment.

"As for you, I want you out of here!" he thundered. He pointed toward the street. "I'm giving you two days to get your shit moved out. And don't you set foot anywhere near my daughter again! You got that?"

Once again, Ricky was living in his car. He had gathered his personal belongings together, but there was no one to help him move his few pieces of furniture. Resignedly, he decided it wasn't worth it, and he let his former landlord keep the bed, chair, and table.

He parked the next few nights at the back of an apartment complex. There was a swimming pool that he used to bathe in at night when everyone was asleep.

A coworker at Church's Fried Chicken who went by the nickname of Slick took him aside a few days later.

Leaving Justiceville: A Life Behind

"I could have told you not to rent a room from those people," he said confidentially.
"Why not?"
"Because they're crooks," Slick said. "That apartment renting thing is a scam."
"A scam how?" Ricky looked worried.
"You got a receipt for your rent every month, didn't you?"
"Well…no," Ricky said hesitantly.
"Oh, boy," Slick shook his head. "Then I'll bet this isn't over."

Robert, another friend from Church's, learned that Ricky was living in his car and insisted that he come and stay with his family for a few days until he found an apartment. Ricky thanked him politely but declined. The young man was persistent, however, stating that his was a Christian family and his parents would never forgive themselves if they allowed poor Ricky to live in his car while they had a perfectly good spare room for him to use. It was their Christian duty to help out a lowly creature such as himself. With a sigh, Ricky finally agreed, albeit reluctantly. With his long work hours, he found it difficult to find time to look for an apartment. During slow times at the restaurants, he made calls to all the apartment complexes in town and found that most of them were out of his price range.
The third night of staying in the guest room of Robert's parents, they confronted him as soon as he walked wearily into the house.

Leaving Justiceville: A Life Behind

"It doesn't seem like you're making much of an effort to look for a place of your own," the mother said.

"This was only supposed to be for a night or two, you know," her husband added sternly. "We aren't running a bed and breakfast here."

Ricky assured them that he had called several places in search of an apartment over the past few days but found nothing he could afford.

"You say that," the man said skeptically. "But I think you just want to sponge off of us. I know your type, always thinking that you should have everything handed to you on a silver platter. We're not made of money, you know."

"You don't fuckin' know me at all," Ricky said flatly. "I only came here because your son insisted. If you think I'm trying to take advantage of you, you're wrong. I'll get my things and leave now."

"Now, there's no need to use foul language," the woman said reprovingly. "After all, we've tried to do the Christian thing here."

"Christian my ass! There's nothing Christian about you. Yeah, you say you're Christians all right!" Ricky snorted derisively. "You're just like all the rest of the people who claim to be so religious, and they're all liars and adulterers and thieves! You act all sanctimonious and shit, but it doesn't mean a thing, because all you do is judge people so you can feel better about yourselves. Christianity is nothing but bullshit!"

Leaving Justiceville: A Life Behind

With that, Ricky went to the guest room and picked up his few things. He had left most of his personal items in his car since he knew from experience that his stint as a guest in this 'Christian' home was going to end badly. He drove away and parked behind the Taco Bell for the night. He settled down in the back seat to sleep with tears in his eyes.

Why did everyone treat him like trash, he wondered? Was it because he *was* trash? Did they see something when they looked at him that said he didn't deserve to be treated with respect and dignity? He knew his family was nothing to be proud of; they were vile people as far as he was concerned. But he wasn't his family. He had fought against everything they were his entire life, and he was determined to be nothing like them. So maybe he came from garbage, but there was no way in hell that he was going to remain garbage!

Leaving Justiceville: A Life Behind

CHAPTER TWELVE

A few weeks later, Ricky was told by his Church's Fried Chicken manager he had a visitor who insisted on seeing him immediately.

"My name is Leonard Butts," the man said with an oily smile. He had thinning, greasy hair and was wearing an ill-fitting cheap suit. "I'm the attorney for Mr. and Mrs. Nelson. I understand you are a former tenant of theirs."

"I rented a room from them until they kicked me out," Ricky nodded uneasily. His friend's warning about them ran through his mind. "What's this all about?"

Mr. Butts pulled a few legal looking papers from his rather battered briefcase and examined them before looking up at Ricky.

"You know, it's illegal to run out on your rent the way you did."

"I didn't run out on my rent," Ricky said. "I paid them two hundred dollars every month. That was the amount they told me to pay."

"I'm afraid you didn't," the attorney shook his head regretfully. "My clients state that you never paid them one red dime the entire time you rented from them."

"I did so!" Ricky said angrily. "They're lying."

"No, they're not," Mr. Butts said. "I've known them a long time, and they're god-fearing people."

"But I paid them, I swear," Ricky said. "I gave them cash."

Leaving Justiceville: A Life Behind

"And can you prove that you paid them?"
"Well, no," Ricky said. "She never gave me a receipt. Most of the time I just pushed the money through the mail slot."
"So you say," the lawyer shook his head disapprovingly. "But a court of law isn't going to be interested in your word alone. It will need proof that what you're saying is true."
"But I don't have any proof," Ricky admitted.
"Oh, dear," Mr. Butts said. "Well, then I'm afraid I have no choice but to proceed with a lawsuit against you, unless you can pay them the money you owe them. Approximately twenty-five hundred dollars."
"Are you out of your fucking mind?!" Ricky exclaimed, his eyes wide. "I'm not paying them another penny! They're fucking liars! This whole thing is a scam, and you're part of it."
"Now, now," Mr. Butts looked offended. "I will not sit here and be accused of wrongdoing from the likes of you."
"Why not? You know I'm telling the truth."
"Are you prepared to pay the Nelson's the money you owe them?" Mr. Butts ignored him.
"I don't owe them anything!" Ricky said.
"Then in that case, I'm informing you that a lien has been placed on your 1964 ½ Mustang in the amount of twenty-five hundred dollars." Mr. Butts leaned in closer with an evil smile. "So you see, one way or another, you will repay the money you owe my clients."

"You can't do that!" Ricky said, outraged. "You can't take my car!"

"I can, actually," the lawyer said. "But I'm willing to let you keep your Mustang as long as you pay five hundred dollars a week until the debt is paid in full."

"That's more than I make in a week," Ricky sputtered. "How can I pay you more than I make?"

"That's not my concern," the man shrugged indifferently. "Either come up with the money, or I take your car. You know, Mrs. Nelson mentioned how much she wanted a car like yours."

"You lying sack of shit!" Ricky yelled angrily. "This was always part of her plan, wasn't it? She wanted my car, and now she's got it."

"So you're relinquishing ownership of your car, then?"

Ricky closed his eyes in anger and despair. Dammit! Why was this happening to him? He'd done nothing wrong; he didn't deserve this! It was more clear to him than ever that there was no god in heaven, because a just and all-powerful god wouldn't let this happen. He would have protected him from the abuse, torment, and cruelty he had endured all of his life.

His shoulders slumped as he handed the keys to his car over to the attorney. He stood among a pile of all of his belongings in the world and watched as Mrs. Nelson drove away in his Mustang with a self-satisfied smile on her face with Mr. Butts sitting in the passenger seat.

Leaving Justiceville: A Life Behind

How could people be so unkind? These unscrupulous charlatans had stolen his only possession of any value right out from under him. That car was his pride and joy, the only nice thing he had ever owned. It was more than just a means of transportation; it was his home. So now he was without a car or a place to live. One step forward and two steps back, the same way things had gone his entire life.

Ricky closed the store that night. He saw his fellow employees out and locked the door behind them. With a sigh, he turned the lights out and settled himself into a padded booth to try to get a few hours sleep. It looked like this was going to be home until he could figure out what to do. First of all, he decided, he had to get another automobile. That took precedence over an apartment because a car could serve both as transportation and sleeping quarters.

Early the next morning, Slick unlocked the back door of the restaurant and began making preparations for the busy day ahead. He switched on the dining room lights and noticed Ricky sleeping uncomfortably in one of the booths.
"Hey!" he called out.
Ricky stirred, yawning and rubbing his tired eyes. He suddenly realized where he was and looked up at Slick with alarm.
"Oh, damn!" he said. He jumped up and straightened his clothes as best he could.
"Did you sleep there all night?" Slick asked him.

"Uh, no," Ricky lied. "I got here early and –"
"Save it," Slick said. "It's obvious you've been here all night."
"I didn't have anyplace else to go," Ricky shrugged. "You can't tell on me. I'll get fired, and I need this job."
"I'm not going to tell on you." Slick frowned. "But you can't stay here. You'll have to come stay with me and my wife."

That afternoon, Ricky walked across the street to another restaurant called Ron's Barbecue. Thirty minutes later, he left the establishment as its newest employee. He regretted having to leave Taco Bell, but felt he had no choice in the matter. It was simply too far to walk every day. Besides, his jobs with Church's and Ron's paid better wages than what he was making, and with his desperate need to save money for a car, he had to go where the money was. He worked as much overtime as he could get at both restaurants over the next several weeks. Often he would run across the street from one job to the next just in time to begin another eight or nine hour shift. He was dog-tired, but at least he was saving some money toward a car. After several weeks of sleeping on the sofa at Slick and Debbie's small trailer, which was thirty minutes away, Ricky had saved back a few thousand dollars, enough to make a down-payment on a cheap car.

Leaving Justiceville: A Life Behind

It was at this time that a coworker from Ron's BBQ, a somewhat surly young man named Brian suggested the two of them get an apartment together. He knew of a place that was renting just a few blocks away from work, he said. He had a car and would be glad to drive Ricky to and from work until he could buy one for himself.

Since the rent was cheap and the apartment so close, Ricky agreed to the idea. Ricky thanked Slick and Debbie for their kindness, and that night he and Brian drove to their new apartment. Ricky paused in the driveway to look up at the dilapidated building with a sinking feeling in his stomach. Oh god, he thought with a sigh. No wonder the rent was so cheap. The place was a dump with its peeling paint, sagging roof, and cracked and dirty windows. There were weeds all around it and trash bags piled up against one side.

"This is it?" Ricky wrinkled his nose.

"Yeah," Brian grinned. "Isn't it great? Our own place. We can party every night, bring chicks back here to screw, drink 'til we pass out, you name it!"

"I'm not much of one for drinking or dating," Ricky frowned. "I work too much."

"You're into girls, though, right?"

"Oh, uh, sure," Ricky said. "Definitely into girls."

"That's good, 'cause I don't want to shack up with no fag," Brian said. He studied his new roommate suspiciously for a moment. "When's the last time you fucked a girl?"

"Uh, it's been a while," Ricky shrugged. "I'm too tired from working so many hours."

Leaving Justiceville: A Life Behind

Well, that much was true, he thought. He was weary down to his bones from the ninety plus hours he was working each week. He had neither the time nor the energy to have much of a sex drive. Besides, all of his sexual experiences had been either forced or with a man who was a drunk and ashamed of what they were doing.

He wasn't ashamed of being gay, but he knew better than to reveal to anyone his true sexuality.

Homosexuality, especially in Texas or anywhere else in the south, was considered just about the most evil sin with which a person could be involved. People believed that, of course, because they were ignorant and judgmental of anyone different from themselves. All gay people knew to keep the truth hidden or face the consequences, such as getting beat up, murdered, or losing their loved ones or jobs.

The apartment itself was no better than the exterior of the building. It reeked of cat urine, the carpet was torn and stained, and there were holes in the drywall, where a former tenant had apparently hit it with his fists. The small refrigerator worked, but the ancient stove was non-functional, and there was no washer or dyer. Ricky didn't have the money for the laundromat, so he was back to washing his clothes by hand in the rust-stained bathtub. He had no furniture or dishes, so he slept on the floor in a sleeping bag and ate his meals at the two restaurants.

Brian was a complete slob. He threw his clothes everywhere and refused to take out the trash or dust the shabby living room furniture, which consisted of

Leaving Justiceville: A Life Behind

a malodorous and worn sofa, an old club chair with no seat cushion, and a thirteen inch black and white television. Since Ricky never used the kitchen, he was tempted not to clean it and let Brian deal with it, but after a while, the smell became too much to tolerate.

Not surprisingly, he ended up walking every day to work through the dangerous streets from his apartment. It wasn't unusual to see police chases or hear gunshots as he walked along the cracked sidewalks as quickly as he could. Brian only worked one job and had no intention of living up to his promise to drive Ricky to work. He spent his evenings watching pornography on his VCR, and often times Ricky would arrive home to the sounds of energetic sexual intercourse issuing from Brian's room. Brian would purposely leave the bedroom door open to show off his latest conquest, usually a woman he had picked up at a bar or on a street corner. Ricky would go into his room, close the door, and try to drown out the noise from next door with a pillow over his head.

On an afternoon that Ricky wasn't scheduled to work, he walked a few blocks from the restaurants to the Chevrolet dealership. He looked the cars over carefully until a salesman wearing a wide tie and plaid slacks approached him.

"Well, hello, young feller," he said jovially. "What can I do for you?"

Leaving Justiceville: A Life Behind

"I'm looking for something cheap," Ricky told him tentatively. "Something with a backseat."

He knew that he would more than likely be living in his car again soon enough, and he needed that backseat in which to sleep at night.

"Oh, a backseat, huh?" the salesman winked and grinned broadly. "I get it. A young buck like you wants someplace to be with his girl."

"Uh, yeah, that's it," Ricky agreed.

God, it was difficult being a gay man in a straight male dominated society! Always pretending and lying just to protect himself.

"Well, I just got this baby in today," the salesman told him, pointing to a used, dark blue Chevy Citation. "I think it's the perfect car for you. Now, will that be cash or check?"

"Uh, I only have enough for a down-payment," Ricky said uncertainly.

"Well, let's go inside and make the deal," the salesman put an arm around Ricky's shoulders and herded him into the office. "You've got good credit, right?"

"Uh, I don't know," Ricky gulped. What was he getting himself into here, he wondered worriedly? "Besides, I'm not sure that's the right car for me. I haven't even driven it."

"Of course it's the right car for you," the salesman said. "Why do you need to drive it? Once you've bought it, you'll get to drive it all you want. Now let me get my manager in here, and we'll write it up."

Leaving Justiceville: A Life Behind

The sales manager and salesman talked fast and firmly to Ricky for the next fifteen minutes. A familiar sensation came over him as they worked as a team to convince him to buy the car. It was that of a mouse being cornered by a predator. He had felt that way from his parents, his brothers, teachers, and practically every other adult his whole life. As their haranguing reached its pinnacle, Ricky finally stood up and backed away from them.
"Stop it!" he shouted. "Just shut up!"
The two men looked at him with astonishment.
"You're not going to gang up on me like this!" Ricky said angrily. "If either of you say another word, I'm leaving here, and I won't be back."
"Why, Ricky," the salesman looked wounded.
"We're just telling you the truth."
"No, you're like everyone else, telling me what you want me to do," Ricky spat. "You don't give a shit about any truth!"
He crossed his arms defiantly.
"Now," he said in a calmer voice. "I want to look at all your cars and drive whichever one I want. And you're going to give me a good deal, or I'll tell everyone what shysters you are."
The two men looked at each other and shrugged resignedly.
"Fine," the salesman said. "Let's go back out and take a look."
Ricky carefully examined all the used cars on the lot. He felt a sense of self-satisfaction at having stood up for himself. These guys were like all the other men

he'd ever known, ready to overpower and take advantage of someone they saw as naïve and defenseless. Well, he wasn't going to allow it this time. He was an adult now and could stand up for himself.

After a few hours of looking the inventory of automobiles over with an increasingly impatient salesman, Ricky decided that the Citation was indeed the best car for him. It had low miles, was in good condition, and was reasonably priced. Even so, he pointed out every tiny flaw he could find to his salesman.

"You'll have to come down off the price," he told the man. "I'm not paying that much for a car in this kind of shape."

After a few more hours of dickering, the sales manager wiped the sweat from his brow and shook Ricky's hand. Once a price was finally agreed upon, the next step had been to get financing for the few thousand dollars his down-payment didn't cover. Since Ricky had virtually no credit, it took quite a bit of convincing by the sales manager to get the bank to finance the automobile. The bank finally agreed to do it, but at an extremely high interest rate. Ricky knew he had little choice, so he agreed to the terms, and the sales manager handed him the keys with a sigh of relief.

One evening, Ricky came in from work just before midnight. He fixed himself a peanut butter sandwich and dropped down heavily onto the old sofa instead

of going into his room. He just needed five minutes to sit on something soft instead of his hard bedroom floor or the hard plastic stools at Ron's BBQ. He turned on the tiny black and white television and watched a rerun of 'Gilligan's Island' while he ate his sandwich. The apartment was stiflingly hot, and the smell of cat urine was overwhelming. Ricky was sweating in the heat, and he had to cover his nose and mouth with his hand just to breathe. Before he knew it, his eyelids drooped, and he fell fast asleep.
He awoke with a start a little later and immediately shielded his head with his arms as his roommate hit him with his fists.
"You goddammed fucker!" Brian shouted at him. "You're fuckin' sweating all over my sofa."
"Stop hitting me!" Ricky yelled as he jumped up and moved out of his reach. "And this sofa isn't yours. It came with the apartment, so it's just as much mine as it is yours."
"That don't give you the right to sweat all over it!" Brian shouted angrily.
"It's hot in here," Ricky retorted. "I can't help but sweat. Look at you; you're sweating as much as I am."
"Don't go looking at my body, ya faggot," Brian shouted. "I knew you were queer."
"Then why did you want to room with me?" Ricky said. "Maybe you're a fag too!"
Brian's scowl deepened, and he ran at Ricky. Ricky was too quick and ran into his bedroom and locked the door. Brian pounded on it with his fists and feet,

yelling and cursing until he finally grew tired of his efforts. He threatened to beat him up and called him names such as fag, queer, or girl. Ricky sat up much of that night, listening for any sound of further threats from his roommate, but all remained still.

The next morning, he cautiously opened his door a crack and peered out into the hall. The only sound he heard was some loud snoring coming from Brian's room. He quietly gathered up his things and slipped silently out the door and down to his car. Before he left, he placed his key on top of the television with a note that said 'fuck you'.

And so Ricky was back to living in his car yet again. He had decided not to burden Slick and Debbie with his problems; it wasn't fair of him to take advantage of their kindness.

On the bright side, the Citation was a bit roomier than the Baja Bug or Mustang, so it was a little more comfortable. And at least there was no odor of cat urine in it. He resumed parking at the back of an apartment complex and bathing in the swimming pool.

At times his life seemed unbearable. He was working long, hard hours at the restaurants just to pay his bills, he had no home, few friends, and it looked like his future was going to remain that way. No matter how hard he tried to get his head above water, someone was always there to push him back down. Even with his innate desire to not only survive, but to

thrive, the struggle – that is, life – was getting wearisome.
Once again thoughts of ending the struggle crossed his mind. Maybe this miserable existence wasn't worth it in the long run. If it was always going to be difficult like this, what was the point?

A new manager took over at Church's Fried Chicken. He and Ricky had both been up for the promotion.
"Ricky," his former manager took him aside one day, "I've taken a job at the new Kentucky Fried Chicken over in Grapevine."
"Oh, no," Ricky said unhappily. "Does that mean you're leaving?"
"It does," his manager gave him a fatherly smile.
"But that could mean good news for you."
"It could?" Ricky said, not understanding.
"I'm going to recommend you to take my place," his boss's smile broadened.
"Me?" Ricky's eyes opened wide. "Are you kidding me?"
"Ricky, you're my best employee. You're never late, you never miss a single day, you're always willing to work over, and you manage your shifts better than any other shift manager. You know every aspect of the job, and I can't think of a better replacement."
"Thanks," Ricky's face turned pink with pleasure.
"It means a lot more money," his boss said. "I'm sure you could use that."

Leaving Justiceville: A Life Behind

Just think, Ricky mused, enough money to afford a decent apartment, new clothes, nice furniture, and proper foods like lettuce and vegetables and fruit.
"But the decision isn't up to me," his manager cautioned him. "I can only give corporate my recommendation, you understand."
"I understand," Ricky said, trying to reign in his excitement.
Wow, just when he was feeling his lowest, the universe came along and gave him a little boost. Maybe his future was going to be more promising than he had thought!

The promotion was announced a few days later, but it wasn't the news Ricky was expecting and hoping for.
"Everyone," his boss said to the employees at large, "I have an announcement. As some of you know, I've taken another job, which I'm going to start in two days."
There was a chorus of disappointed 'awww's' from the assembled workers.
"I know, and I'm going to miss all of you too. But I'm moving on, knowing that I'm leaving you in good hands."
Ricky flushed with excitement. This was it, the moment to which his whole life had been leading.
"You have a new manager, and he's someone you all know because he's one of you."
Ricky's boss gave him a rueful look for a few seconds.
"Paul, would you come up here, please?" he said.

Leaving Justiceville: A Life Behind

A slightly overweight young man with crooked glasses and greasy hair stepped forward to stand beside him. Ricky's smile faded, and a look of puzzled disappointment took its place.

"Everyone, please welcome your new store manager," the boss said. "Paul has been with us for six months now, and the corporate officers have decided that he is the best person to take my place. I know he'll do a good job for you, so I hope you'll support him and do the same good job you've all done for me."

A little later, the boss took Ricky aside.

"I'm sorry, Ricky," he said regretfully. "I told them that you were the best man for the job, but I'm afraid they had ideas of their own."

"How could they think that Paul would be a better manager than me?" Ricky said angrily. "He's only been here a few months, and he doesn't have any managerial experience!"

"I know," his boss agreed. He added dryly, "It probably has something to do with the fact that his uncle works in the corporate office."

"No hard feelings, I hope," Paul said a little later.

"Why would there be hard feelings?" Ricky scowled at him.

"Well, I know you were up for this job too," Paul smirked. "It has to be a bit upsetting to know that you still weren't good enough, even after all the years you've been here. That has to hurt."

Leaving Justiceville: A Life Behind

"It doesn't hurt at all," Ricky said. "Because I know that I was recommended for this job, and the only reason you got it was because your uncle works at corporate."

Paul's oily smile faded.

"That's not true!" he said. "My uncle had nothing to do with this."

"That's not true, and you and I both know it," Ricky said. "And everyone else knows it too. And let me tell you something else. You don't have what it takes to be a manager, and you'll end up falling flat on your face. Just don't look to me to pick you up when you fail."

That was the beginning of the end for Ricky at Church's Fried Chicken. When the next schedule came out, Ricky was stunned to see that his hours had been cut dramatically.

"I'm sorry, Ricky," Paul said with feigned sympathy. "I just couldn't find anyplace to put you."

"There are holes in this schedule all over the place!" Ricky exclaimed. "You're leaving us shorthanded during our busiest times."

"I'm doing the schedule the way I was shown," Paul said defensively. "If you don't like it, find yourself another job."

Ricky worked his twenty hours a week at Church's for the next two weeks. When his hours were cut to sixteen hours in split-shifts, he knew it was time to make a move.

Leaving Justiceville: A Life Behind

"I can't do split-shifts," Ricky told Paul. His hateful manager was sitting at his battered desk in the restaurant office. "You already know that I work at Ron's BBQ."

"Are you refusing to work?" Paul said.

"I'm telling you that I can't do it because I have a second job," Ricky said evenly, doing his best to hold his temper in check.

"Well, you either do the job, or I'll have to fire you," Paul shrugged. "It's up to you."

Ricky stepped farther into the office and closed the door. He grabbed Paul by the shirtfront with both hands and hauled him to his feet.

"You slimy, worthless pile of shit!" he seethed. "You don't have to fire me because I quit!"

He sucker-punched the other man, sending him reeling back into his desk chair.

"Fuck this job, and fuck you!"

"I could have you arrested!" Paul shouted at him.

"For what?" Ricky said. "I never hit you." He looked around the small room. "Let's see you prove that I did!"

He left the room, gathered his few personal belongings, and said goodbye to his coworkers. He got in his car and drove to Kennedale on the southeast side of Fort Worth to Slick and Debbie's trailer. They were properly outraged at the situation, and Debbie told him to sit down at the table while she fixed dinner.

Leaving Justiceville: A Life Behind

"You're staying here tonight," Slick told him. "We're going to eat some supper, drink some margaritas, and talk about this."

The three of them stayed up late that evening, talking and laughing and imbibing more than a few drinks. Ricky had to admit that he felt just a little better when he awoke on their sofa the next morning.

The next day, Ricky met with the manager of Ron's BBQ. After explaining the situation at Church's with him for five minutes, an agreement was reached. His boss was only too happy to work with Ricky since he was his best employee by far. In exchange for working double shifts with no overtime pay, Ricky would receive a twenty cent raise, making the three dollars and ten cents an hour the highest wage he had ever received.

Leaving Justiceville: A Life Behind

CHAPTER THIRTEEN

One day while Ricky was wiping down some vacated tables in the Ron's BBQ dining room, a regular customer called him over to his table.
"Ricky, you're here every time I come in here," the man smiled at him. "Is that all you do is work?"
"Just about," Ricky shrugged.
"Well, your boss told me you're his best employee, the only one of these kids he can count on."
"That was nice of him to say," Ricky said politely.
"You ever thought of doing something other than restaurant work?" the man asked.
"I don't know," Ricky frowned. "I never gave it much thought."
"Well, why don't you think about it?" the customer said. "There ain't no future in this kind of work. I work over at Heller Brewing Company in Fort Worth. We're always looking for good people."
"You are?"
"You bet," the man said. "You got a CDL license?"
"CDL?"
"A commercial driver's license," the man explained. "I've got a job in mind for you, but you need a CDL to do it."
"How do I get one?" Ricky asked.
"You study for it and then take a test at the DMV."
He wiped his mouth with his paper napkin and stood up. He handed a business card to Ricky.

Leaving Justiceville: A Life Behind

"You get your CDL and then come see me," he said. "I'll give you a job that pays double what you're making here."

Double the pay, Ricky thought excitedly! He could go from eighty hours a week down to forty hours like normal people! He could have a life!

The next day during his lunch break, Ricky drove to the DMV and got the information he needed to study to obtain his commercial license. At night and during his breaks, he would study the manual determinedly until, after a few months, he felt he had a reasonably good grasp on it. It seemed rather difficult to him, but decided it was because he had never taken Driver's Ed. in school. He dipped into his meager savings and rented a U-Haul truck for the next two weeks. He drove it everywhere, on city streets, highways, the Interstate, and even into downtown Fort Worth. It was challenging to him at first and more than a bit intimidating, but he was persistent. He was going to get his CDL and that job at Heller Brewing, and nothing was going to stop him!

Ricky took his CDL exam and driving test and walked proudly out of the DMV with his brand new commercial driver's license. He drove straight to the Heller Brewing main offices and asked to speak with Phil, the customer who he had spoken to at Ron's BBQ. The man greeted him with a smile and a handshake and, as promised, gave him a job cleaning beer lines in the local bars to which they sold beer. Ricky said goodbye to his boss and coworkers with a

Leaving Justiceville: A Life Behind

mixture of relief and regret. It wasn't as if he had gotten close to any of them, but they had been his constant companions for quite some time. Also, it was a bit frightening to be making such a big change in his life. He believed it was going to be good for him, yet he couldn't help but worry just a little.

At this point, Ricky was five feet, ten inches tall, with a weight of one hundred thirty pounds and a waist of twenty-five inches; all the years of hard work and eating very little had taken its toll on his body. On his first day of work, Phil showed him the locker room

Leaving Justiceville: A Life Behind

and handed him the smallest uniform they had in stock. It hung loosely on his thin frame. Ricky didn't own a belt, so Phil looked around for something to keep his pants up. He finally found a bit of rope, and Ricky tied it around his waist. Phil shook his head and chuckled before opening his wallet and handing Ricky some cash with instructions to buy a belt before the end of the day.

Ricky worked Monday through Friday cleaning out the beer lines on all of the south side and downtown bars. It was his job to disconnect the kegs and clean the lines with a cleaning solution and then rinse them with water. It was hard work, but Ricky enjoyed it. It was his first time in a bar as an adult, and he was surprised to meet some nice people. Many of these establishments catered to college or upper income clientele. The bartenders and wait staff were usually friendly to him and offered him free alcoholic drinks, which he always declined. He did accept Cokes and pretzels or peanuts from them, however. Now that he was no longer working at a restaurant, his food source had disappeared, so he ate whatever he could find cheaply at the local grocery stores.

After a few weeks on the job, Ricky had saved back enough money to get an apartment. This was big income as far as he was concerned: two hundred-fifty dollars a week! He found a one bedroom apartment in a very nice complex near to his work. A few more weeks of sleeping in his sleeping bag on the floor, and when he had enough money, he leased some

Leaving Justiceville: A Life Behind

bedroom and living room furniture. They weren't the best quality sofa, chairs, and tables, nor necessarily his style, but to him they looked like something out of a palace; it felt as if he was living like a king. With kitchen appliances that actually worked, Ricky began buying actual groceries that he could put away in the cabinets and refrigerator. He cooked himself mostly simple meals like spaghetti and hamburgers and salads. It wasn't the most balanced of diets, but it was the best that Ricky had ever eaten. For the first time in his life, he was eating on a regular basis.

Phil oversaw his work and liked what he saw, and eventually Ricky was promoted to the position of keg driver, which paid fifty dollars a week more than his previous job, plus a small commission on every keg he sold. It was a strenuous job lifting the heavy kegs, which outweighed him by thirty pounds, but Ricky wasn't going to complain. The other drivers laughed at him and told him he was too scrawny to handle the job, but that only made him all the more determined. He had a two-wheel hand truck to help him move the kegs to and from the truck, but it still required a considerable amount of lifting and ingenuity on his part. After a week or so, he had devised a system of using his right leg as a swing to heft the heavy metal containers up into the truck. As a result, he was developing some sizeable muscles. He was always exhausted after his shifts, but at least it was only ten hours instead of sixteen.

He continued to work as much overtime as possible, even working on Saturday mornings answering the

Leaving Justiceville: A Life Behind

telephones to earn an extra seventy-five dollars a week. At one point, he was told he was going to start delivering beer to four of the gay bars in town. Phil told him that the other drivers didn't feel comfortable going to those places – they didn't feel 'safe'.
Safe, Ricky frowned? What was it about a gay bar that these big, burly truck drivers were afraid of? Did they seriously think a gay man was going to molest them? He had to chuckle a bit at that thought. Most of these guys were overweight, unhygienic, unattractive, and uneducated, so why did they think that any gay guy would want them? But then again, why had his father had so many affairs when he was just about the most unappealing man Ricky had ever seen? One day he would realize that apparently most heterosexual men, even the homeliest and most disgusting among them, seemed to believe that all straight women and gay men were just dying to get in their pants. Must be the arrogance and sense of superiority that straight men, especially the white ones, felt society had imbued them with over all other minorities.
Sometimes Ricky was so horny he felt he might burst if he couldn't be with a man, but there was no way he would have considered going to bed with any of these guys or any other straight man, for that matter. He only wanted to be with a man who wanted to be with him in return. Sex wasn't just about getting off, at least not for him. It was important to him that it be meaningful and beautiful. And since he knew no gay

people, it seemed he would have to take care of his libido at home, alone.

Ricky unloaded a couple of kegs onto a hand truck and wheeled them in the back door of Spinner's, a popular gay bar near downtown Fort Worth. There were several similar bars located in the same neighborhood, such as the Six-Fifty-One, Inc, and the Corral. Taking a deep breath, Ricky rolled the heavy hand truck up to the back door and pushed the buzzer. A moment later, he smiled nervously at the young man who opened the door to let him in.
"It's on through that door over there," the man said in a friendly voice, pointing at a curtain covered opening.
Even from the backroom Ricky could hear the bone-shakingly loud music coming from the bar. He nervously pushed the curtain aside and paused for a moment, his eyes wide and his mouth open as he looked around in awe.
In many ways, this bar was very similar to all the straight clubs he had been in. That is, it had loud music, a dance floor, a long mirror-backed bar, a couple of pool tables, and a dart board. What took him by surprise was the sight of the five scantily clad young men dancing on wooden boxes and both ends of the bar. As he watched, one of the attractive youths knelt down and allowed the suit-clad gentleman standing in front of him to place a dollar bill inside the strap of his silver G-string bikini. He

bent down and gave the man a brief kiss and then stood up to resume his dancing.

Oh my god, Ricky thought! Two guys kissing! In public! In front of other men! Obviously he knew this sort of thing must happen in gay bars, but it was the first time that he had ever personally witnessed such a monumental event. His gaze traveled across the large, dimly lit room to the dance floor, where several gay men and a few lesbian couples were dancing to the lively pop music. Men dancing with men, women dancing with women; it almost seemed too good to be true. Guys were standing in the shadows along the walls or at tables, kissing passionately and fondling each other. Over the deafening music, he could hear even louder conversations and laughter as people yelled to make themselves heard.

This is amazing, Ricky mused. I wouldn't have believed it if I hadn't seen it with my own eyes. My first time being around openly gay men, and it feels incredible and wonderful and even rather frightening. He frowned as that thought occurred to him. What did he have to be afraid of? He pondered the situation for a few minutes and realized that it wasn't fear he was feeling. It's just that it was so new to him. He was unsure how to react to it. On the one hand, he was rather shy and accustomed to keeping to himself, but he also longed to join in with these happy people. But would they accept him, he wondered? They were his people, his own kind, but what would he do if they rejected him and decided he was unworthy like

Leaving Justiceville: A Life Behind

his own family had? The more he thought about it, the more he realized that there was a lot at stake here. These people were very different from his family. Everyone here was laughing or smiling, at least those that weren't making out with each other, Ricky noted. They were all having a marvelous time, enjoying each other's company and the music and alcohol. This was a place – one of the very few places – where they could come and just be themselves. For once, they didn't have to pretend to be the good little straight boys and girls that society insisted they be. Out in the world, they had to fake it, but not here. How liberating it must be to spend time here, Ricky thought. But he was here to do a job, not to fraternize.

The young man who had let him in the building showed him where the taps were, and Ricky set to work. It didn't take long for him to switch out the kegs and load the empty ones onto his hand truck. As he walked behind the bar to the end, he heard a couple of guys talking.

"Will you look at that," the first man said with a low whistle. "Now that's a cute ass."

"Yes, it is," the other man agreed.

Ricky looked around to see who they were talking about and was surprised to see them looking in his direction.

"What's your name?" one of them asked.

"Who? Me?" Ricky frowned.

"Yes, you, cutestuff," the other said.

"I'm…I'm Ricky," he stammered nervously. "You think I have a cute ass?"

"Well, come on over here and let us buy you a drink," one of the men grinned, "and we'll show you what we think."

"Those kegs are bigger than you are," the other chuckled. "Come sit on my lap and let daddy rock you."

Ricky backed away a couple of steps.

"Uh, thanks, but I've…I've got to go," he said. With that, he turned and hurried from the bar, awkwardly pushing the hand truck in front of him.

He loaded the kegs and the dolly into his truck and climbed, trembling, behind the wheel. Did that really just happen, he asked himself? Were those men coming on to him? That was a bit disconcerting, but also flattering, he mused as a smile crossed his face. It faded as another thought occurred to him. Were they flirting with him, or were they making fun of him? The more he thought about it, the more convinced he became that their attention had been nothing but mockery. Was he so homely that other gay men would never find him attractive? Would all of them take one look at him and reject him out of hand?

Still, whatever the two men's intention had been, it had been an interesting experience setting foot in a gay bar for the first time. Even if no one looked at him or spoke to him, he had finally been among his own people.

Leaving Justiceville: A Life Behind

At Ricky's next stop, a somewhat more sedate country and western bar called the Six-Fifty-One, he watched in awe as a group of about twenty men line-danced to some familiar sounding country song. They were all wearing well fitting Wrangler jeans and western shirts, with cowboy boots and hats to complete the ensemble. Wow, Ricky thought, these guys are so sexy, and the way they're dancing in unison is very erotic.

He walked around the edge of the dance floor until he was standing off to the side of the dancers. After observing them for several minutes, he began trying to imitate their steps as unobtrusively as possible.

An attractive man in his thirties dancing nearby noticed him. He had dark hair and a handlebar mustache, and he took Ricky by the hand and pulled him over to stand beside him. Ricky tried to pull away, but the man was adamant.

"I'm supposed to be working," Ricky frowned anxiously.

"You've got time to line dance with me," the man said.

"I don't know how."

"Come on," he smiled at the youth. "I'll teach you. Watch me and do what I do."

Slowly he went through the basic steps of this particular line dance, while Ricky did his best to follow along.

"That's it," the man said encouragingly. "You're getting it."

Leaving Justiceville: A Life Behind

This was a first for Ricky. He'd never done any dancing in his entire life, and he felt awkward and exposed, like everyone was staring at him. It was embarrassing, he thought, but it was also kind of exhilarating.

"Relax," the older man said. "Just let your body move to the music."

Ricky strove to do as he said, and by the end of the song was already getting the hang of it. When the music ended and another song began, the bar patrons moved off the dance floor and returned to their drinks and conversations.

"I'm Mike," the man shook Ricky's hand. He led him over to a tall table with a pair of bar stools pulled up to it. They sat down. "And you are…?"

"I'm Ricky."

"I haven't seen you here before," Mike said.

"I'm not really here," Ricky said hesitantly. "I mean, I'm here, but I'm working. I'm the new keg driver for Heller Brewing."

"I got that from your uniform," Mike said dryly.

Ricky stood up and prepared to leave.

"I have to go," he said.

"When are you coming back?" Mike asked him. He grinned enticingly. "There's more dance steps I can teach you."

"Uh, I don't know," Ricky said. "Maybe…tomorrow night?"

"Great," Mike said. "I'll see you here tomorrow night. Nine o'clock."

Leaving Justiceville: A Life Behind

Ricky continued his deliveries. All the bars he visited were busy and filled with dozens of cheerful men and women, who were having a ball dancing and laughing and visiting with their friends. At the Inc. club, he was startled when a group of young men whistled and catcalled at him. He looked over at them bashfully and several of them gave him a thumbs up sign. He supposed he should be offended by their inappropriate attention, but he couldn't help but blush and grin back at them.

By the time he finished his route that evening, he had received more than a few offers of free drinks or to dance, wolf whistles, or pinches on the ass from bar patrons. Well, at least he knew the attention he was getting was positive, and he felt an inordinate amount of pleasure at the complimentary words, even if they were sometimes crude and suggestive.

The next evening, Ricky finished his shift and then hurried home to put on his new Wranglers and cowboy boots. He had to admit that his ass looked particularly good in his jeans. Somewhat nervously, he stepped into the Six-Fifty-One and took a seat at the end of the bar. He ordered a Coke and sipped on it while he looked warily around the room. Mike was sitting across the dance floor from him at a table with a couple of other guys about his age. He glanced up and noticed Ricky sitting by himself. Ricky quickly dropped his gaze and turned away. Mike said a few words to his companions and then walked over to the bar.

Leaving Justiceville: A Life Behind

"Hey, Ricky," he said with a smile. "I've been watching for you."

"You have?" Ricky gulped.

"Yeah. Come on over and sit with me and my buddies."

Somewhat reluctantly, Ricky followed him back to his table, where Mike introduced him to his friends, Bill and Frank. It turned out that Bill and Frank were a couple, a concept that was new to Ricky. He had never thought about two men actually living together in a committed relationship before. He had assumed that gay guys hooked up for sex and then went about their business with no attachments. But here was proof that two men could truly fall in love, just like straight people. Of course, he'd never seen any straight couples that really loved each other, either. Certainly not his parents or any other members of his family, nor anyone else he could think of. But here were Bill and Frank, with Bill's arm around Frank's shoulders and Frank's hand tucked into a back pocket on Bill's tight Wranglers.

"So you guys…live together?" Ricky asked, trying to ascertain if he was understanding the situation correctly. "Like a man and a woman?"

"We are not like a man and a woman," Bill chuckled. "But we live together because we love one another, and we've made a commitment to each other."

"We live like a married couple," Frank explained. "Just because the government doesn't recognize our relationship doesn't mean that we can't love each other and promise to always stay faithful."

Leaving Justiceville: A Life Behind

"You look doubtful," Mike grinned at Ricky.
"No, I think it's great," Ricky said hastily. "It's just new to me. All of this is so…new."
A popular country song began to play over the speakers.
"Come on!" Frank said eagerly. He pulled Bill and Ricky onto the dance floor. Mike took his place next to Ricky and showed him the dance steps. In a matter of moments, Ricky was moving to the music as best he could, lagging behind just a little as he learned the correct steps. Bill and Frank laughed at his clumsiness, and he laughed with them.
This is so much fun, he thought happily! These are nice guys who seem to really like me. And they're sharp and educated and attractive, too, and they're treating me like I'm one of them! How wild is that? Do they not realize that I come from trash and have spent half my life living in my car or ditches or on heating grates?
These sweet and funny men were just the opposite of all the ignorant and redneck men and women with whom he had grown up. So perhaps he truly was more than the trash that his parents had told him he was. If these guys liked him, then maybe he was worthwhile, after all.
Ricky spent the next several hours laughing and talking and dancing with Mike and many of his friends. He was introduced to a dozen men and women that night, and he did his best to remember all of their names. They all greeted him with welcoming

smiles and handshakes, and they treated him like part of their group without question.

He stepped into the bathroom to relieve himself at one of the urinals and looked in wonder at all the names and phone numbers written on the wall in front of him. He took a moment to examine them closer and was startled when a voice spoke over his shoulder.

"You don't want to call any of those guys," Mike said with a grin. "You don't know what you might be getting yourself into."

"I wasn't going to call them," Ricky said. "I was just curious."

Mike pressed against him from behind.

"You're very cute," he said. "You know that?"

"I'm not really cute, am I?" Ricky said. "You're just messing with me."

Mike turned him around and placed his hands on either side of his head. He pulled his face up and kissed him. Ricky tried to cover his exposed groin with his hands, but Mike pushed them away so that he could fondle the younger man. A few seconds later, he dropped to his knees and took Ricky's length into his mouth. Ricky looked around in a panic at being exposed and doing such a thing in public, but soon realized that no one was paying them any attention, other than a few interested bystanders who were cheering them on, that is.

It took only a couple of minutes for Ricky to climax under Mike's expert ministrations.

Leaving Justiceville: A Life Behind

"Will you come home with me tonight?" Mike asked him. "I'd like to really be with you."
"You would?"
"Yes, I would," Mike said. "Wouldn't you like to be with me?"
Ricky started to answer, but Mike held up a hand to stop him.
"Just for sex," he clarified. "And just as friends."
"Just as friends?"
"That's right," Mike grinned at him. "You're just a baby; you're too young to be in a relationship, especially with someone who's probably fifteen years older than you. But I like you. You're sweet and adorable."
Ricky said good night to all of his new friends and walked a few blocks with Mike to his apartment. It was a small space but nicely decorated. Mike and Ricky undressed somewhat diffidently and climbed into Mike's bed where, for the next hour, they made love to one another. It was a lovely experience for Ricky, and he savored the male contact. Mike was a kind and generous lover, and it was clear that he enjoyed their time together as much as Ricky did. After that night, Mike and Ricky remained friends, as they did with all in their small circle. They never slept together again, however, because it was about that time that Mike met a gentleman named Clyde. The two of them started dating, and Ricky watched somewhat enviously as the two developed their new friendship into a loving relationship.

Leaving Justiceville: A Life Behind

He continued to frequent the Six-Fifty-One club every weekend and a few other nights during the week. It was quite a change for him since he had spent most of his life as a solitary figure. He was quite content to be alone, but he found to his surprise that he was savoring his new friends. Each night that he set foot inside the bar, a chorus of welcomes would meet his ears, and he eagerly looked forward to that greeting.

Dancing, laughing, and sharing the details of their lives with one another; it was the first time in his life that he actually thoroughly enjoyed himself and other people.

He was popular with the bar crowd, and not just because of his appealing looks. No one was more surprised than he was to find that he had a sense of humor. There hadn't been much to laugh at until now, so this was a new aspect to his personality that he and the world were discovering.

Life for Ricky was good for the next couple of years. He continued to work long, tough hours; after a lifetime of toil and strife, he didn't know how to do anything else but work hard. At least now, thankfully, he had a social life as well as a professional life.

He began to open up somewhat to his coworkers, and he developed some friendships there. He was invited to parties and out to dinner, so much of his free time was taken up these days.

Quite a number of men at the clubs were interested in Ricky, but he found that most of them merely wanted

one thing. After meeting Bill and Frank, and Mike and Clyde, he felt that he wanted more than just casual one-night hookups. Not that he was judging the guys that wanted that, because he himself was intimate with some of these guys. He had, like most young men his age, a very strong libido, and every so often it needed more than just jerking off to a picture of Robert Redford or Burt Reynolds.

His efforts were rewarded at Heller Brewing. Within a year, he was promoted once again, this time to the position of Draft Supervisor, making the most money he had ever earned in his life. It was his responsibility to set up new accounts and install all the apparatus required for the bar to sell their product. He also managed signage in the clubs, oversaw the keg drivers, and took over their routes when one of them would call in sick. It was a lot of responsibility, but Ricky was up to it, and he took his job very seriously. As always, he put everything he had into his work, which pleased his bosses greatly.
"You're the best Draft Supervisor we've ever had," one of them told him one day. "One of these days you'll be running the company, I'll bet."

Ricky became good friends with one of the women who helped answer phones on Saturday mornings during that time. Going from no friends ever to having lots of friends was a bit jarring to him, but he relished it. Her name was Tara, and she lived with her doting mother Mary Ann in a very nice house in

Fort Worth. She was a few years older than Ricky, a stocky woman with short dark hair cut in a masculine style.

Whenever Ricky wasn't at the Six-Fifty-One with his friends, he spent time with Tara and her mom. Ricky had never laughed so hard in his life than when the three of them would sit in their kitchen, talking and drinking beer. He rarely spent any time at his apartment anymore, and oftentimes would sleep in Tara's guestroom rather than drive across town.

"Why the hell don't you move in here with us?" Tara asked him one evening at the kitchen table. "We've got the extra room, and you sleep here half the time anyway."

"It's silly for you to keep your apartment," Mary Ann added. "Save your money. It'll be cheaper for you to live here, and you can save for a down-payment on a house of your own."

Ricky considered their offer for a few weeks. It made sense, he thought, since he was renting an apartment and furniture that he rarely used. Splitting the bills with Tara and her mother would help them out and allow him to save money too. It was a win-win situation for all of them, the more that he thought about it. He would still have his privacy, with his own bedroom and bathroom. The three of them got along beautifully, so he wasn't worried about there being any conflicts. Eventually he made the decision and moved in with them.

It was at this time that Ricky received another promotion at Heller Brewing. He became the

Leaving Justiceville: A Life Behind

Advertising Manager, which meant that he oversaw the day to day advertising sales for the managers, supervisors, salesmen, and drivers. This was a job that Ricky thoroughly enjoyed.

He even hired his friend Slick to be an advertising representative. Now that he saw him again on a daily basis, their friendship grew even stronger. Slick was a hard worker, and Ricky gave him the unofficial job as his assistant. They joked and laughed and worked hard, causing the hours on the job to fly by.

With his professional and personal lives going well, Ricky was more relaxed and slept better than ever before. He felt more content and satisfied with his life. Tara and Mary Ann were like family to him, although nothing like his own family, of course.

He had seen and heard nothing from them since his mother's visit to the drive in at Taco Rio. When he thought of them now, he noticed that he was no longer quite as bitter and angry. He still harbored a grudge against them for unfairly stealing his childhood from him, but at least that was no longer in the front of his mind every day. With all the good things and people in his life now, he found that they were no longer as important to him. The past was the past and could not be changed, so why dwell on it, he decided.

Tara and Mary Ann and Ricky lived together harmoniously for the next few years. Ricky was making the most money he'd ever earned, but Tara and Mary Ann were struggling to make ends meet.

Leaving Justiceville: A Life Behind

Mary Ann answered phones for an answering service and made barely more than minimum wage, so often times Ricky paid more than his share of the bills.
As a favor to them, Ricky hired Tara to work as a beer line cleaner, the same job that he had done when he first started with the company. While running her route, she met a rather heavy-set woman named Gloria, and the two became good friends. Gloria began spending more and more time at the house, and the four of them laughed and enjoyed each other's company.
Gloria complained about her job as a checker at the Winn-Dixie store, saying her boss was unfair and the pay was lousy. Eventually Ricky found Gloria a job at Heller Brewing. It was a fairly low paying job, but it was better than her previous one.

Leaving Justiceville: A Life Behind

CHAPTER FOURTEEN

One Saturday evening, Gloria held a party at her house with her roommate Tammy, and Tara and Mary Ann and Ricky were invited. Ricky drove himself there after running one of his driver's routes. He stepped inside the rather rundown house and took his jacket off. He stepped into the living room and was surprised to find that all the guests were women, and that they were all looking askance at him. It suddenly dawned on him that this was an all female gathering, and he was the only man present.

He greeted a few of them with a friendly nod and made his way to the kitchen. Tara and Mary Ann were talking with Gloria and the woman who he assumed was her roommate. Gloria turned to him and frowned.

"What are you doing in my kitchen?" she demanded. "I don't like men in my kitchen."

"What?" he said, taken aback at her tone as well the question itself. "I...I just wanted to get something to drink."

"Come into the pantry for a second," Gloria said, taking his elbow and guiding him into the small room. She lowered her voice. "You need to leave."

"Why?" Ricky frowned.

"I've got a party going on," she said.

"I know. You invited me, remember?"

"I know, but you need to go," she said impatiently.

"But why?"

Leaving Justiceville: A Life Behind

"I don't want you here," she said. "You don't fit in with my guests. Can't you see they're all women?"
"I know that," he said, his temper beginning to flare. "But if you didn't want me to come, why the hell did you invite me?"
"I was trying to be polite. But this isn't the place for you. So go."
Ricky slammed his drink down on the counter and stormed to the entryway, where he snatched up his coat and ran from the house. He sped away with angry tears in his eyes. He drove straight to the Six-Fifty-One club and spent the rest of the evening with his friends.
After a while, he felt better, but his feelings had been hurt at being basically thrown out of a party to which he had been invited, and for no good reason!

It wasn't long before Gloria began spending most nights with Tara in her bedroom. When questioned about it by her mother, Tara insisted that there was nothing going on between her and Gloria. She told them that she was having an affair with the man who lived across the street, a young man with a live-in girlfriend. Ricky and Mary Ann gave each other a look with raised eyebrows, knowing that Tara wasn't telling the truth.
"You're gay," Ricky said. "Just admit it. There's nothing wrong with being a lesbian."
"That's right," Mary Ann chimed in. "You have nothing to be ashamed of."

Leaving Justiceville: A Life Behind

"I'm not ashamed and I'm not a lesbian!" Tara snapped. "The neighbor and I have sex all the time."
"You do not," Ricky snorted. "You don't like guys. I've always known that."
"You have not! And I do like guys, or I wouldn't be sleeping with him."
"So what's Gloria doing sleeping in your room?" Mary Ann asked pointedly.
"Her roommate is abusive to her, so she needs someplace safe to sleep," Tara said. "That's all she's doing. Sleeping!"
"Uh, huh," Mary Ann said dryly. "You're sharing a bed with a gay woman and nothing's happening."
"Well, believe what you want," Tara said. "I'm not gay."

It wasn't long before Gloria moved into the house with the three of them. Her demeanor toward Ricky changed immediately. Whereas he had considered them friends, she suddenly became cold and distant whenever he was around.

One day, she and Tara knocked on Ricky's bedroom door. Without waiting for him to answer, they opened the door and strode into the room, continuing a conversation they were apparently in the middle of. Ricky looked up from his bed, where he was listening to some music on his cassette player.

"See," Gloria said, pointing to the wall that abutted the kitchen. "We can put the washer and dryer here. It wouldn't cost that much to run new plumbing from

the kitchen. And over here we could put a folding table and wash-sink."

"What are you guys talking about?" he asked with a frown.

"Gloria wants to turn this room into the laundry room," Tara explained.

"My bedroom? You want to turn my bedroom into the laundry room?" Ricky said, not believing his ears.

"You could still sleep in here," Gloria shrugged. "Your bed can stay where it is, and you can still have half of the closet."

"This is my room!" he said. "You can't just come in here and take it away from me. I pay a big part of the bills here, you know."

"Yes, but it isn't your house, now is it?" Gloria said. "It belongs to Mary Ann and Tara, so you have no say on what goes on here."

"This is my home," he said indignantly. "I do have a say on what goes on here."

Gloria looked at Tara and rolled her eyes.

"You see, it doesn't pay to have a man in the house," she said. "They think they own the place, and they always ruin everything."

"I'm not trying to ruin anything," Ricky said defensively. "But you can't turn my bedroom into a laundry room without my saying it's okay, for god's sake!"

The two women glared at him and left the room.

"We'll see what Mom has to say about this," Tara said.

Leaving Justiceville: A Life Behind

"No!" Mary Ann said emphatically. "You are not turning Ricky's room into a laundry room!"
"He'll still have a bed," Gloria said irritably.
"This is his house as much as it is mine or Tara's," Mary Ann said.
"No, it's not," Gloria said. "His name isn't on the deed, so he has no say."
"And neither do you," Mary Ann glowered at her. "You're not going to come into my house and –"
"It's my house too," Tara interjected. "And this is no big deal. So Ricky has the washer and dryer in his room. What's wrong with that?"
"Because it's my bedroom!" Ricky said. "If you want a bigger laundry room so bad, turn your room into one."
"Don't be ridiculous," Gloria snorted. "There are two people sleeping in our room."
"Sleeping," Mary Ann said. "Yeah, right."
"Don't start, Mom," Tara said warningly.
"Look," Mary Ann said, trying to remain calm. "Ricky is like a son to me, and I will not treat him this way. That's all there is to it."
The arguing continued for a while until finally Ricky had had enough.
"Stop it!" he shouted. "I'm done with all of this."
He looked at Tara.
"If your new girlfriend is more important to you than me, go ahead and do what she wants," he said. "I've had enough of all of this. I'm moving the fuck out."
"Fine," Tara shrugged indifferently.

Leaving Justiceville: A Life Behind

"Now, Ricky, you are not moving out," Mary Ann said. "You were here long before Gloria. If anyone's moving out, it's her."

That's when the shouting and cursing really began between the three women. Ricky backed away and returned to his bedroom, where he began packing up his things. Once again, he was out on his ear with no place to stay except his car.

Well, he told himself, it's your own fault. You should have known that something like this would happen eventually. You can never, ever count on other people, even the ones who claim to be your friends. That was a lesson you learned as a child, and apparently you're still naïve enough to think that people are decent and good. They will always let you down, every goddamn time!

The only people so far that hadn't let him down were his friends at the clubs. True, they were more casual friends, but they were all he had. He stopped at the Six-Fifty-One club, and before the evening was over, he had a half dozen places to stay for a while until he got back on his feet.

Ricky was making well over thirty thousand dollars a year now, an extremely good wage for that time, and he decided it was time to buy a house of his own, something that no one could kick him out of or take away from him. Over the next week or so, he worked with a realtor to buy a brand new house in North Richland Hills. He borrowed enough money from the bank to purchase furniture.

Leaving Justiceville: A Life Behind

"Now, you understand that this mortgage has a fluctuating interest rate," the loan officer said as Ricky signed the paperwork.
"What does that mean?" Ricky asked him.
"Oh, nothing you need to worry about," the man assured him. "It merely means that your monthly payment may go up or down a little, depending on the current interest rate."
"How much are you talking about?" Ricky asked worriedly.
"Just a few dollars," the loan officer smiled. "Don't worry about it. With your income, you'll have more than enough money to pay it, no matter how much it goes up. You do want the loan for your new house, don't you?"
"Yes, but –"
"Just sign the papers, Mr. Blain," the man said. "Once you're living in your new house, none of this will matter."
And so Ricky signed the papers.

For the first year, Ricky reveled in his new house. It was a small brick ranch located in a very nice, new subdivision. Wow, he thought with a sense of awe, his very own house! And it was new and clean and classy, so different from the way he had grown up. It had new carpeting and appliances, fresh paint on the walls, nice light fixtures, two bathrooms, and even drapes and blinds on the windows. Once he added his new furniture, he felt like the richest king living in his castle. And there was an attached garage that he

could put his car in. Where before he had been forced to live in his car, now even his car had a house! To most people, that was just ordinary life, but to Ricky it was thrilling and almost beyond belief!

Ricky occasionally saw Tara and Gloria at work, and he was pleasant and courteous to them, but their friendship was not the same now. It wasn't in his nature to hold a grudge or be unkind to anyone; he knew only too well how it felt to be on the receiving end of other people's cruelty.
He also understood Tara's need to put her girlfriend first, even though she had yet to admit that they were indeed in a relationship. If he ever had a boyfriend, a possibility he deemed unlikely, he would have to come first above everybody else. That's the way relationships were meant to be, he thought.
How nice it would be, he sighed wistfully, to have a partner to share all of this with; someone to love and to love him, someone to come home to, who was happy to see him. Stranger things had happened, he supposed, but he didn't expect there to be anyone like that in his future. Still, as long as he had his work and his friends at the clubs, he was good. Don't ever rely on anyone else for your happiness, he told himself sternly. You alone are responsible for that.

About a year into living in his new house, he opened his mailbox one day to find a letter from the bank which held his mortgage. His eyes opened wide as he read through the short document. It was unfortunate,

Leaving Justiceville: A Life Behind

it said, but since the interest rates had suddenly skyrocketed, his monthly payment on his home was going to more than double. But, the letter went on, he had agreed to the terms of the loan, so he was obligated to pay whatever amount the rate dictated. Basically, it informed Ricky that they were sorry for his bad luck, but he was screwed! Either pay an amount that he could not afford each month, or lose his home, the first thing of any value that he had ever owned.

He dropped heavily down on his front stoop and looked around with tears in his eyes. What the hell was he going to do now? His gut feeling when he had signed the papers for his loan was that the bank was being dishonest with him, and yet he knew that the fault didn't lay with them, but with himself. He had been suspicious when the loan officer assured him that said his monthly payment would only fluctuate by a few dollars at the most over the term of the loan, but he had not pressed the issue. Instead he had signed the papers willingly, so he was to blame for all of this.

The next day, a co-manager at work suggested he find a roommate to help make his mortgage payment. It wasn't an ideal solution since Ricky enjoyed living alone, but at least it would help him keep his house. "Dan is looking for a place to rent," his friend said, referring to one of the delivery drivers. "Why don't you talk to him about it?"

Leaving Justiceville: A Life Behind

Ricky spoke to Dan later that day, and an agreement was reached. Dan was a decent guy, Ricky thought, reasonably attractive, clean and reliable. He dated one of the women in the office off and on, so Ricky knew he was straight. That was good, he thought, since that way there could be no complications developing from any sexual tension.

Dan worked full time while he was going to college in Fort Worth, so he was rarely at home. He usually came in late at night and kept to his bedroom to either sleep or study. That suited Ricky just fine and made his home still feel like his own.

This arrangement worked well for a few months until late one night when Dan knocked on Ricky's bedroom door.

"Ricky?" he called out. "Are you still awake?"

"Yeah," Ricky answered sleepily. "What do you need?"

Dan slipped into the dark room and closed the door behind him. Ricky looked around but didn't see him in the blackness. A moment later he felt the covers on the bed lift over him and a warm body slip into the bed behind him.

"Dan, what are you doing?" he asked with a frown.

"I just want to talk to you," Dan whispered. "There's something I need to tell you."

"Okay," Ricky said warily.

A moment later Dan's naked body was lying on top of him, and he was kissing him passionately. Ricky tried halfheartedly to push him away for a few seconds but finally gave in to the lust he was feeling.

Leaving Justiceville: A Life Behind

The two made love to one another for several hours, with Dan moving slowly and sensually in and out of Ricky's body until he climaxed mightily at last. Ricky experienced his own orgasm at the same time, and then the two of them lay side by side, panting for breath.

"That was great," Ricky grinned. "It was a total surprise, but it was fun. All this time I assumed you were straight."

There was no answer from his bed partner.

"So what did you want to tell me?"

"Uh, nothing, I guess," Dan mumbled. "Good night." Without another word, he climbed out of bed, picked up his clothes, and quietly left the room.

The next morning, Dan was sound asleep when Ricky left for work, judging by the snoring coming from behind his bedroom door. Last night had been a lot of fun, Ricky thought with a smile as he drove to the office, although totally unexpected. He had had no inkling that Dan was attracted to him, or even gay, for that matter. Maybe they would do it again sometime. Dan was a nice looking man, and they got along well together; he was an ideal roommate since he was rarely at home.

Ricky didn't see Dan for the next couple of days, although it was evident from the bathroom and kitchen that he had been there. On the third day, Ricky came home from work to find all of Dan's things gone and his house key lying on the kitchen

counter. The next day, when he spoke to the co-manager who had recommended Dan as a roommate, he was informed that he hadn't seen Dan either, but that he had requested the DFW Airport route. That was a nightly route and in the opposite direction of most of Ricky's accounts.

"Well, he moved out without a word to me," Ricky said with annoyance.

"Did something happen between you two?" the other manager asked with a knowing look. "I mean, did you two have a fight or something?"

"No," Ricky shrugged. "Nothing happened. I thought everything was fine."

"Well, I heard he's going to ask that girl from the office he's been seeing to marry him. Maybe he's planning on moving in with her."

"Yeah, that's probably it," Ricky said dryly.

He did see Dan a few times in passing after that, but Dan avoided him, and the two didn't speak again.

Thanksgiving week arrived, and Ricky was barely keeping his financial head above water. Without a roommate, he was nearly drowning under his outrageous mortgage, his car payment, and his other bills. He kept on the lookout for a new roommate but so far had had no luck.

Mary Ann called Ricky the day before and insisted that he come for dinner.

"Now I won't hear any arguments," she said firmly. "You're like a son to me, and I want you here for Thanksgiving."

Leaving Justiceville: A Life Behind

"What about Gloria?" Ricky asked hesitantly.
"What about her?" Mary Ann said. "She may live here, but this is my house, and Tara and I want you here. We miss seeing you."
"I miss you too," Ricky said, swallowing hard.

Thanksgiving Day arrived, and Ricky drove over early per Mary Ann's instructions so they could watch the parades on television together. Gloria was cool but cordial to Ricky, and he was friendly back to her.
The day passed by pleasantly. The four of them cooked a turkey and stuffing with mashed potatoes and gravy, green been casserole, and hot rolls for their holiday meal. They talked and laughed together, and it almost felt like old times to Ricky.
Late in the day, Mary Ann fixed them turkey sandwiches and leftovers, after which Ricky said his goodbyes and headed home.
He was unusually tired when he walked into his kitchen from the garage, and he felt a bit nauseated with a sharp pain in his lower abdomen. I hope I'm not catching a flu bug, he thought. Wearily, he took a shower and then dropped heavily onto his bed. He was asleep within seconds of his head hitting the pillow.

Around two o'clock in the morning, Ricky awoke in intense pain. His color was ashen, and he was diaphoretic. Something's seriously wrong, he thought fearfully. Forcing himself out of bed, he fell to his

knees. He tried to stand, but when he did, the pain increased even more. So he crawled from his bedroom down the hallway to the living room. It took all of his strength to reach for the phone and call Tara and Mary Ann. Through gritted teeth, he tersely explained the situation and asked them to take him to the hospital. He tried once more to stand, and the sudden jolt of intense pain that seared through his belly caused him to black out. He lay unconscious on the floor, the phone receiver on the floor beside his hand, beeping its alert to his unhearing ears.

He was to learn later that it took Tara almost an hour to find his house since she had never been there before. She finally located the address and, together with her mother, got Ricky's limp form into their car and raced him to Fort Worth Osteopathic hospital. Ricky awoke briefly in the backseat of the car.
"What's going on?" he asked weakly.
"We're taking you to the hospital," Mary Ann explained gently.
"Owww!" Ricky doubled over with pain again. "Oh god, it hurts!"
That was all Ricky remembered for the next few days.

Tara and Mary Ann stayed with Ricky in the Emergency Department of the enormous facility. The nurses explained that Ricky was going to be taken for a CT scan. About an hour later, the doctor came into the waiting room to speak to them.

Leaving Justiceville: A Life Behind

"Mr. Blain has a mass of some sort in his lower abdomen near his appendix," he said gravely. "At this point, we don't know what it is, but it has apparently caused a blockage, an obstruction in his bowel. That is the reason for his severe pain."
"What can you do?" Mary Ann asked worriedly.
"We're going to take him into surgery so we can better determine what we're dealing with."
"Is he going to be okay?" Tara asked.
"I don't have enough information to answer that question right now," the doctor said regretfully. "But I'll come back and talk to you as soon as I can."

Four hours later, the surgeon returned to the waiting room and spoke to Mary Ann and Tara.
"Mr. Blain is very fortunate," he began. "The bowel was obstructed, as we expected, and he had developed a rather large abscess as a result. Also, there was a tumor on his appendix which I suspect to be benign. We will send it for biopsy, and it will take a few days to get the results back."
He gave them a very serious look.
"If you hadn't gotten him here when you did, I don't believe he would have survived. If the abscess had ruptured, it would have poisoned the entire abdominal cavity, and the situation would have deteriorated very quickly if that had happened."

Ricky remained mostly unaware of his surroundings for the next several days. The nurses kept him medicated for severe pain, but his discomfort

continued due to the JP drain the surgeon had inserted into the wound to help suck out the remaining pus and blood that had collected in the abscess. He also had multiple IVs and a catheter inserted into his bladder, which was extremely uncomfortable to him.

He had a few visitors from work and from the clubs, but he didn't remember any of them being there. Much to his astonishment, Mary Ann told him later that his sister had even come to see him, as well as one of his cousins and an aunt and uncle. He never learned how any of them knew he was in the hospital. Ricky remained a patient for just over two weeks. It took several more weeks for his wound to heal, and the doctors insisted that he be off work for at least a month. With no income coming in, and no prospects for a suitable roommate, Ricky made a tough decision. One of his managers at work was looking for a place to rent with his family, so Ricky leased his house to them while he rented a very inexpensive little house down the street from Mary Ann and Tara. The mortgage on his house had steadily increased to the point that he simply couldn't afford it. With the rental income and the cheap rent on his house, Ricky was able to pay his bills much easier.

His recovery went as expected with no complications. The surgeon told him that the tumor they had removed was indeed benign, much to his relief.

By now, his car was getting a little worse for wear. He put a lot of miles on it with work and the clubs

Leaving Justiceville: A Life Behind

and his friends, so he decided, now that he could afford it, he was going to treat himself to his dream car. After all, he reasoned, he worked hard, and his job was secure, so why not?
It was with a great sense of pride and pleasure that Ricky drove off the lot at Haggerty Ford in his new red Mustang GT! He drove it around town to show it off to his friends, all of whom were very pleased for him.

Life for Ricky was good, he thought with satisfaction. He lived in a decent place, even if it was an older home, and he owned his dream car. He had good friends and a great job with frequent raises and bonuses. What else could he possibly ask for? He had come so far from his awful childhood in Justiceville, and life was better than he ever would have dreamed.

CHAPTER FIFTEEN

Work at Heller Brewing continued going well, and he was now an executive with the company, albeit a lowly one compared to the vice-presidents and other top employees. Practically every worker knew and liked him. They were fully aware that they could count on him to do his job well or to help them out whenever they needed it. Even the owners of the company knew they could rely on him. Whenever there were high profile parties, such as entertaining the Governor or other highly placed officials, Ricky was requested to work the events. He always left a good impression with the important guests, which in turn reflected well on the owners and the company and its products.

Every time there was a special event planned at one of the local bars, restaurants, grocery stores, and Catholic churches, Ricky was asked to be in charge. It was surprising to him, but all of the Catholic Church events in South Arlington always served beer at their gatherings. Soon there wasn't an occasion where Heller Beer was being served that Ricky wasn't asked to attend and supervise.

Ricky sat behind the pilot in a Cessna 182 airplane as it flew a few hundred feet above the flat Texas landscape. What the hell am I doing, he thought anxiously? This is crazy! He and two of his friends from Heller Brewing had parachutes strapped to their

Leaving Justiceville: A Life Behind

backs and were waiting for their instructor to tell them when to jump.

"Oh, come on," his friend Mack said to him one day a few weeks ago. "It'll be fun.

"Are you out of your mind?" Ricky asked him good-naturedly. "There's no way I'm jumping out of a plane!"

And yet, here he was. He still couldn't figure out how the man had convinced him to do something so foolish.

The instructor opened the door of the plane and Ricky instinctively shrank back away from it.

"Okay," the man yelled. "Remember what I told you."

He went on to reiterate the lessons they had learned in their skydiving classes.

"Okay, Mack," he shouted. "You're first."

With a grin, Mack stepped up to the door and fearlessly jumped out of the plane. Ricky watched in horror, knowing that he was going to have to do the same thing in just a few seconds. His other friend stood in the doorway and leaped out into the rushing air.

"Okay, Ricky," the instructor said. "Come on."

Ricky made his way to the opening in the side of the plane, reaching out all the way for something solid to hang on to.

"One, two, three," the instructor yelled. "Jump!"

Ricky hesitated and moved away from the door in fear.

"I can't," he said. "I can't do it."

Leaving Justiceville: A Life Behind

"Yes, you can," the man said patiently. "You know what to do, and once you've jumped, you'll love it." Ricky nodded shakily and stepped up to the door. "Hey, Bert!" his instructor yelled to the pilot.
The next thing Ricky knew, the plane tilted sharply and he slid helplessly out of the doorway. He screamed in panic as he fell at one hundred twenty miles an hour toward the ground. It took a moment for him to bring his terror under control, but as soon as he could think, he pulled the ripcord, and the parachute deployed above him. His rate of descent slowed dramatically, but he remained almost paralyzed with fear. The ground still seemed to be approaching at an alarming rate of speed, he thought. He had about ten seconds to look around and try to appreciate the scenery, but a new sense of dread filled his mind as he looked down to see where the wind was carrying him. Oh my god, he thought! I'm not over the landing site! I'm going to land on the freeway!

Dozens and dozens of cars zipped along the divided highway beneath him. He was helpless to stop himself or guide the parachute to an alternate spot. As the pavement grew closer and closer, Ricky forced himself not to close his eyes since he knew he needed to see where he was landing. The cars and trucks that had appeared as tiny little dots now looked huge and intimidating.

Okay, it was time to land, he told himself, trying his best to remain calm. He brought his legs up as the instructor had taught him so that his body was in an

Leaving Justiceville: A Life Behind

L-shape. There was nothing he could do about the traffic; all he could do is hope that he didn't get run over by a car or semi. The paved road hurtled toward him, and he hit it more forcefully than he expected. In a moment he was rolling along the pavement, getting entangled in the parachute lines and the parachute itself. He heard squealing brakes all around him, but he couldn't see anything because of the billowing fabric that surrounded him.

When he finally rolled to a stop with cuts and abrasions all over him, he took a moment to regain his senses. He fought through the parachute material until he could look out. There were cars and trucks all around him sitting sideways in the roadway or in the ditch. A few people had alit from their vehicles and were running in his direction. Several of them helped him out of his harness, and he clumsily got to his feet. One of the people assisting him held him up when he seemed unable to stand on his own.

It was only a few seconds later that a police car shrieked to a stop nearby, lights flashing and sirens blaring.

"What the hell's the matter with you, you stupid punk?" the grim looking officer yelled at him as he strode over to him. "Do you know that you could have caused a lot of innocent people to die from a stunt like this?"

"It wasn't his fault, Officer," someone said. "It was out of his control."

"Let me see some identification," the cop demanded.

Leaving Justiceville: A Life Behind

Ricky shakily reached into his back pocket and tried to open his wallet. A woman standing next to him kindly helped him extract his driver's license.
"Don't you even want to know if he's okay?" another person asked. "Can't you see how shaken up he is?"
The policeman didn't seem to hear either of them as he pulled out a ticket pad and began writing out a citation.
"I'm giving you a ticket this time," he said sternly. "But if you ever pull anything like this again, I'll see to it that you're thrown in jail! You got that, kid?"
"Yes, sir," Ricky said tremulously.
The gentleman supporting him strengthened his grip as Ricky's knees gave out on him.
"Officer, I think he needs to go to the emergency room," the man said.
"Get in the car," the officer said gruffly.
A couple of people helped Ricky into the backseat of the police car and, once traffic had resumed, the officer drove Ricky to the airfield to pick up his car. He drove away without a word, leaving Ricky to sit in his car until his nerves had calmed enough for him to safely drive. Instead of going to the hospital, he drove home and treated his multiple wounds himself.

One day in 1989, Ricky was called into the president's luxurious office.
"Sit down, Ricky," Mr. Paine said, indicating a leather upholstered chair in front of the massive mahogany desk. "I'd like to talk to you."
"Sure, sir," Ricky said respectfully.

Leaving Justiceville: A Life Behind

The man had a reputation for being racist, misogynistic, and homophobic behind closed doors, but Ricky never witnessed that kind of behavior from him. He had always treated Ricky well. He and his two brothers owned the company; he served as president with one brother acting as vice-president, and the third as operations manager. All three men seemed to be decent guys, as far as Ricky was concerned.

"I've heard a rumor floating around," Mr. Paine said. "I'm curious if it's true."

"A rumor?" Ricky said uneasily.

He had a sinking feeling that he knew where this conversation was headed, and it turned out he was correct.

"Are you gay?" the president asked him point blank.

"Me? Gay?" Ricky did his best to look surprised. "No, I'm not gay."

He knew better than to admit anything to anyone in management. Everyone was aware of the gay employees who had been fired in the past, just for being seen going in and out of gay bars. Of course, that wasn't the official reason they had been terminated; some other excuse was fabricated, but everyone knew the truth. Heller Brewing was a very homophobic company, like most other Texas businesses at that time. How ironic, Ricky thought, that they should hate gay people so much, and yet a good portion of their income came from the gay bars that they serviced. Talk about hypocrisy!

"It's okay if you are," Mr. Paine said quickly. "It doesn't bother me in the least."
"I know," Ricky said. "But I'm not gay."
"Oh," his boss said. "It's just that Dan mentioned something that he thought you were that way."
Dan, Ricky thought disgustedly. He should have known. The biggest closet case in the company had ratted him out, that low life sonofabitch!
"Well, he was wrong," he said emphatically. "I don't know why he would say such a thing."
Ricky left the office with his face red and his fists clenched. He was furious that another gay guy, who obviously had serious issues with his own sexuality, had pointed fingers at Ricky so that attention would be directed away from himself. Well, he would have to be careful from now on; if anyone in management knew he was gay, then he would end up without a job, and he couldn't afford that.

Soon after his conversation with the company president, Ricky became aware of subtle changes in how he was treated by other employees.
Inappropriate jokes would be made, and Ricky would be forced to laugh them off.
"Hey, Blain," someone would say as they grabbed their crotch, "come over here for a minute. I got something for you to suck on." Or "Hey, Ricky, meet me in the showers." Or "Blain, I bet you'd love to lick the crack of my ass, wouldn't you?"

Leaving Justiceville: A Life Behind

One of the managers, Mick, the same man who had suggested Dan rent a room from him, approached him one day in the office.
"Hey, Ricky," he said with a genial smile. "Whatcha doing?"
Ricky looked up from his desk.
"I'm working," he frowned. "What's it look like I'm doing?"
"Working," Mick chuckled. "I just wondered if you'd like to take a break with me."
"Uh, yeah, I guess I can," Ricky set his pen down and closed the folder on which he had been working.
The two men walked outside, where his friend lit up a cigarette. They chatted for a while until Mick looked around to make sure no one was around to overhear them.
"I'm so fucking horny," he said, rubbing his crotch with his hand. "Aren't you?"
"Uh, no," Ricky frowned, startled at his friend's conduct. "Besides, we're at work. If you're horny, wait until you get home and jerk off."
"Or we could jerk off together," Mick suggested with a lascivious look in his eye. "We could go out behind that old magnolia tree and jerk each other off. I'd jerk your dick, and you could jerk mine. Wouldn't you like to jerk me off? You'd get to touch my dick."
"I don't want to jerk you off, and I don't want to touch your dick!" Ricky exclaimed indignantly. "What's the matter with you?"
"I just figured that since you're gay..." Mick shrugged.

"I'm not gay!" Ricky snapped.
"It's okay," his friend grinned cajolingly. "You can tell me. I won't tell anyone."
"Okay," Ricky said, looking around cautiously. He leaned in closer and spoke softly. "You tell me you're gay, and I'll tell you."
"I'm not gay," Mick looked both startled and annoyed.
"You just wanted to jerk me off," Ricky reminded him. "That sounds pretty gay to me."
"That was just a joke," Mick said. "But if you're not gay, why don't you ever date women?"
"I date women all the time," Ricky lied.
"I've never seen you with one. And you never talk about being with a woman."
"So?" Ricky shrugged. "Just because I don't talk about it doesn't mean I don't do it."
"What's your girlfriend's name?"
"Why does it matter what her name is?" Ricky said. "What, you want to ask her out too?"
"Just tell me her name," his companion said impatiently.
"Lisa," Ricky said. "Her name is Lisa, and she works at Taco Bell."
Wow, he thought angrily, this is turning into a witch hunt! They know, or at least suspect I'm gay, and they're all working together to find out for sure so they can fire me. Dammit!
"So this 'Lisa' is a woman? That's not code for some guy?"

Leaving Justiceville: A Life Behind

"You know, I've had enough of this conversation," Ricky said coldly. "I've got to get back to work."

The curiosity into Ricky's sex life seemed to dwindle down for a while, and he began to relax just a bit. The company owners didn't question him again, but Ricky was not naïve enough to think this was the end of it. He was sure that further inquiries would come from them, albeit indirectly.
"So how's Lisa?" one of his coworkers asked him one day.
"Lisa?" Ricky looked confused for a moment, and then he remembered. "Oh, Lisa. Uh, we broke up."
"Really?" the man said. "Well, that's great."
"It is?"
"Yeah, 'cause I got the perfect girl for you!"
And so for the next several weeks, Ricky found himself set up on blind dates with many different women, mostly by Mick and his manager friends, as well as a few other executives in the company. To allay any suspicions about his sexuality, Ricky agreed to go out with these young women, most of who seemed very nice. Naturally, nothing ever happened with any of them, and he never called them again.
As a result, the questions began to surface again, and most of them came from Ricky's fellow executives. He knew, however, that the people behind them were the three Paine brothers. Ricky kept his guard up at all times. He watched his surroundings carefully whenever he went out to the clubs, just in case he

was being observed by anyone from work. He could always use the excuse that he was merely checking on his accounts, but he realized that might not be enough.

In early 1990, the gay bars in Fort Worth, Arlington, and surrounding areas formed a boycott against Heller Brewing for their public support of an antigay ordinance that the local Republicans were trying to railroad through the city government. As a gay man and a Heller Brewing company employee, Ricky was naturally very conflicted on the matter. He couldn't support anything antigay, obviously, and yet at the same time, he didn't want to lose his job. He knew the men and women who owned these establishments, as well as their clientele, and most of them were friends of his. He could never, ever betray them! If he did, then he would be betraying himself as well.
As the boycott began to grow in popularity, and Heller Brewing began losing a significant amount of revenue, the Paine brothers turned to Ricky. None of them or any of the other managers or executives had ever set foot in any of the gay clubs.
"Ricky, you have to do something," one of the Mr. Paines said to him. "We're looking like the bad guys in all of this, not to mention that we're losing money."
And money is all you care about, you homophobic prick, Ricky thought.

Leaving Justiceville: A Life Behind

"There's nothing I can do," he shrugged. "You're supporting discrimination against your customers. What else can they do but boycott? I don't blame them."

"We're not out to hurt anybody," Mr. Paine shrugged. "We just believe in traditional values."

"And so do they," Ricky said.

"They most certainly do not!" Mr. Paine said indignantly. "They're perverts and sicko's."

"But you're still willing to take their money," Ricky said dryly.

"Whose side are you on here?" his boss scowled.

"I'm on both sides," Ricky said. "I support you and Heller Brewing because this is my job, and I can't afford to lose it. But I support them because I know them, and I know that they are good people. They are not perverts or sicko's. All they're asking for is to be treated like everyone else."

"Then they should act like everyone else," Mr. Paine snapped.

"What does everyone act like?" Ricky frowned. "We're all different from each other. Just because my tastes are different from yours doesn't mean that either of us is right or wrong. We're just different. And that's what I support: our differences! You have a right to believe what you want, but they have the right to stand up against you for their civil rights."

"I don't have time for this," Mr. Paine said. "Just fix this situation, and do it soon."

"Well, it would help if you'd withdraw support for this ordinance," Ricky said. "You don't have to

change your beliefs, just pull back and stay out of it. If you want all those gay people to continue drinking your beer, that is."

Ricky spent many hours planning events at many of the gay clubs that Heller Brewing supposedly sponsored. Actually, the Paine brothers knew nothing of what Ricky was doing, but he did it without their approval anyway. There were wet jockey-short contests, dart tournaments, pool competitions, half-price drinks, all designed to show the gay community that Heller Brewing wasn't the monster he knew them to be. It pricked his conscious a bit to try to convince his gay friends of this falsehood, but at the same time, he felt that maybe he could make a difference. To that end, he started a petition in all the clubs to demand that Heller Brewing withdraw their support of the antigay ordinance. Over a few weeks time, he collected more than a thousand signatures, and it was with a great deal of satisfaction that Ricky presented the signed documents to the Paine brothers. They dismissed the petitions as nothing more than rabble-rousers who just wanted some publicity, but one evening, as Ricky was sitting on a barstool at the Six-Fifty-One club, the news on the television at the end of the bar announced that Heller Brewing had withdrawn its support of the potential law. The crowd around Ricky cheered and hollered, and he was clapped on the back and hugged more times than he could count.

Leaving Justiceville: A Life Behind

The measure failed in the city council, and nothing was ever mentioned about it again, including all the hard work that Ricky had done to bring an end to the boycott. However, the questions into his sexuality began again in earnest. And this time, things were about to get ugly.

Joe Paine, the operations manager, began insisting that Ricky provide a detailed itinerary each day. He wanted to know where he was, who he was with, and what they were doing at all times, including his off times. Ricky resented this intrusion into his private life, and he entertained himself by making up some ridiculous activities, such as horseback riding, snow skiing, scuba diving, and so on.

Ricky noticed, too, that he was being followed now, usually by Mick or one of the other managers. He would see their cars behind him, or notice them parked down the street or outside of his house, waiting for him to go out.

A new club opened in Arlington, called Britches and Bloomers, a place that catered to both gay men and women. It was open Thursday through Sunday nights. Ricky landed the account and noticed right away that the owners of the place were in over their heads as they tried to manage staff, billing, customer demand, and more.

He would leave work late at Heller Brewing and drive to the club to help the grateful owners out with whatever he could do. It was thanks to him that

things ran smoothly. Several of his friends visited the club, and he would stop acting as bartender long enough to go out to the dance floor and party with them for a while.

Unbeknownst to Ricky, a few members of upper management were parked outside in their Mercedes when he went into the bar one Friday night. He didn't notice them peer in the front door until they spotted him dancing erotically with a couple of his closest friends.

On Monday morning, Ricky was called into Joe's office and asked pointblank if he was gay. Once again he denied it, and nothing more was said. But from that point on, things began to deteriorate even more. Ricky did his best to reign in his temper and remain patient, but it was becoming increasingly difficult.

Joe's brother, Patrick, who was the company vice-president, appointed himself as Ricky's direct supervisor. Even though Ricky was considered an executive, Patrick began demanding that he do a wide variety of jobs that were typically reserved for the lowest paid employees. For instance, he would call Ricky on a Saturday evening and tell him that there were pallets of beer that needed to be restacked immediately at some of the liquor stores. That happened on at least a dozen different occasions. Other times he would call Ricky in the middle of the night and tell him the alarm was going off at the office, and he needed to get over there right away.

Leaving Justiceville: A Life Behind

More often than not, there was no alarm going off, but Ricky was obligated to go check it out anyway. One of the more menial jobs he was ordered to do was to come in at five o'clock in the morning to sweep out the delivery vans before the drivers arrived to load them. He was told to clean toilets, drive forklifts in the warehouse, and stay up all night answering the phones in the front office in spite of having an answering service.

But the worst job, the very worst of all, was being paged overhead by Patrick to come to his office and empty his spit cup, a disgusting Styrofoam cup the odious man would fill with tobacco juice a half dozen times a day. And he didn't just partially fill it with the nausea-inducing spit and tobacco; he filled it clear to the top.

"Now you spill one drop of that on this expensive carpet and you'll be paying for it out of your salary for the next ten years," Patrick would gloat.

He was still required to work events since the public knew him so well and asked for him. One of the ruder famous people he served beer to was George W. Bush, then owner of the Texas Rangers and a good friend of Patrick's.

Ricky knew what the man was doing, and he was determined not to let it beat him. And he noticed something different as time went along. At first it was only him that Patrick was treating badly. But eventually Ricky saw that the man was cursing and yelling and berating a lot of employees.

Leaving Justiceville: A Life Behind

He was to learn later that the man had some serious marital problems, along with some significant personal issues. Still he knew he had been singled out because he was gay, and the Paines were just itching to fire him.

One day as he was emptying the disgusting spit cup, Patrick began yelling and shouting obscenities at him for no good reason.

"You know," he glowered, "I fucking love people like you; you owe so much goddamn money to everyone that you can't afford to quit. I own you!"

Okay, that did it! That was the final straw to Ricky; he had taken all the abuse he was going to take from this homophobic company and these miserable sons of bitches. With a feeling of satisfaction, he held up the cup and let it drop from his fingers. It splattered all over Patrick's desk and the carpet underneath.

"You don't own me, you hateful fuck!" Ricky yelled at him. "No one owns me! And if you think I can't afford to walk out of this hellhole, then you are seriously stupid! I fuckin' quit! And I hope you and your brothers rot in hell!"

Patrick's face turned beet red, and he tried to shove him, but Ricky was too quick for him. He sucker punched the older man, sending him reeling before he stalked out of the office and slammed the door behind him.

Ricky was literally trembling as he climbed into his Mustang and drove away, tires squealing on the pavement as he roared out of the parking lot for the

last time. Oh holy god, what had he done? What was he going to do now?

Well, he forced himself to calm down a little, he wasn't completely broke. He had the Power Partnership Plan with Heller Brewing, and that would get him by for a short time. There was also his savings account, but that wouldn't last long. He considered his bills for a moment: house rent, car payment, and utilities. He had enough money to last him a few months, maybe three if he was careful. But after that, he was screwed.

Don't panic, he told himself. You'll get another job easy enough. You did a great job with Heller, there's no reason why you couldn't do the same thing with one of the other beer companies in town. There were Coors, Anheuser-Busch, and Pabst Blue Ribbon, to name a few. One of them would definitely give him a job.

Dammit, he should have known this was going to happen. Life was always determined to kick him in the teeth, and sure enough, it had done it again! It was all so unfair, but that wasn't surprising to Ricky. And even though he had been kicked to the curb, he was going to pick himself up and beat life at its own game!

Over the next few weeks, Ricky applied for a job – any job – with each of the beer companies, but he was given a resounding 'no thanks' from all of them. How could that be, he wondered? He was extremely

qualified for any position they had, from janitor to driver to top executive.

The interviews were all the same:

"So why did you leave Heller Brewing?"

"I felt I had gone as far with the company as possible," Ricky said. Well, he thought, that was the truth; there was no way he was going to go any higher since the owners were so homophobic.

"I see. Are you married?"

"No."

"Do you have a girlfriend?"

"Is that pertinent to this position?"

"No girlfriend…" the interviewer would make a note on his application. "I see. Well, thank you for coming in to see us. We'll call you if anything opens up."

After interviewing with the third brewing company, Ricky was beginning to suspect that something was going on. Just from the way the interviewers looked at him, it was becoming clear that the Paine brothers had gotten to these companies before him. He knew that all these rich white beer company owners were buddies, all conservative, and all homophobic, racist pigs. In short, he'd been blackballed by the bastards!

So his career in the beer industry was over. Not that he was so passionate about beer, but he did care about doing a good job and being paid well for his work.

"Something else will come up," one of the bartenders at the Six-Fifty-One club told him one evening as Ricky sat at the bar. It had been a month since he had

Leaving Justiceville: A Life Behind

left Heller, and he was beginning to think no one was ever going to hire him. "You'll find a job, so don't worry. You're too good at what you do."
It had been another discouraging day of interviewing, calling, and mailing out applications to companies of all sorts in the Fort Worth area. The responses had all been the same: don't call us, we'll call you.
"What is it that you do?" the man next to him asked curiously.
Ricky took a moment to study him. He was in his forties, attractive, with short brown hair and a slim build.
"I was an executive with Heller Brewing Company," Ricky told him hesitantly.
"I'm Ted," the man smiled and shook his hand.
The two struck up a casual conversation for the next hour or so. It turned out that Ted owned and operated a boarding and grooming kennel in Norman, Oklahoma, a city located about three hours from Fort Worth. He was a friendly and gregarious man, and Ricky listened to him with interest as he described, as Ted described it, his five acres of heaven out in the rolling hills of Oklahoma, away from the hustle and noise of the city.
Finally, Ricky took a final sip of his beer and stood up to leave.
"Nice meeting you, Ted," he said. "Maybe I'll see you around sometime."
"So you're looking for a job?" Ted said.
"Yeah."

Leaving Justiceville: A Life Behind

"Well, I'm looking for someone to hire," Ted said. "I'm starting up a dog shampoo business to cover a four state area, and I need someone to go on the road and sell shampoo. You'd set up accounts with vets and kennels and grooming shops. I think you'd be perfect for it."

"I don't know the first thing about dogs or shampoo," Ricky shook his head. "Thanks, but I think I'll pass."

"No, wait, Ricky," Ted persisted. "Listen to me for a minute. This is the same sort of thing you did with Heller Brewing: selling product, setting up new accounts, calling on existing accounts, customer service. The only thing different is that you're selling dog shampoo instead of beer."

Well, Ricky mused, Ted was correct. If there was one thing he knew after his years with Heller, it was customer service. If a bar or liquor store told him they needed something other than beer, Ricky would do his best to find it for them. He figured a happy and satisfied customer would only buy more product and make his company even more money.

"Think about it over tonight," Ted said. "If you're interested, come by my hotel room tomorrow morning at nine o'clock. I'm at the Econo Lodge over on Twenty-Eighth Street."

He handed Ricky his business card.

"I hope you'll do this," he said sincerely. "I can tell that you've got what it takes; you're the type that's going to do well no matter what."

Leaving Justiceville: A Life Behind

Ricky considered Ted's offer the rest of that night and the next morning. Did he really want to leave Fort Worth and all of his friends? After all, this had become his home. What about his house and furniture?

Weren't his options better in a big city like this instead of some rural community? It was true that no other offers were falling into his lap, but maybe he needed to give it more time.

Everything within him was telling him to say no to this offer. You don't even know this guy. What if he's a psycho, or a drug user or alcoholic, or a serial killer even? You have no idea what you might be letting yourself in for! Don't do this!

He called Mary Ann and Tara early the next morning and explained the situation.

"I don't know what to do," he said. "Am I crazy for even considering this?"

"I don't think so," Mary Ann said.

"I'd be giving up my house and all my things," he said. "Moving away from everyone I know."

"So?" she said. "What's wrong with that?"

"Maybe this is the beginning of something really good," Tara added.

"Or something bad," Ricky said ominously.

"Now don't look at the dark side of things," Mary Ann admonished him in a motherly voice. "If things don't work out for you there, you can always come back here."

"What have you got to lose?" Tara said. "Nothing ventured, nothing gained."

Leaving Justiceville: A Life Behind

"And maybe it will do you good to get away from Fort Worth and Texas," Mary Ann said. "You may find that you like Oklahoma."
"I doubt that very much," Ricky said.

Leaving Justiceville: A Life Behind

CHAPTER SIXTEEN

Ricky drove to the Econo Lodge and knocked on Ted's door. Ted answered it a moment later with a cheerful smile and in the company of a familiar bar customer, who was still pulling on his shirt. The man gave Ted a little kiss and then grinned impishly at Ricky.
"Hey, Ricky," he chuckled "I got him all warmed up for you."
A red flag went up in Ricky's mind, but he sighed resignedly. He was already here, so he might as well talk to the man. Besides, it wasn't his place to judge who Ted slept with or anything else about his private affairs.
The two men sat down to discuss the particulars of the job that Ted was offering. Basically it would be the same job Ricky had done with Heller, except he would be selling shampoo and covering a four state area: Oklahoma, Missouri, Arkansas, and Texas. Room and board was included along with a salary, commission, and paid insurance.
"Now, I have a partner," Ted told him. "His name is Matthew, and I think he's about your age."
"So I'd be living with you?" Ricky said uneasily. "I'm not sure I want to do that."
"It's just until the business gets up and running," Ted explained. "I can't afford to pay a big salary at first. But look at it this way; you'll be getting in on the ground floor with this. I expect to start turning a profit within a couple of years. Until then, you can

live for free. I've got a very nice house. Matthew's a nice guy and a good cook, you'll have your own room, and you can come and go as you please." He added enticingly, "No expenses, no responsibilities except selling shampoo."

Well, that sounded tempting, Ricky thought. No bullshit to put up with from anyone, only Ted to answer to. Of course, he didn't know this Matthew person, but he was probably a decent fellow. Ted, after all, seemed like a happy, likeable kind of gentleman. Although, what was he doing sleeping with this random guy from the bar if he had a partner at home? Perhaps they had an open relationship, he mused. Lots of gay couples had an arrangement like that.

"Tell me about your partner," he said.

"Well, he's fifteen years younger than me," Ted shrugged. "Nice looking, big dick. He's a nurse, but he takes care of the kennel now. I'm on the road a lot lately, so he handles things at home."

"All by himself?"

"Well, I have a groomer, a girl named Dorothy," Ted said. "Matthew handles the rest."

"So he doesn't mind that you sleep with other guys?" Ricky frowned.

"I can do what I want," Ted said. "Besides, he's mostly a business partner/employee than a partner, if you know what I mean."

"Oh," Ricky's expression cleared.

"So what do you think?" Ted asked him. "Are you in or not?"

Leaving Justiceville: A Life Behind

"I...I'm not sure," Ricky said hesitantly.
"I'll tell you what," Ted said cajolingly. "Come up for the weekend. Meet Matthew, see the place, and then decide. I think once you've visited it, you'll want to stay."

Ricky considered his friends' advice and finally made his decision. With great apprehension, he made the three hour trip to Ridgeview Kennels, located a few miles from Norman, Oklahoma. Norman, he soon learned, was a very nice town of approximately one hundred thousand people. The University of Oklahoma was there, and the Sooners football team was a huge source of pride for the town and the entire state. Apparently there was a lot of oil money in this town, based on some of the nice neighborhoods and shopping malls he drove through.

He followed the directions that Ted had given him and pulled tentatively into the rural driveway of a small beige house with brown trim. There was a vast cement block and metal kennel building with its own driveway located to the left of the fenced lawn. Another metal building that housed ten dog runs sat to the right of the house, and there were a half-dozen outdoor kennel runs with dog houses located behind it.

He parked the car near the house and walked up the two steps to the concrete porch. Warily he knocked on the door, and a moment later it was answered by a tall, dark haired man with glasses and a goatee.

Leaving Justiceville: A Life Behind

"Hi," the man said with a smile. He reached out his right hand. "I'm Matthew. You must be Ricky."
"Hi," Ricky said tentatively. "I guess I'm in the right place."
"Yes, you are," Matthew grinned. "Ted's told me all about you. We're glad you're here. Let's put your bag in the spare room and then I'll show you around."

Leaving Justiceville: A Life Behind

Ted joined them, and the three men walked around the five acres with Ted doing most of the talking. He explained in detail as he led them through the modern and spotless seventy-five run kennel buildings, the grooming building, the pasture with the pecan tree grove, where Ted's two Arabian mares were grazing, and finally back to the house. It was a pleasant two bedroom building with newly refinished woodwork, a modern kitchen, and comfortable traditional furnishings.
Ricky had to admit that it was a very nice place. Obviously the kennel business was quite good; Matthew and Ted had a lovely home that was nicely decorated and had a swimming pool and hot tub, and they drove a beautiful light yellow Cadillac with plush white leather seating.

There was also a new John Deere tractor with matching brush mower, an eighteen foot Sea Ray speedboat, and a fairly new Class-A Winnebago motor home.

That evening, Matthew prepared a delicious meal of ribeye steaks, baked potatoes, and salads for the three of them. They sat at the round oak dining table to eat, and Ricky took the opportunity to study his companions. There was Ted, older, cheerful and talkative; and then there was Matthew, who was younger and more reserved. He looked to be about Ricky's age; Ricky was to learn later that their birthdays were a mere four days apart.

Leaving Justiceville: A Life Behind

There was something about Matthew, he mused. He didn't have movie-star good looks by any means, but he was attractive with a nice slim build. He also seemed very sweet and had a good sense of humor. Matthew was a registered nurse and had a Bachelor's of Music Education degree, but instead of working in the medical or music fields, he managed the kennel, while Ted concentrated on his other interests. He had started a mobile flea-dipping business, did pest control, and owned a few other operations besides the kennel and the dog shampoo business. Ricky noted that Ted was a great idea man, but that he seemed to get bored with things that didn't make him a lot of quick money. He would just shrug and move on to other endeavors. He was content to leave the kennel and the grooming to Matthew and his groomer, a talented woman named Dorothy.

"Why don't you work as a nurse?" Ricky asked Matthew.

"I did for a while," Matthew shrugged. "It wasn't for me. I'd much rather work with dogs than people. But tell us about you; we want to know everything."

Ricky reluctantly told them a little about his life, but he avoided any personal details. He knew better than to trust strangers, and as nice as these two guys seemed, he didn't know them yet. Perhaps in time, he would share things with them, but not now.

"You have a really nice place here," Ricky changed the subject.

"It's Ted's," Matthew said. "The only thing that's mine, or at least partially mine, is the car."

Leaving Justiceville: A Life Behind

"Oh," Ricky said. "I thought…"
"I came here with a car and some furniture and my piano," Matthew told him. "The rest is Ted's."
The piano he spoke of was a magnificent shiny black Samick six foot grand that Matthew had recently bought and which stood proudly in a corner of the living room. After dinner he played a mini concert for Ricky, who was impressed indeed with his musical talent.

The weekend passed pleasantly. On Saturday evening, Matthew and Ted invited a number of friends, all gay men, out for hamburgers and hot dogs and to swim in the pool. Ted introduced Ricky as their new employee, who was going to be staying with him and Matthew. There was much laughter and teasing and cheerful conversation with these agreeable men, and Ricky found himself joining in the merriment and having a great time. For a while, he forgot about all of his troubles. By the end of the evening, many of the swim trunks had been discarded as the men frolicked and played in the warm water. There was nothing sexual going on between any of these guys; they were all just good friends, who were enjoying fellowship with people like themselves. Ricky watched Matthew throughout the evening, and more often than not found the man looking back at him. Matthew would jump on him and dunk him under the water, and they would thrash about playfully in the water.

Leaving Justiceville: A Life Behind

On Sunday, Ricky said a reluctant goodbye to Matthew and Ted. He told Ted that he would let him know his decision, although in his mind he had pretty much decided to accept the position. There was nothing for him in Fort Worth anymore, especially since the Paine brothers had blackballed him from getting work. True, he had his friends there and his house, but the majority of his friends were bar friends. There was nothing wrong with that, and they were all great guys, but much of what they had in common with one another had more to do with their sexuality and alcohol than any true bond. As for his house, it was rented out since he could no longer afford it. His other belongings had no sentimental value to him, so it wouldn't bother him to get rid of them.

He returned to Fort Worth and talked again with Mary Ann and Tara.

"It sounds to me like you've already made your decision," Mary Ann said sagely.

"Just be careful," Tara warned him. "I can tell you like this Matthew guy, but remember that they're a couple. Don't let yourself get hurt."

"I don't know that they are a couple," Ricky said. "I think they were at one time, but now it's just business. Ted goes out and picks up guys when he's traveling, after all."

"But does Matthew know that?"

"Ted says he does."

"Tell me this," Mary Ann said. "Do they sleep in the same bed?"

Leaving Justiceville: A Life Behind

"Well…yeah," Ricky admitted reluctantly. "But that was probably only because I was there. There are only two bedrooms, you know."
"Just don't fall for someone who's not available," Tara said. "You don't want a broken heart."
"I'm not going to fall for anyone," Ricky snorted disdainfully. "I'm not looking for a boyfriend. The last thing I need is an attachment to some guy."
"Then I say go for it," Mary Ann said. "It sounds like a good opportunity. It's better than your options here."
Well, that was true, Ricky thought. What did he have to lose?

Ricky spent the week disposing of his belongings. He sold some of his furniture to his renters and landlord, and gave the rest to Mary Ann and Tara. He made a deal with his tenant to do a rent to own on his house. The only things he kept were his car and his clothes. He said one last goodbye to his friends at the clubs and to Mary Ann and Tara, and with a deep breath, drove away from Fort Worth for the last time.

Oh god, he asked himself, what the hell was he doing? He had to be out of his mind moving in with two guys who were virtual strangers to him, in a new state away from all he had known, leaving behind all of his friends. He must be freaking nuts!

Matthew greeted him with a smile and a hug and helped him carry in his few things and place them in

his room. The second bedroom was smaller than the master, but it was nicely decorated with an antique oak bedstead and matching dresser. It was right next to the bathroom and down the hall from the master bedroom.

"Nice Mustang," Matthew said admiringly. "I'm really into cars. I've always wanted a Mustang.

He studied the sporty red coupe with a careful eye.

"If you like a Mustang so much, why are you driving a Cadillac?" Ricky asked.

"Well, I've never owned a Cadillac before," Matthew said. "I never thought I ever would. This was probably my one chance. Besides, it was part of a deal that Ted made when he sold his truck and fifth-wheel, so I didn't have much choice."

"I see," Ricky said. "Where is Ted, by the way?"

"Oh, working on some business deal or another, I suppose," Matthew shrugged "You want to go for a swim?"

The two men lazed for an hour or so in the pool until Ted returned home in the kennel van with the name emblazoned on both sides. Matthew returned to his work in the main kennel building, and Ted and Ricky went over Ricky's new responsibilities. They talked about the existing accounts that Ted had already established and the new territory that Ricky was expected to cover each week. The job seemed a bit daunting, mostly because it covered a four state territory, but Ricky wasn't afraid of a challenge. Hell, his entire life had been nothing but challenges!

Leaving Justiceville: A Life Behind

For the next few weeks, Ricky and Ted worked the routes together so Ricky could get a feel for the products and the businesses to whom he was selling. On the weekends, Ricky would work at the kennel with Matthew. Their tasks included cleaning and disinfecting the runs each morning, feeding and watering the dogs and cats, exercising the animals during supervised playtimes, and waiting on customers.

"How do you do this every day by yourself?" Ricky asked.

"I just do it," Matthew shrugged. "Someone's got to, and I don't mind. It's better than working with people."

"You're not a big fan of people?" Ricky said.

"Hardly," Matthew chuckled. "People are liars and cheats; but dogs are honest. With them, what you see is what you get."

"Are you talking about your family?" Ricky frowned.

"No, my family is great, for the most part," Matthew said. "At least my parents are, and my brother and sister. My cousins and aunts and uncles are okay, I guess, but they wouldn't like it if they knew I was gay. They're all religious; I can only imagine how they'd react. I don't think my sisters would take the news well, either."

"Don't they know that you're living with a man?"

"Yes, but they think he's just a roommate or a business partner," Matthew said.

"So Ted is more than that?"

"Well, no," Matthew said hesitantly. "I mean, we started out as lovers, but now we're mostly just friends. I'm more the kennel manager than anything to Ted at this point. And that's okay. Our relationship has kind of run its course, and it's all good."

Ted's mother, a wealthy elderly lady who lived in Tulsa, bought herself a new car and gave Ted her very nice Oldsmobile Cutlass Salon. He in turn sold it to Matthew's niece, who lived in Illinois, Matthew's home state.
"If your family is in Illinois, how did you end up in Oklahoma?" Ricky asked.
"I got my music degree in Springfield, Missouri and then got a job at the Oral Roberts hospital in Tulsa after graduation," Matthew explained. "I worked there for a while and then took a job as a music minister at a church up in Byron, Illinois so I'd be closer to family. The church found out I was gay and fired me, so I moved back to Tulsa, met Ted and moved down here."
"What made you want to be part of anything to do with the church?" Ricky shook his head in disbelief. "They're all a bunch of judgmental hypocrites that just want your money!"
"I know that now," Matthew smiled ruefully. "But I was raised in the church, so I believed what they taught me. I was a really naïve kid. It took me a lot of years to finally realize that the church didn't want me, in spite of preaching that God loves everyone."
He took a moment to chuckle and shake his head.

Leaving Justiceville: A Life Behind

"The funny thing is that it was while I was attending a Christian college that I came to understand that being gay is not a sin, that it's just part of nature. They wouldn't be very happy if they knew that."
The more Ricky talked to Matthew, the fonder he became of him. He was still leery about getting close to him or anyone else, but found that his heart wasn't necessarily cooperating with what his mind told it to do.
Was he falling for the guy, he wondered, or was he just horny? He'd been with enough guys to know that what he was feeling for Matthew was different than anything he had experienced before. But was it just attraction, or was there more to it? He would just have to wait and see, he supposed. Either way, he was going to proceed very cautiously where Matthew was concerned.

Matthew's niece and sister, Charlotte and Joyce, drove down from Illinois to pick up the car that Ted had sold to them. It was the first time that any of Matthew's family had made the long trip from Illinois, although he spoke to his parents every weekend by phone.
The two women were suitably impressed with their brother/uncle's place, although he reminded them that it all belonged to Ted. Ricky took an instant liking to them because of their bright personalities and witty senses of humor. The women spent a few days lounging by the pool under the hot Oklahoma sun, and Ricky and Matthew joined them when their

work allowed. Ted spent much of his time out and about, running errands or making business contacts, but they were all together in the evenings.

The first night that Charlotte and Joyce were there, Ricky graciously gave up his bedroom to them and slept on the living room sofa.

"So where are you and Ted going to sleep?" Joyce asked her brother with a frown. "I mean, there are three of you living in this house and only two bedrooms. What are the sleeping arrangements?"

"Uh, I'll sleep with Ted," Matthew said evasively. "It's not a big deal."

Once everyone was settled in their beds and the house was dark, Ricky heard a stealthy noise and saw a shadowy figure tiptoe across the living room to Ted and Matthew's bedroom door. He watched with surprise as Charlotte knelt down and tried to peek through the keyhole into the room beyond. A moment later, he saw her sneak back to the second bedroom. Hmm, he thought, that was a bit weird.

The next morning, he stood in the kitchen at the back door of the house with a cup of coffee. He listened to a conversation between Matthew and his sister on the patio. It was wrong to eavesdrop like this, he knew, but his curiosity got the better of him.

"So did you sleep okay?" Matthew asked her as he sat down in a patio chair. She was already reading a magazine and sipping on a cup of coffee.

"Not really," she said.

"Oh, because of the strange bed, I suppose," Matthew nodded knowingly.

Leaving Justiceville: A Life Behind

"No, because I was trying to figure out how I'm going to deal with having a gay brother," she said. He saw Matthew look at her with both surprise and annoyance.

"What's there to 'deal with'?" he asked. "I haven't changed any. The only thing that's different is that now you know one more thing about me."

"But that makes you different," she said.

"No, it only makes your perception of me different," he said firmly. "I'm still the same person I've always been."

"But –"

"Look, my being gay has nothing to do with you or anyone else," Matthew said. "As far as I'm concerned, it nobody's business but mine and the guy I'm sleeping with."

"You're sleeping with Ted," she said. There was an accusatory tone to her voice.

"Well, we do sleep together, but we're not a couple anymore," he admitted. "Is that why one of you was trying to peek through the keyhole last night?"

Ricky stifled a laugh at that. Good for you, Matthew, he thought. Stand up for yourself, and don't let her or her daughter get away with trying to make you feel bad about who you are! God knows, that's all his family ever did, only they were much harsher in their methods of tearing down his self-esteem.

"What if you get sick? You now…" she asked. "What if you get it?"

"I don't sleep around," Matthew frowned indignantly. "We don't all sleep with every gay guy we meet!"

"But are you sleeping with Ricky too?"

"Of course not!" Matthew said. "I hardly know him. And I don't even know if he's gay or not."

He shook his head and waved his hands about to stop the direction the conversation was going.

"None of this matters," he said firmly. "I'm gay, always have been, always will be. It shouldn't make any difference to you one way or another."

"Listen, your being gay affects those around you whether we like it or not, and I have to decide how to deal with it."

"There's nothing for you to deal with," he reiterated heatedly. "All you have to do is accept me for who I am. If you can't do that, then we have nothing more to talk about."

"I accept you and I love you," she said quickly. "It's just that I have to get used to things."

"I know," he said. "I love you too. I'll see you later."

With those words, he arose from his chair and walked away toward the kennel to begin his day's work.

Later, Ricky took Matthew aside as he helped him clean the dog runs in the main kennel building. "You know, it doesn't matter what your family thinks," he said earnestly. "Fuck them if they don't accept you for who you are."

Leaving Justiceville: A Life Behind

"I know," Matthew said. "I just don't know why people have to make my life all about them. What does it matter to anyone else if I'm gay?"

Ricky thought about his childhood and his experience at Heller Brewing, and all the other times he had been more or less discarded simply because of his sexuality.

"It shouldn't matter," he said. "But that's how people are. They aren't very nice."

"My family's nice," Matthew said. "A lot of them are just…overly religious."

"Religious people are the worst," Ricky asserted firmly. "They say they are good so they can judge anyone who's different. Believe me, I know that for a fact."

"They're not all like that," Matthew said. "I know people who are Christian and are good and honest and kind. Like my parents. They're good people."

"People that believe in God are just stupid," Ricky said. "All that stuff in the Bible is nothing but bullshit!"

"Well, I agree with you there," Matthew said. "But I still believe in God."

"Why? It's not worth it."

"It is to me," Matthew shrugged. "It makes me feel good to believe in something bigger than myself. It may not be the god of the Bible, but there is a Force behind the universe and our existence. It all has to mean something."

Leaving Justiceville: A Life Behind

One weekend, Ricky, Ted, and Matthew visited the Habana Inn, a gay resort in Oklahoma City, about thirty minutes away. It contained a hotel, an adult store, a couple of clubs, and an upscale restaurant that had excellent food. The three men ate their delectable London broil and listened to the pianist play a variety of tunes on the small grand piano. Afterwards, they made their way to one of the two nightclubs located on the premises. This particular bar played country and western music, so Ricky felt right at home. It didn't take but a few minutes for a number of men to approach him and ask him to dance. He was unaware of it, but Matthew watched enviously as Ricky two-stepped around the dance floor with a variety of guys. Finally Ricky returned to their table and dropped into a chair, breathless but happy.

"Why don't you get out there and dance?" Ricky asked him. "Ted's dancing."

The two looked out where Ted and a skinny, much younger man were moving across the floor arm in arm.

"I'm not much of a dancer," Matthew said ruefully. "And I have no idea how to two-step."

"I'll teach you," Ricky grinned. "Come on."

With that, he grabbed Matthew by the wrist and pulled him out to the dance floor. After stumbling a few times, Matthew began to get the hang of the steps involved, and he and Ricky reeled around the parquet-wood floor.

Matthew typically drank very little alcohol, so Ricky encouraged him to try something light and sweet, like

a Tom Collins. Matthew sipped on the drink while they laughed and talked with each other and some of the other patrons. As the evening passed, a small group gathered around them. They played a few rounds of pool in spite of Matthew's protestations that he wasn't particularly skilled at the game.

An attractive middle aged man watched leeringly as Matthew clumsily attempted to put a ball in the corner pocket. Ricky was behind him, helping him point the cue, and the two were laughing together at Matthew's terrible aim.

"Here, let me show you," the older man said, pushing Ricky aside to take his place.

He rubbed his body against Matthew's back and reached around him so that his face was next to the younger man's head. He kissed him gently on the neck.

"This is how you do it," he whispered seductively. Matthew looked up and grinned at Ricky, clearly enjoying the attention and the physical contact with this nice looking man. As Ricky observed them, the other man pressed even closer and ground his groin against Matthew's ass. Ricky scowled at the two of them.

He felt something unusual in his chest, an unpleasant sensation that he was not accustomed to feeling. He was uncertain as to what it was exactly, but he noticed that it increased when he looked at Matthew and this stranger. In fact, that's when it had started, when this man started showing Matthew attention. He felt annoyed and angry and…well, jealous!

Leaving Justiceville: A Life Behind

Matthew was his friend, and this guy had no right to be doing what he was doing. And what made it even worse was that Matthew obviously liked what was happening.

Dammit, he thought angrily! He turned away and strode to the bar and demanded a Smirnoff's Ice from the bartender, who handed it to him with a wink. When he returned to the pool table area, Matthew and his new acquaintance were nowhere to be found. He looked around until he spotted them on the dance floor, two-stepping to the lively music. Matthew was grinning from ear to ear with pleasure at being in the arms of a good-looking guy. Ricky understood that he was unaccustomed to dancing and gay bars; this was all a new experience for him, and he appeared to be having the time of his life.

The evening progressed, and Ricky and Matthew danced a few more times. Many more men came up to them to ask them to dance, including Ted. Every time that Matthew moved off with another man, Ricky's stomach clenched a little tighter. Even while he was dancing with his own partner, he would watch Matthew laugh and snuggle up with his various partners. One man in particular was especially handsy with him, caressing his ass and nuzzling his neck.

Ricky had little to say to Ted or Matthew on the drive back to Ridgeview kennel. When they arrived at the house, he went straight to his bedroom and shut the door without saying good night. He lay in his bed in

Leaving Justiceville: A Life Behind

the darkness as he tried to figure out what was happening with these confusing emotions. One feeling was perfectly clear to him: he liked Matthew a lot, more than anyone else he had ever known. The man was sweet and gentle, but also had a slight edge to him when he was provoked. He was genuinely nice and honest and trustworthy. In short, he was different than almost everyone he had ever known. He treated everyone with the same respect and dignity regardless of their social standing or economic worth.

It had bothered him greatly to see Matthew with other men tonight. Some of them had even tried to make out with him. True, he had received a great deal of attention himself this evening, something he took in stride after his years in the gay club scene. He even felt jealous whenever Ted and Matthew would go to bed at night. He knew there was nothing going on between them, but it still irked him that the two men still occasionally had sex. Of course, that was understandable since they had been a couple at one time and still shared a house and a bed. Things like that were bound to happen between two men.

But why couldn't one of the men be him instead of Ted? Why didn't Matthew see him as a potential bed partner? Tears filled his eyes as he thought about the days ahead. He sensed that he would go on having feelings for Matthew, only to have him always out of his reach.

As he lay in his bed, quietly crying into his pillow, a tentative knock came at his door.

Leaving Justiceville: A Life Behind

"Ricky?" Matthew called out. "Are you okay?"
Ricky dried his eyes.
"I'm fine," he said, his voice shaky from his tears.
The door opened and Matthew came into the room. He switched on the bedside lamp and sat down on the bedside.
"Why are you crying?" he asked gently.
"I'm not crying," Ricky said scornfully. "I'm fine."
He looked up into Matthew's hazel eyes, and his tears threatened to return. What was it about this man that attracted him so? Why was he so different from any other guy? Why did he want more than anything in the world to be with him and make love to him? And why was it breaking his heart knowing that Matthew didn't feel the same way about him?
His eyes scrunched closed as tears flowed from them and across his nose to the pillow below.
"Hey, it's okay," Matthew said, rubbing his arm soothingly. "Whatever's bothering you isn't that bad. Just tell me what it is."
"What's wrong?" Ted called from the doorway. He spoke to Matthew as he pointed at the sobbing man in the bed. "Why's he crying?"
"I don't know, Ted," Matthew frowned. "Go on back to bed. I'll be there in a minute."
Ricky's weeping became even stronger as he pictured Matthew lying naked in bed with another man.
"Ricky," Matthew said worriedly. "Tell me what's wrong, please. I want to help if I can."
Ricky tried to stem his tears in vain, and Matthew moved closer and gathered him into his arms to rock

him gently back and forth. For the next fifteen minutes, Matthew held him, softly offering words of comfort until Ricky's tears finally abated. He pulled away from him and turned over to curl into a fetal position facing the other direction.
"Are you okay now?" Matthew asked him with concern.
"I'm okay," Ricky said, his face red from his tears and embarrassment at having put on such an emotional display. Matthew must think he was a complete fool by now.
"Okay then," Matthew stood up and turned out the light. "Good night. I'll see you in the morning."

Leaving Justiceville: A Life Behind

CHAPTER SEVENTEEN

The next several weeks and months hummed along smoothly enough for Ricky. His job was going well, and he was already building up a strong following among vet clinics, pet stores, and grooming shops. With his genial personality, he developed an instant rapport with most of his customers, and he was usually able to joke around with the majority of them. Business was booming, and he stayed on the road much of the time, staying in motels whenever he was too far out across the four state territory. He found that it was easier for him emotionally and psychologically being away from Matthew, so he didn't mind the long days of driving and calling on accounts.

How the hell had he let this happen, he wondered? He had always been able to keep his emotions in check before, so what had changed? He was the same guy he'd always been, the boy and man who was ever able to keep other people at a safe distance. Of course, that hadn't been a difficult task because most people in his life had been horrible creatures: dishonest, cruel, unkind, vicious, backstabbing pieces of shit that he was thankful to be rid of.

It was Matthew that was the difference, he realized. There was something special, something endearing and unique that made him want to know him better.

Several months after Ricky moved to Oklahoma, Ted and Matthew sat him down at the kitchen table.

Leaving Justiceville: A Life Behind

"We need to make some changes," Ted told him. "You're doing great with selling shampoo; business is good, and we're already turning a profit in our first year. A lot of that has to do with you."
Uh, oh, Ricky thought wearily. Here we go again. He was about to be screwed over one more time.
"But...?" he said.
"Now that you've established the groundwork," Ted went on, "I'm going to take over the routes."
"So I'm out of a job," Ricky said coldly. "Now that I've built up your business for you, you want to save all the profits for yourselves. I should have known. You're no different than all the rest."
"No, that's not it," Matthew said. "We want you to stay."
"How can I stay here if I'm out of a job?" Ricky said. "I have a car payment, you know."
"Why don't you sell it?" Ted suggested.
"I'm not going to sell my Mustang," Ricky said indignantly. "I have to have a car."
He stood up from the table.
"I'll pack my stuff and leave," he said stiffly.
"Ricky, wait," Matthew pleaded. "I have a proposal for you. Or rather, we do."
"What is it?" Ricky remained standing as he eyed them suspiciously.
"Why don't you stay and work the kennel with me?" Matthew said. "Dorothy just quit, so I'm going to have to take over all the bathing. I know a little about grooming from watching her the last several years, so I might be able to do some of that too."

Leaving Justiceville: A Life Behind

"The kennel is so big that it's just too much for him," Ted said. "Why don't you work with him since the two of you work well together, and you already know the work?"

"You'll still pay me?"

"Well, we can talk about that," Ted said evasively. "You'll still get room and board, and if you sell your car, I'll promise to buy you another one if it becomes important that you have one of your own. In the meantime, you can drive the Cadillac or the truck or the kennel van. This will save you money in the long run."

"So basically I'll be working for you for free," Ricky said dryly. "Yeah, that sounds like a good deal for me."

"It won't be for free," Matthew said. "I'll make sure you have all the spending money you need, anything you want. It will be just like what I'm doing. I don't get a salary, either, but it works out fine because I have a beautiful place to live and nice vehicles to drive."

"But you also have no salary and no future," Ricky added.

"How can you live here like that?" he asked Matthew later as the two worked in the kennel. "You're basically an unpaid employee. None of this is yours; you don't own anything except your piano. You're completely at Ted's mercy."

"I'm not at anyone's mercy. I'm here because I want to be. And Ted's a good guy," Matthew said. "He

would never treat me badly. Besides, I like the work. I like living in the country, away from other people. It's a good life with hardly any worries. And I think it's even better with you here."

Okay, Ricky thought; that decided it. Those few words from Matthew had suddenly made this an easy choice. To hell with everything and everyone else! Matthew wanted him to stay, so this was where he wanted to be! Whatever future he and Matthew might have together, if any, this was where it would start. At this point, he didn't care about the money, his car, nothing; all that mattered was being here with Matthew.

So Ted went on the road in Ricky's place, and Ricky stayed in Oklahoma at the kennel full time to work with Matthew. Together they cleaned and disinfected the kennel each day, fed and watered the animals, played with the cats and dogs during their exercise periods, and cleaned the house and cooked their meals. They did the laundry for the house, kennel, and grooming shop, which was practically a full time job by itself. There were the hedges and shrubs to trim, the large lawn to care for, the horses to tend to, not to mention the pick up and delivery service the business offered. Matthew was also responsible for doing the grocery shopping. And now was the added responsibility of bathing dogs.

"How the hell did you do all of this by yourself?" he asked him one day. "This is a lot of work!"

Leaving Justiceville: A Life Behind

"I don't know," Matthew shrugged in a vague manner. "I just do what I have to do. It's not a big deal."

Ricky contacted his insurance agent, a nice lady who lived in Fort Worth. She had expressed an interest in his car when he had insured it with her. Sure enough, she was interested in buying the car from him for her son. Ricky hated to let the sporty car go but decided that it was worth it. What did he need with a car anyway? If he had to choose between an automobile and Matthew, he would obviously choose Matthew. Over the next few months, Ricky and Matthew grew closer as they worked together. Virtually all of their time was spent in each other's company, and Ricky was pleased to see how compatible they were. They worked from sunrise until after six o'clock in the evening every day; it seemed there were always jobs of some sort to be done. But they still managed to find time to relax in the swimming pool or hot tub. They rarely left the premises together since someone had to stay within earshot of the animals, if not actually in the kennel buildings then by the intercom that connected all of the buildings with the house.

One night – the fourth of July, in fact – Matthew fixed the two of them some ribeye steaks on the grill while Ricky baked some potatoes in the microwave and put together a couple of salads. They chatted comfortably with one another as they ate the simple but delicious meal.

"You know, it's a lot less lonely having you here," Matthew commented. "Not that I'm the lonely type,

Leaving Justiceville: A Life Behind

but it's good to have some company since Ted is on the go most of the time."

"He is gone a lot," Ricky agreed.

"Well, he's a people person," Matthew said. "Much more so than I am. I'm a homebody, and I'm perfectly content being out here, miles from town and away from everyone. He likes to talk and be around people."

"Not me," Ricky said.

"You like to be around people," Matthew said. "You used to sell for Heller Beer and go to all the clubs. You sold shampoo to hundreds of accounts all over the four state area. You're great with people."

"Yeah, but that's because it was my job," Ricky said. "In reality, I'm more like you than Ted."

The two men talked for a while longer and then put their used dishes in the dishwasher.

"How about the hot tub?" Matthew suggested. He wriggled his shoulders painfully. "I'm really sore. I think the hot tub would help."

Ricky eagerly agreed, and the two stripped down and climbed carefully into the hot tub, which was set at one end of the deck on the back of the house. The only light came from the back door that they had left ajar when they had come outside. They sat down on opposite sides of the tub with the hot, roiling water all around them, soothing their aching muscles. Matthew laid his head back and looked up at the starlit sky.

"Look," he said, pointing upward. "There's the big dipper."

Leaving Justiceville: A Life Behind

"Where?"

"Come over here and look where I'm pointing," Matthew said.

Tentatively, Ricky slid across to sit next to his friend. He looked up to the area of the night sky at which Matthew was pointing. It was getting increasingly difficult for him to hide his attraction to the man, what with them spending virtually all of their time together. But he knew that it would be foolish and possibly ruin everything if he told Matthew how he felt. Matthew probably didn't feel the same about him, and then things would become awkward, and he would more than likely end up having to leave here. He couldn't risk that because Matthew was too important to him.

"See?" Matthew pointed again. "Right there."

"Oh, yeah," Ricky nodded with a smile. "I see it."

He was unaware of it, but Matthew was studying him closely while he stared toward the heavens.

"You've got really cute dimples," Matthew grinned. "Did you know that?"

"I've got dimples?"

"Yeah, and they're adorable," Matthew said. "In fact, all of you is kind of adorable."

"No, I'm not," Ricky frowned.

"Then how come every time we've been out to the bars, dozens of guys ask you to dance or buy you drinks?"

"They don't do that," Ricky said scornfully. "No one even notices me."

Leaving Justiceville: A Life Behind

"Oh, please," Matthew chuckled. "They're all over you. And that's because you're so cute. I'm the one no one looks at."

"Sure they do," Ricky assured him. "You just don't notice it."

"No one ever speaks to me when we go."

"That's because they're shy."

"I'm shy," Matthew said. "That's why I'll probably never meet anyone."

"You met me," Ricky said without thinking. Oh wow, that had been bold of him, he mused. But even as that thought occurred to him, his courage failed him. "I mean, you just have to try talking to people when we're out."

What the fuck am I doing, he frowned? Why am I encouraging him to look for another guy when I'm sitting right here? Stupid, stupid, stupid!

"Nah," Matthew shook his head. "I'm too afraid of getting shot down. No one wants to talk to me, anyway, and my self-esteem is too fragile to take rejection."

"So how did you and Ted meet?"

"I answered an ad in the 'Gayly-Oklahoman'," Matthew said, referring to a popular gay newspaper. "I drove down from Tulsa and met him here. Our first date was watching him groom a customer's dog, take it home, and then go out for Little Caesar's pizza. It wasn't terribly romantic, but I had a good time."

"You must have," Ricky said dryly. "You're still here."

"Yeah, but just as a friend and unpaid employee," Matthew laughed. "Our relationship ran its course, and that's okay because I'm perfectly content. Ted's a good man, and I like it here."
"And I'm here too," Ricky reminded him. "You're not alone."
"No, I'm not," Matthew grinned at him.
He leaned over and gave Ricky a chaste kiss on the cheek, much to Ricky's surprise.
"I'm glad you're here," he said.
The two men stared into each other's eyes for a long moment. Warily, Ricky leaned closer to his friend and kissed him on the lips. Oh god, he thought, this is what I've wanted to do for so long. He was unaware that Matthew was thinking the very same thing.
"Come on," Matthew said huskily. "Let's go inside. I'm turning into a prune in this water."
"Yeah, me too," Ricky said softly.
They wrapped their towels around their waists, and Ricky followed Matthew inside and into the second bedroom. Without a word, Matthew closed the door behind them and dropped his towel.

With their groomer suddenly gone and working for the competition, Matthew and Ricky had no choice but to try to take her place.
"I've watched her groom lots of dogs," Matthew said confidently. "I think I can do it. At least some breeds. I've groomed Ted's English Cocker Spaniels, after all."

Leaving Justiceville: A Life Behind

They found a spiral-bound book on dog grooming in a cabinet in the grooming shop. It contained step-by-step instructions on how each breed should be clipped. It even contained pictures and diagrams to help them as they walked somewhat blindly into this new profession. Matthew did indeed have years of observation and bathing and grooming Ted's dogs, so he wasn't completely clueless. He knew about the various shampoos, dryers, clippers, blades, brushes, and so on that were involved in dog grooming. To Ricky, however, this was a whole new world, one that he was completely unprepared for. But he had never backed down from a challenge in his life, and he wasn't about to start now. Besides, it was too important to Matthew and Ted and the business to do a poor job. Typical of him, he threw one hundred percent of his effort and determination into learning everything he could about grooming. It was the same with the kennel, the shampoo business, Heller Brewing, and the restaurants in which he had worked before. He had gone into those situations without knowing the first thing about them, and yet he had not only done those jobs, he had done them extremely well. The grooming would prove to be no different.

The first few dogs that Ricky groomed were, shall we say, less than optimally groomed. One American Cocker Spaniel went home with its owner looking quite nice, at least on the surface. Once he had a little more experience under his belt he would look back at that particular dog and mentally cringe as he realized

that under that beautifully brushed and trimmed hair lay nothing but solid mats. Oh, well, he mused; it had been a learning experience, and how else would he educate himself and do better in the future if he didn't make some mistakes along the way.

He studied the grooming book for hours from cover to cover, eager to learn all about how he could be the best dog groomer in the state of Oklahoma. Together, he and Matthew critiqued each other's work and provided one another with suggestions to improve their skills.

"You're getting really good," Matthew said one day as they stood back and eyed a miniature poodle that Ricky had just clipped. "That's better than I could ever do."

With Ted gone on the road more and more often, Ricky and Matthew spent all of their time together. Of course, with so much work to be done, most of their time was spent cleaning, or mowing, or bathing, or trimming. It was also their job to process phone orders for shampoo and ship them out. Even so, they enjoyed themselves whether they were working or relaxing.

Overall, it was a very pleasant few months for the two of them. In the evenings they would cook their dinner, an activity they both savored. Sometimes they tried interesting new recipes just for the fun of it, and often times would end up throwing the disgusting results in the trash.

Leaving Justiceville: A Life Behind

For the first time in his life, Ricky felt completely at home with another person. Matthew was easygoing and gentle of spirit. He was loving and funny and agreeable to be around. The two of them got along perfectly, and Ricky felt as if he had known him all of his life. After their first time of being intimate with one another, they took to spending most of their nights together as well as their days.

"My mom and dad are coming here from Illinois," Matthew said one day.
"Why?" Ricky frowned.
The two men were grooming a one hundred sixty-five pound black Newfoundland who, fortunately, was the epitome of the 'gentle giant' title that the breed had earned.
"Well, I talked Ted into giving them the Cadillac," Matthew explained.
The previous week, Matthew had convinced Ted to trade the five year old car for a one year old Cadillac, a beautiful gray Fleetwood sedan with low miles and fender skirts that gave it a classic appearance.

Leaving Justiceville: A Life Behind

"So they're driving down to pick it up?"
"Yes," Matthew nodded. "Their old Buick has like two hundred thousand miles on it, and the Caddy is still in perfect shape."
"That's a nice thing to do for them," Ricky said.
"Well, to be honest, the trade-in value on Cadillacs wasn't that great, so I convinced Ted to give it to them instead of trading it because it would make a terrific tax break for him," Matthew chuckled.
Ricky and Matthew spent a few hours the day before Matthew's parents were due to arrive washing and waxing the Cadillac, polishing the chrome so that it shone with a mirror-like finish and cleaning the white-walls and white leather interior so that they practically glowed.
"It looks like brand new," Ricky said admiringly.
"They're going to love it," Matthew said with a happy grin. "I can't wait to see their faces."

Leaving Justiceville: A Life Behind

Bill and Betty, Matthew's parents, arrived the next day accompanied by Joyce and Charlotte, Matthew's sister and niece. They drove down in the Oldsmobile Cutlass Salon that Ted had sold them a few months earlier. There was a happy reunion between the family members before the two younger women made a beeline for the swimming pool. Ted had already met his parents a few times when he and Matthew had traveled to Illinois in their motorhome. Betty was a pretty woman, slightly plump with blonde hair and a lovely smile. Matthew's dad was an older version of his son; that is, tall and slender with thinning dark hair. He seemed less outgoing than his wife, but still pleasant and friendly.

Ricky watched the family hug and laugh together, just happy to be in one another's company after so long of being in different parts of the country. Wow, he thought, these people really love each other. Matthew was obviously thrilled to see his parents. What must that be like, he wondered, to have parents you could love and who loved you in return? Never before had he witnessed such true affection and respect between members of a family.

"This is Ricky," Matthew introduced him. "He used to sell shampoo on the road, but now he helps me in the kennel."

"Nice to meet you, Ricky," Matthew's mother smiled at him. "Matthew's told us all about you."

Matthew's father frowned suspiciously at Ricky as he shook his hand.

Leaving Justiceville: A Life Behind

"You're living here?" he asked, his eyes narrowed. "With Ted and Matthew?"
"Yes," Ricky said uneasily, sensing the other man's displeasure.
"I see," Bill said. "But in a separate room, of course."
"Yes, of course."
Ricky looked at the ground, feeling guilty even though he knew he had done nothing wrong.
Apparently Matthew's parents didn't understand their son's and Ted's relationship status.
"I've, uh, got to go check on the dogs," he mumbled. With that, he turned and walked across the lawn and through the gate to the main kennel building.

Betty's eyes were shining as Matthew showed his parents their new car, which was parked near the house under a pair of mimosa trees. It sparkled and gleamed in the dappled sunlight. Bill studied it carefully with a more critical eye.
"Oh, my goodness," she cried. "It's more beautiful than I imagined!"
"Ricky and I got it all waxed and polished for you," Matthew said. "Dad, what do you think?"
"It looks nice," Bill said. "As long as your mom likes it, that's good enough for me. But who are we to be driving a Cadillac? That's awful fancy for someone who's just a farmer."
"Why shouldn't you drive a Cadillac?" Matthew frowned. "You're as good as anyone else. And you're not just a farmer. You're a farmer, and that's something to be proud of."

Leaving Justiceville: A Life Behind

"I reckon," Bill nodded thoughtfully. "As long as your mom's happy, that's all I care about."
Betty walked over and gave her husband a kiss and a hug.
"How could I not be happy?" she said.
Wow, Ricky thought, Matthew's dad's primary concern was for his wife's happiness. That was another side of a relationship he had never witnessed before. His own parents had always put their selfish wants and needs first, above their spouse or their children's interests every time. Neither of them had given a damn about making each other or their family happy. Of course, that was because they were miserable, detestable, horrible people to begin with. People like them should never have procreated, he had often thought. Just look at his two disgusting brothers. He had heard through the grapevine that both of them had been in prison for a number of infractions, deservedly so. They had both married and divorced, most likely because they had learned too well from their father how to mistreat a woman.
But Matthew's parents truly loved one another. They spoke with respect to each other and their children and granddaughter. In fact, they had loaned their rather decrepit Buick to another granddaughter for months so she could attend college. The couple had made due with Bill's old Ford F-100 farm truck, a vehicle that was a challenge to drive, even for Bill. The more he watched Matthew's family interact, he realized all over again how terrible his own family was. They were nothing like this. Bill and Betty

loved their family, and though they clearly didn't have a lot of money, they were clean and cared about their appearance.

That's how a loving relationship is supposed to be, Ricky mused. Showing respect and support and affection for one another, putting each other's needs above their own, wanting nothing more from life than to see each other happy. He supposed their relationship wasn't perfect, since that wasn't possible, but it was by far the best one he had seen in his entire life. People could be good and decent, after all.

Matthew's family stayed for five days, and Ricky got to know them a little better. Betty was a sweet, warm, motherly person, who he took to right away. Bill was a bit more standoffish, and it was clear that he had his suspicions about Ricky's relationship with his son. Still, he was friendly enough. Joyce and Charlotte were fun to be around, and he laughed and joked around with them quite a bit.

Ted was home for part of the visit, but he left to go back on the road. Ricky and Matthew slept in the motorhome at night, which allowed their guests to have the run of the house and the two bedrooms. They all went out for dinner or got pizzas, and sometimes they would grill steaks or hamburgers on the grill. Matthew's family was anything but fancy; they were a meat and potatoes kind of group, which suited Ricky just fine. Those were the kind of people to whom he related the best.

Leaving Justiceville: A Life Behind

Matthew wanted to show them the city of Norman and the Cowboy Museum up in Oklahoma City, so several day trips were planned. They even drove down to the southwest corner of the state to the town of Lawton, where they climbed to the peak of Mount Scott, the tallest point in Oklahoma. As they stood on the rounded rocky top of the mountain, Bill made his way over to where Ricky was standing, staring out at the terrain twenty-four hundred feet below them.
"You and Matthew seem to get along well," he said casually.
"Uh, yeah," Ricky said. "He's my best friend."
"I see," Bill said. "That's fine, as long as you don't interfere with him and Ted."
"I'm not interfering with anything," Ricky said with a hint of indignancy.
"I'm glad," Matthew's father said. "Because I don't want anyone to spoil the good thing that Matthew has going here with Ted."
"What thing?"
"He's living in a beautiful home, with a successful business," Bill said. "He's even driving a Cadillac and can afford to give his old one to us. He's got it made here."
"There's more to life than Cadillacs and beautiful homes," Ricky pointed out. "There's love."
"I don't want to know anything about what goes on between him and Ted," Bill frowned. "Just make sure you don't ruin things for him."

Leaving Justiceville: A Life Behind

Ricky thought about Matthew's father's words to him the rest of that night. Was he interfering with Matthew's life by being here? He didn't believe so, but perhaps he was just being selfish. After all, Matthew was the first guy he'd ever really had feelings for. And Matthew seemed to care about him too. His relationship with Ted had gone from a committed intimate partnership to one of friendship and companionship. Both men had told him that, so he knew it was true. Matthew was here for convenience, mostly. Even though Ted owned the property and nearly everything on it, Matthew enjoyed the work and the home they shared. He was comfortable and at ease here, and he was free labor for Ted. Ted knew that the kennel business and property were in good hands with Matthew caring for everything.

Wouldn't you just know it, he thought despondently. As with everything else in my life, this isn't going to work out, either. Things were going too well! I'm happy for the first time, and I'm with a guy I really like, so naturally the Universe is going to take it all away from me, dammit.

"Are you awake?" Ricky whispered in the darkness.

"I'm awake," Matthew replied softly. "Why are you still awake?"

"I can't sleep."

"Why not?"

"Matthew, I want to ask you a question, and I want an honest answer," Ricky said.

"Okay," Matthew frowned.

Leaving Justiceville: A Life Behind

"Am I causing problems for you and Ted by being here?" Ricky asked hesitantly.

"Problems?" Matthew said, confused. "What kinds of problems could your being here cause?"

"I don't know," Ricky shrugged. "You tell me."

"I don't know what you're talking about," Matthew said. "Everything's better with you here. I can't do all of this by myself; I need you here."

"I know. But am I coming between you and Ted?"

"No, of course not," Matthew said. "You know better than that."

"I don't want to interfere with your life, or spoil things for you here."

"You're not spoiling anything," Matthew chuckled. "Where did you get a crazy idea like that?"

"Nowhere," Ricky shrugged. "Just forget I said anything."

But Ricky couldn't forget about it. He cared very much for Matthew, and the thought of causing him pain in any way was unbearable. Perhaps he had overstayed his welcome and should start looking into moving on, probably back to Fort Worth.

As if in response to what he was thinking, Ted came home from one of his trips with little to say to him or Matthew. Ricky would look up from his plate at the dinner table or away from the television to find Ted frowning at him. He would watch Ricky and Matthew in the pool or hot tub, or fixing dinner together with a suspicious gaze. There was some

jealousy and anger in that look as well, Ricky thought.

After a few days of silent treatment, Ted took Ricky aside to speak to him privately.

"I think you need to move out," he said abruptly.

"Move out?" Ricky echoed, surprised.

"It's too crowded in this small house for three people," Ted said.

"But you're hardly ever here," Ricky reminded him. "It's not like I'm putting anybody out by being here."

"There's a trailer down at Ed's house," Ted ignored him.

He was referring to the neighbor, an elderly couple who lived on a small water moccasin infested lake. On most mornings, you could step out the front door and hear Ed shooting the poisonous creatures.

"You can live there and walk to work," Ted continued.

"Why?"

"I don't want you living here any more," Ted said, as if that was explanation enough. "This is my place, and that's the way I want it."

"Are you going to pay me a salary?" Ricky asked. "Because so far I haven't seen any money or a car of my own since I sold the Mustang."

"We'll talk about it," Ted said evasively. "For now, you need to plan to go."

"What did Ted say to you?" Matthew asked him while they were grooming dogs the next day.

Leaving Justiceville: A Life Behind

"He wants me to move out," Ricky said. "Is that what you want too?"

"No, of course not!" Matthew exclaimed. "That's not what I want at all."

"I'm supposed to move down to that trailer down at Ed's house."

"There is no way you are moving down to that snake trap!" Matthew snapped. "You are staying right here!"

"Maybe I should just go back to Fort Worth," Ricky said unhappily.

The very thought of that made him feel sad, as sad as during his childhood.

"No, you can't do that," Matthew said quickly. "I mean, you can't leave me here with all this work."

"Maybe I should leave and you come with me," Ricky suggested.

"I don't want to leave," Matthew said. "And I don't want you to leave, either. You like it here, don't you?"

"Of course I do," Ricky said. "But if it's going to be like this…"

"Look, I haven't told you this," Matthew said tentatively. "But part of the reason I've stayed here is because Ted is leaving all of this to me in his will."

"You mean you're staying here for the money?"

"I know it sounds like I'm a gold-digger," Matthew said ruefully. "But I've put a lot into this place. I refinished all the woodwork in the house, I take care of it, and I've helped build up the business to where it's grossing over a hundred thousand dollars a year.

Leaving Justiceville: A Life Behind

And Ted and I have a history together. All of that matters to me; I don't want to just walk away from the last six years like they meant nothing."

As it turned out, Matthew didn't have to worry about making that decision, because Ted made it for him. Ricky overheard the two men arguing about him, with Ted still insisting that Ricky had to leave and Matthew arguing just the opposite. For a few weeks, nothing more was said on the matter, and he and Matthew continued their work with the kennel and the grooming.

Finally one day, Ted took Matthew aside and sat him down in the living room while Ricky listened from his bedroom.

"I want you to know that I've changed my will," he said without preamble.

"You did what?" Matthew said, not believing his ears.

"I've decided to leave everything to my family," Ted said.

He was referring to his well-to-do sister, his multi-millionaire brother, and their children.

"Why?"

"It's just the right thing to do," Ted shrugged. "All I've built up here should stay in the family."

"I've helped build it up too," Matthew protested.

"But family comes first," Ted insisted. "That's the way it should be, and that's the way I want it. End of discussion."

Leaving Justiceville: A Life Behind

"I know you haven't gotten a paycheck from Ted," Matthew said a few weeks later.

"Neither have you," Ricky shrugged. "And you've been here a lot longer than I have."

"True," Matthew agreed with a sigh. "But that's not the point."

"The point of what?" Ricky looked confused. "I don't know what we're talking about."

Matthew handed him a fat envelope with an enigmatic grin.

"What's this?" Ricky said, frowning as he thumbed through the stack of bills. "There's a lot of money here!"

"I know," Matthew said excitedly. "Isn't it great?"

"Yes, it's really great," Ricky agreed. "But what's it for? Why are you giving it to me?"

"For a car," Matthew said, as if the answer should have been obvious. "I've been saving this back for a while now so you can put it toward a car."

"Wow," Ricky said, his eyes wide with surprise. "I can't believe you did that."

"Well, you gave up your own car," Matthew said. "So this will help go toward another one."

Leaving Justiceville: A Life Behind

CHAPTER EIGHTEEN

A week later, Ricky answered an ad in the Oklahoma City newspaper for a fourteen year old Oldsmobile Cutlass Supreme that was for sale. The owner was an elderly gentleman, who offered to bring the automobile to the kennel for Ricky to see. Ricky eagerly agreed and, within a few hours, a light blue coupe pulled into the driveway. He examined the car closely and was pleased to find that it was in mint condition with extremely low miles. The owner had all the car's records to show that it had had excellent care, and within a matter of minutes, a deal was struck.

"Isn't it exciting?" Matthew said. "Your very own car. I mean, I know it's not your Mustang, but it's still very nice."
"It's great," Ricky said. "At this point, I'm just glad to have a car of any kind. Thank you for helping me get it."

Leaving Justiceville: A Life Behind

"Don't thank me," Matthew shrugged. "You've more than earned it. There's no way I could have kept up with all the work around here without you."
"We make a pretty good team, don't we?"
"You bet we do!" Matthew grinned and gave him a peck on the cheek.

Leaving Justiceville: A Life Behind

"There's nothing for me here anymore," Matthew told Ricky a few days later.
The two men were cleaning the deck on the back of the house. Matthew had been rather morose and had had little to say to him since Ted's revelation regarding his will.
"I think maybe," he took a deep breath, "maybe it's time to consider moving on. I can't keep working here for nothing, with no future, no benefits, no savings. If something happens to Ted, I'm out on my ass with nothing to show for it. His family would take everything and leave me with nothing. They'd just sell the business and the property and there's no way I could afford to buy it. I'd be stupid for staying."
"I agree," Ricky nodded. "You should leave."
"I'm going to tell Ted that I'm leaving as soon as I can figure out where I'm going and what I'm going to do."
"Well, when you leave, I'm going with you," Ricky said firmly. "I'm sure as hell not staying here!"

Matthew gave the matter of his future considerable thought, with Ricky offering ideas of his own.
"I think I'd like to go back to Illinois," Matthew said thoughtfully. "It'd be closer to Mom and Dad. And there's a really nice area where I used to live, up along the Rock River. I think it might be good to go back there."
"What would we do?"
"Well, I still have my nursing license," Matthew said. "I could get a job as a nurse, not that I'm crazy about

going back into nursing. I could also teach piano lessons. I did that when I lived up there before. Or maybe I could groom dogs, now that we know how to do that."

"And I know I can get a job at any fast food restaurant," Ricky added eagerly.

"So I think the first thing to do is make a trip up there and see what's available as far as jobs and places to live," Matthew said determinedly. "Once we get that settled, we're out of here!"

Two days later, Ricky and Matthew set out for Illinois in the gray Cadillac. It was a long and tiresome drive, but the two men drove straight through to the small town of Oregon, a town of three thousand people located in the north central part of the state on the beautiful and scenic Rock River. They rented a room in a small motel on the north edge of town, across the highway from the Paddlewheel Inn and the wide, placid river. Matthew had lived in this area a few years before. After graduating with his Bachelor's of Music Education degree in Springfield, Missouri, he had moved to Tulsa for a year and then accepted a position as a music minister in the small town of Byron, about ten miles northeast of Oregon on the river as well. That job had lasted a year until the congregation discovered that he was gay and fired him immediately. Having no other options, Matthew had accepted a job as an RN at the Osteopathic Hospital in Tulsa and moved back to the Sooner

Leaving Justiceville: A Life Behind

state. It was shortly after that that he had met Ted and moved to Norman.

Since he was familiar with the area, he was able to navigate their trip easily. They had planned to stay one week, during which time they hoped to find jobs and a place to live. Ricky interviewed at a few fast food restaurants in nearby Rockford and within a day had a few options to choose from. With his work experience and personable demeanor, most of the interviewers were eager to snatch him up. He ultimately decided to accept the position of the Alpine Street store manager for a well-known fast food chain that had three stores in the city. Meanwhile, Matthew took a part time job as a dog groomer at a small grooming salon in Byron. He had not planned on moving back to Illinois, so as a result he had unknowingly allowed his Illinois nursing license to lapse by one month. While he reapplied for it, he decided he could supplement his income with private piano lessons and grooming out of whatever residence they ended up with. He and Ricky spent a considerable amount of time figuring out what their expenses would be and how much income they would need to survive once they made their move.

"I think we can just make it," Ricky sighed as he wearily tossed the pad of paper aside. The two were sitting cross-legged on the motel bed after having eaten supper at the Blackhawk Steak Pit. It had been a productive but exhausting day of traveling all over Rockford and the surrounding areas. At least they

were both gainfully employed, although they were certainly going to be anything but rich.

"I don't care," Matthew said. "As long as we can pay our bills and get the hell out of Oklahoma, I'm good to go."

Ricky and Matthew settled down under the covers in the air conditioned, knotty-pine paneled motel room. They lay in silence for a while.

"It's kind of scary," Matthew said softly, staring up at the dark ceiling.

"What is?"

"Starting over like this," Matthew said. "Everything's going to change."

"Yeah, it is," Ricky acknowledged. "But that's a good thing."

"I guess," Matthew shrugged. "I just thought that I was where I was supposed to be at the kennel. I didn't plan on ever leaving there."

"Well, I thought that too," Ricky said. "But once I found out you were leaving, there's no way I could stay there."

"Doesn't that scare you to start over?"

"No. Do you know how many times I've started over in my life?" Ricky said wryly. "The first time was when I was eleven."

"I still don't know how you were brave enough to do that," Matthew said. "I mean, when I was eleven, I was playing with Matchbox cars and Lincoln Logs. There's no way I could have ever survived on my own like you did."

Leaving Justiceville: A Life Behind

"I wasn't brave at all," Ricky said. "I just did what I had to do."

"Oh, you were brave, all right," Matthew said. "You are the bravest person I've ever known. If I'd gone through what you experienced as a child, I would have curled up in a ball and died. But not you; you not only survived, you thrived. You worked all those jobs and got a car before you were even twelve. And you were still a kid when you became an executive with Heller Brewing. Look at all you've accomplished in your life, and all because you had the courage to stand up and do it."

"It wasn't a big deal," Ricky said. He hesitated a moment and then spoke in a tentative voice.

"So…since we're planning all of this – you know, moving here and living together and all – what exactly does it mean?"

"What does it mean?" Matthew looked puzzled.

"Yeah. We've been living together, working together, sleeping together, and now we're moving here together and buying a place of our own. It sounds like we're a couple or something."

"Is that what you want? For us to be a couple?" Matthew asked him.

"Do you?"

"I asked you first," Matthew said evasively.

"I asked you second," Ricky said.

Matthew thought for a moment.

"I guess the more important question, the one we should be asking, is do we love each other?"

"Yeah, I guess that is the important question," Ricky nodded thoughtfully.

There was a moment of silence as the two men considered this.

"Sooo…how do you feel about me?" Matthew said.

"I…I like you a lot," Ricky said uncomfortably.

"I like you, too," Matthew said. "I…maybe…more than like you."

"You do?"

"Yeah."

"What does that mean, exactly?" Ricky frowned.

"Look, if I tell you how I feel, and you don't feel the same way, that won't mess things up between us, will it?"

"No, it won't. But I probably do feel the same way."

Matthew took a deep breath.

"I think I love you," he said, letting his breath out in a rush. "I know we haven't known each other all that long, but –"

"I love you too," Ricky said.

Wow, he thought with a sense of wonder, I really do love him. I love another man, really love him! It's almost unbelievable, but it's true. The thing that I never dreamed would ever happen has actually occurred. I've fallen in love, and the person I've fallen in love with has fallen in love with me! What are the odds of that happening?

"You do?" Matthew grinned. He leaned over and gave him a kiss before settling back on the bed beside him. "So then I guess that makes us a couple."

"I guess it does," Ricky said with a satisfied grin.

Leaving Justiceville: A Life Behind

"Maybe we should do something special," Matthew said. "You know, since this is an important moment."
"Okay," Ricky said. "What did you have in mind?"
A moment later the two were making ardent love to one another.

The next day, Matthew contacted a realtor. The woman was very friendly and helpful, but most of the houses she showed them were simply too expensive, even the cheaper ones.
"Well," she said at last, "I'm afraid that's all I have available."
She thought for a moment.
"Although, now that I think about it, I do know of a place that would work for you."
"We're desperate," Matthew said.
"We're not desperate," Ricky shook his head. "Just tell us what you had in mind."
"Well, there's a place in Mount Morris that I think would be perfect, as long as you're willing to keep an open mind."

After lunch, the realtor took them to a large mobile home park on the east edge of the small town of Mount Morris, five miles west of Oregon.
"A trailer park?" Matthew wrinkled his nose. "Do we have to live in a trailer park?"
"Now don't take that attitude," Ricky said. "At least let's keep an open mind, like the realtor said."
They drove slowly through the development, and Ricky had to admit that it wasn't bad. As far as trailer

parks went, this one was actually quite nice. The mobile homes were all widely spaced and neatly maintained, with tidily trimmed lawns and shrubs. The streets were paved, and there were lots of trees scattered throughout.

The mobile home that was for sale was typical of the park, except this one had a large addition built onto it, and it had a car port, a new storage shed, and even a fireplace. It had a more rural feel to it since it backed up to a cornfield, making it seem less claustrophobic.

"This is great," Ricky told the realtor. "Let us talk about it for a few minutes."

"You won't find a nicer mobile home in the area," she told him. "But if you do decide to buy it, you have to be approved by the owners of the park."

She leaned in closer.

"They're elderly and rather…shall we say, conservative," she added confidentially.

"In other words, they're homophobic pricks," Ricky said dryly. "And they don't want any fags living in their trailer park."

"I'm afraid so," she said. "If I was you, I'd tell them you're brothers or cousins or something."

A deal was soon struck with the trailer's owner, and Ricky and Matthew met with the park's owners, who lived in a trailer at the far end of their street. Ricky took an instant dislike to the pair.

"Won't you sit down?" the old man pointed to a chair.

Leaving Justiceville: A Life Behind

Ricky and Matthew sat down side by side. A rather plain and unattractive middle-aged woman sat primly in a living room chair.

"This is our daughter, Esther," the man said. "I'm Jacob, and this is my wife Naomi."

"Nice to meet you," Ricky said with a strained smile.

"Now, I'm sure your realtor explained the purpose of this meeting," Jacob said.

"Yes, she explained it," Ricky said. "But we've already bought the trailer, so I don't see –"

"Whether you've bought the trailer or not is of no importance to me," Jacob said sternly. "You will not move into it if we find you undesirable."

"Undesirable?" Matthew frowned.

"We don't want the wrong sort living in our mobile home community," Naomi explained. "You know, criminals and black people and Mexicans and Jews."

Ricky and Matthew glanced uncomfortably at one another. God, these were the worst sort of people, intolerant and hateful like so many of the people he had known back in Texas, yet who claimed to be devoutly religious. There was nothing Christian about them, he realized.

"And especially no homosexuals," her husband added ominously. "You know all of those people are destroying this great nation of ours."

"Tell us about yourselves," the elderly woman said.

"Well," Matthew said hesitantly. "We're moving here from Oklahoma to be nearer my family."

"Our family, that is," Ricky interjected quickly. "We're cousins."

Leaving Justiceville: A Life Behind

"I see," Jacob said. "I was wondering why two young men such as yourselves were living together. We can't be too careful, you know. For all we knew, you were a couple of queers shacking up and moving in to convert the whole town."

"Oh, yes, we know," Ricky said with a smile. "We are definitely not here to take over the town. We just want to live close to my dear Uncle Bill and Aunt Betty."

"My parents," Matthew said.

"And what does your father do for a living?" the old man asked Matthew.

"He's a farmer," Matthew answered.

"And your mother's a housewife, I take it?" Naomi asked.

"Of course," Matthew said truthfully.

"That's good, because we don't believe in the wife working outside of the home," Jacob said. "God put the man in charge and the woman is to obey. Don't you agree?"

"Do you read your Bible on a regular basis?" Naomi asked before Ricky or Matthew could answer.

"Oh…yes, of course," Ricky said. "There's nothing we enjoy more than reading our Bibles."

"I'm glad to hear it," Naomi said. "You know, our daughter here is single. If either of you are interested in taking her out…"

Matthew and Ricky looked briefly at the grim, sour-faced woman sitting silently nearby and then at each other.

"Uh, you know what?" Ricky said. "We both have girlfriends."

"Yes, we're dating," Matthew added. "Uh, girls, that is. That's another reason we're moving here from Oklahoma. Our girlfriends are here. "

"Oh, that's a shame," Naomi frowned, obviously disappointed.

"What do you boys do for a living?" Jacob asked.

"I manage a fast food restaurant," Ricky said. "And Matthew has a degree in music and teaches piano."

"And you both plan to keep the property neat at all times?" Naomi said. "Jacob here is very strict when it comes to cleanliness."

"An unclean home leads to an unclean mind," Jacob said piously.

He handed Ricky and Matthew each a pamphlet from their church extolling the horrors of hell and damnation.

"Now be sure and go to church every Sunday," Jacob said. He turned to his wife. "I think we can approve of these boys. They look okay to me."

"Well, if you can please Jacob," Naomi said to the two young men, "you must be okay. He's a very good judge of character, you know."

"I'm sure he is," Ricky said politely. "We're all brothers and sisters in Christ, you know."

Ricky and Matthew walked back to the Cadillac, which was still parked at the trailer they were buying. They waited until they were out of eye and earshot of

Jacob and Naomi's trailer and then burst out laughing.
"Brothers and sisters in Christ?" Matthew practically doubled over with mirth. "Oh my god, that's hysterical! I can't believe you said that with a straight face!"

Leaving Justiceville: A Life Behind

CHAPTER NINETEEN

Ricky and Matthew spent the next few days visiting the three state parks which were located in the vicinity: White Pines, Lowden, and Castlerock. Two of those parks were located on the lovely Rock River, while the third sat a few miles southeast of Mount Morris. There were lots of trails to traverse, rocky bluffs to climb, and even a rustic lodge with a dining room and delicious home cooking. Several of the small towns in the area had picturesque downtowns with lots of interesting antique shops.
What a beautiful area, Ricky thought. Lots of rolling hills and woods and fields of corn and soybeans and wheat. Everything seemed cleaner and brighter here than in Texas or Oklahoma. The grass was greener, the sky bluer, the trees taller and straighter. Even the heat of the late summer day was less oppressive and stifling. It was warm and humid, but nothing like this time of year in Texas. He remembered walking from his house to his car at four-thirty in the morning when he had worked at Heller, only to be covered in sweat by the time he walked the twenty-five feet to the curb. Often times the temperature was already near one hundred degrees. No wonder the trees were more stunted and the grass a dreary green; they were exhausted from just trying to survive in that miserable heat.

With jobs and a place to live taken care of, Ricky and Matthew returned to Oklahoma and made their

arrangements to move. They planned to take some of the furniture from the house, and they bought a washer and dryer and a refrigerator with Ted's money since neither of them was being paid. Once they felt fairly comfortable that they had most of the necessities of daily life, they rented a big U-Haul truck with a car carrier to tow behind. The Cadillac was carefully loaded onto it, leaving Matthew to drive the truck and Ricky to drive his car. The incredibly heavy and awkward grand piano was dismantled, tipped onto its side, and stowed first into the truck, where it was strapped securely to the sides and bed of the vehicle. The appliances and furniture followed, and soon the truck was filled to capacity. They set out early the next morning for Illinois after Matthew said a heartfelt goodbye to Ted and Ridgeview Kennels. It was a long, tedious trip, so they decided to make it easier by driving it in two days. Ricky was used to working sixteen hour shifts, so he wasn't intimidated by making such a long trip all at once. However, he knew it would be a bit too long for Matthew, and he didn't want to push him any harder than necessary. The emotional aspect of the situation alone was wearing on him, Ricky realized, so he did his best to remain cheerful and optimistic for Matthew's sake. This was a big change for him, and he was dealing with the unpleasant feelings of trepidation, loss, and grief. Ricky was naturally a bit apprehensive himself about moving to a completely new place and starting a brand new job. He wasn't concerned about the new job itself since it

was similar to work he had done before. And he wasn't afraid of the challenges he knew they would face. Nothing had ever stopped him in the past, and it wasn't going to now. His main concern was for Matthew, who was clearly more emotionally fragile at this difficult time. This was a tough time for him, and he wanted to make the transition as easy as possible.

The two-day trek was uneventful, although driving a big truck while pulling a trailer behind it was a bit harrowing as they drove among the crowded and fast paced traffic of St. Louis. Matthew's parents met them at the trailer park in Mount Morris and helped them with the daunting task of unloading the truck. The most difficult job for the four of them was to move the six hundred pound piano and set it up. Kind of ironic, Ricky thought; here they owned a grand piano and a late model Cadillac and yet were moving into an older mobile home in a small town trailer park.

Matthew's dad was decidedly cool toward Ricky, but was at least civil.

"It's a shame you had to leave Oklahoma," he said to Matthew. "Are you sure you couldn't have worked things out with Ted?"

"No, Dad," Matthew said patiently. "That whole thing was over a long time ago. I only stayed there because I was comfortable there, and I thought I…I thought that was my future. But it wasn't."

Leaving Justiceville: A Life Behind

"His future's just starting," Ricky said. "And it's with me."
"We're glad Matthew's not alone," Betty said with a warm smile.
"I'm only saying –" Bill began.
"Honey, just let it go," Betty said gently, placing a restraining hand on his arm. "Let's just be glad that Matthew is back in Illinois instead of so far away."

"I don't think your dad likes me," Ricky said as they lay side by side that night in their bedroom at the back end of the trailer.
"He likes you," Matthew said. "It's just that he thought I belonged there at Ridgeview Kennels, that my future was all set. I don't think he understands the personal side of the situation."
"He barely spoke to me."
"Just give him some time, and he'll come around," Matthew said. "I promise."

Ricky began his new job a few days after they settled into their new home. It was very similar to the work he had done at Taco Rio and Taco Bell, although with a different menu, of course. As with his other jobs, he took to the work easily and learned the ins and outs of the position very quickly. It paid decently, but considerably less than his job at Heller Brewing. Still, at this point he was just thankful to have work of any kind.
While Ricky was working fifty hours a week in Rockford, which was located nearly an hour away

Leaving Justiceville: A Life Behind

from Mount Morris, Matthew was grooming dogs at The Menagerie in Byron, making even less money. By coincidence, the shop was located just two doors down from the house where Matthew had lived when he had been fired from the local Assemblies of God church a few years before.

To supplement their income, Matthew advertised for piano students in the local papers and, within a few weeks, had twenty piano students, which he taught in the late afternoon hours five days a week.

Fortunately, their bills were not enormous; there were the mortgage, the Cadillac payment, Matthew's student loan, piano payment, groceries, utilities, gas, and a few assorted credit cards. With their combined income, they were just able to meet their monthly obligations, but there was nothing left over for extras. Still, Ricky didn't care. He was working at a job he enjoyed, he was living in a nice place; granted, it was a trailer, but that didn't matter. He was sharing it with the man he loved.

God, that was still surreal to him! He, Ricky Blain, was in a relationship! And it was with Matthew, a really terrific, educated, smart, funny, talented, attractive guy. How the hell had that happened? Matthew came from a good family, and he was always using big words, he had two degrees, and he played the piano.

"You know, sometimes I feel dumb when I talk to you," Ricky frowned.

Leaving Justiceville: A Life Behind

"You?" Matthew said incredulously. "How could you possibly feel dumb? You're like one of the smartest people I know."
"But I don't know all your fancy words," Ricky said. "You have all kinds of education that I never had."
"Just because I have more formal education than you doesn't mean anything," Matthew said. "You are so smart, much smarter than you know. I feel dumb compared to you sometimes."

Money was extremely tight for Ricky and Matthew. There was no money for movies or restaurants, so they entertained themselves by decorating their trailer, walking the trails at the three beautiful state parks, visiting lots of antique stores (from which they bought nothing, but it was still fun to look), and occasionally driving over to Savanna on the Mississippi River to go to the Mississippi Palisades State Park so they could climb the steep hills that rose a couple of hundred feet above the wide expanse of water. From there they would drive up to the picturesque village of Galena in the northwest corner of the state and visit the myriad of unusual specialty shops located there. They would climb the tall Long Hollow Scenic Overlook tower located a few miles from town, from which they could see into Illinois, Iowa, and Wisconsin.
Often times on these little excursions, they would have no money for lunch, so they would use Ricky's Phillips 66 gas card to buy prepackaged sandwiches, Hostess pies, candy bars, potato chips, and soft drinks

and then enjoy their little feast in their car or on a picnic table in the parks. When the snow fell, they would use the floor mats from the car to go sledding down the steep hills at White Pines Park.
On rare occasions, they would drive to Woodfield Mall in Schaumburg, a suburb of Chicago, or to Cherryvale Mall in Cherry Valley on the east edge of Rockford. They never bought anything on these trips but enjoyed window shopping and spending the time together.

The grooming at The Menagerie didn't work out for Matthew, so he finally quit and started grooming out of the trailer. While that business slowly built up, Ricky hired him to work two days a week at the restaurant with him. Matthew did his best, but he was a bit too slow and borderline incompetent; he may have held two degrees, but he clearly wasn't cut out to work in the fast-food industry. Ricky was patient with him, as well as the other employees. Ricky was unaware of it, but during the short time that Matthew was employed there, he took the time to study his partner and boss.
Ricky was very good at his job, Matthew observed. He was extremely organized and knew what he was doing. He was very fair and treated all of his employees with dignity, and they all liked and respected him. Maria, his assistant manager, and Ricky became quite good friends, and the two of them ran a tight ship.

Leaving Justiceville: A Life Behind

On one occasion, however, Ricky had reached the end of his patience.

"I've told you all time and again to clean this shelf," he said in a loud voice to the employees. "Just look at it. It's filthy!"

His staff stopped what they were doing and looked at him blankly.

"Whose job was it to clean this?" he asked them.

The workers looked at one another uneasily, but no one answered him.

"So it's no one's job to clean it?" Ricky said. He waited, but still no one responded. "Well, fine."

With that he grabbed the shelf in both hands and yanked roughly on it until it finally tore loose from the wall. All the while his employees looked on in astonishment, with wide eyes and open mouths.

Ricky kicked the back door open and threw the metal shelf out onto the parking lot.

"There," he said, breathing heavily from the exertion. "Problem solved."

Maria just stared at him for a moment and then burst out laughing. Soon they were all overcome with mirth; it took several minutes for them to settle down and get back to work.

"I can't believe you did that," Maria wiped her eyes, still giggling.

"Hey," Ricky shrugged and grinned. "I told them repeatedly to clean it. Since they didn't do it, they'll just have to live without it!"

In a moment, they were doubled over with laughter once again.

Keeping the help, the vendors, his managers, and the public happy was a monumental task, and Matthew couldn't help but admire the strength and humor, not to mention the restraint (except for the shelf incident, of course), that Ricky showed while working in such a difficult job.

Matthew quit the job at the restaurant once the piano lessons and grooming picked up. It was a relief to him to be away from that environment, especially since rumors were beginning to spread regarding his and Ricky's relationship.

After several months, eventually the hour drive to Rockford five to six days a week became tiresome to Ricky. He enjoyed the job for the most part, but it was a long trek to make so frequently. Often times he would get home after a twelve hour day only to be called by the security company that a burglar alarm was going off at the store. He would sigh heavily, climb into the car, and drive back to Rockford.
"You can't keep doing this," Matthew told him late one night as Ricky crawled wearily into bed. He had only been home for thirty minutes and eaten the supper that Matthew made for him and heated up in the microwave.
"I just want to sleep," Ricky sighed. "I have to be up at five."
"See, that's what I mean," Matthew said. "You're working way too many hours and driving all that way. You're exhausted."

Leaving Justiceville: A Life Behind

"What other choice do I have?" Ricky said. "We've got bills to pay."
"Why not check into a job at Kable News here in town?" Matthew suggested. "It's like five minutes from home."
Kable News was a New York based business that employed hundreds of local workers. It distributed books, periodicals, and newspapers across the United States.
"One of my piano students works there," Matthew went on. "I'll bet she could get you a job."
"I don't know anything about the publishing business," Ricky protested with a yawn.
"So?" Matthew said. "As smart as you are, you could learn it in a second."
"It probably doesn't pay as well," Ricky said. "We can't afford that."
"The lessons and the grooming are picking up more and more," Matthew said. "We'll get by somehow."
"I'll think about it," Ricky mumbled. Two seconds later, he was sound asleep.

Three weeks later, Ricky said goodbye to his friends at the restaurant in Rockford and started his new job as a list management technician for Kable News. Within fifteen minutes of greeting the head of personnel with a handshake, Ricky was hired. The salary was less than what he had been making, but he soon decided it was worth it. The job was enjoyable, and he liked his coworkers for the most part. The best aspect of it was that it was literally five minutes from

Leaving Justiceville: A Life Behind

home. No more hour long trips everyday, no more managing employees and dealing with the public. What a relief!

Life moved along contentedly for Ricky. He was in a loving relationship, had an enjoyable job, and lived in a nice home. The mobile home wasn't exactly ideal, of course, but it was serviceable and comfortable, not to mention inexpensive in which to live. Money remained extremely tight for him and Matthew, but at this point, neither of them cared. Once the bills were paid each month, there was no money left, and yet the two of them were quite satisfied in general.
One day Matthew got a call from Ted. He hung up the phone and turned to Ricky with a frown.
"What'd he want?" Ricky asked.
"He's coming to Janesville to visit his brother," Matthew said. "He wants to meet with me."
"Why?" Ricky asked suspiciously.
"Probably to talk about something to do with the kennel, I guess," Matthew shrugged.
"If it's something to do with the kennel, why can't he just say it over the phone?"
"I don't know. He said he needs to see me in person."
"But…why do you have to meet with him while I'm at work? Make it at a time that I can go with you."
"This is the only time he's got," Matthew said.
"Listen, it's no big deal. I'll just go talk to him and see what he wants. Nothing to worry about."
"Yeah…I suppose not," Ricky said worriedly.

Leaving Justiceville: A Life Behind

What was this whole thing about, he wondered? Why would Ted need to see Matthew in person if he just wanted to talk about the kennel? Something potentially bad was happening here, he could just sense it.

The next day, Matthew made the hour and a half trip from Mount Morris to Janesville, Wisconsin. Ricky kissed him goodbye that morning and went to work at Kable News with his heart in his throat. Deep down, he was certain he knew why Ted was making this trip to see his brother; he wanted Matthew back. No, he didn't believe that he loved him. He was just being a typical man, wanting a toy simply because someone else was playing with it. In this case, that particular toy was Matthew. In Ted's mind, Matthew still belonged to him and Ricky had no right to play with him. He was coming to get him back, Ricky was sure. And what if Ted succeeded? What would he do then? How could he live with a broken heart? Because he knew without a doubt that if Matthew left him, his heart would be shattered beyond repair. He had never allowed himself to love anyone in his entire life. Of course, there had never been anyone in his life thus far who was worthy of love except for Matthew.

As he sat at his desk at Kable News, he found it almost impossible to concentrate on his work as he pictured Ted and Matthew together. God, just the thought of that was excruciating to him. He couldn't lose Matthew, he just couldn't! He loved him, and he knew that he would never be able to give his heart to anyone else if Matthew ever left him.

Leaving Justiceville: A Life Behind

Now, just calm down, he told himself sternly. Matthew loves you; he's not going to leave you for Ted, even if they do have a history together. They haven't been a couple for a long time. The only reason Ted would want Matthew back was because he was so good with the kennel, and Matthew would surely realize that.

But would he, he thought worriedly? Matthew could be so naïve sometimes. Ted was a smooth talker and was usually able to convince anyone of just about anything. Matthew would be putty in his hands, especially without Ricky there to intervene.

Whatever happened – if Matthew chose to leave him, that is – Ricky would need to have a plan. What would he do all alone again? Would he stay in Illinois or go back to Texas? There was nothing for him here, that was for sure, other than his job and a half interest in a mobile home. But then again, what was there for him back in Texas? Even less than here. Well, he would wait until he knew for sure that Matthew was leaving him or not and then make his plans.

At four o'clock that afternoon, Ricky drove the few blocks to the trailer park and sighed with relief at the sight of Matthew's Cadillac sitting in the driveway. Wait, he told himself cautiously, just because he's home doesn't mean he's decided to stay. Maybe he's inside right now packing his things so he can head back to Oklahoma with Ted.

With great trepidation he stepped inside the trailer and looked around.

Leaving Justiceville: A Life Behind

"How was work?" Matthew called out from the kitchen.
"It was fine," Ricky said. He stepped into the kitchen and Matthew gave him a brief kiss. "How, uh, was your visit with Ted?"
"It was okay," Matthew shrugged.
"What did he want?" Ricky asked hesitantly.
"Well, I'll tell you," Matthew frowned. "But I think we'd better sit down first."
"Just tell me," Ricky said. "I don't need to sit down."
"Come sit down anyway," Matthew said.
The two men sat down on the camelback sofa in front of the fireplace.
"He wants you back, doesn't he?" Ricky said, swallowing hard.
"Yes, he does," Matthew looked surprised. "How did you know?"
"I just knew," Ricky gulped. He forced himself not to cry. "So what are you going to do?"
"What do you mean?"
"Just tell me," Ricky said. "If you're going to leave, that's fine. I just need to know so I can make my plans."
"I'm not leaving, you dope," Matthew frowned. "Why would you think that?"
"Because I know how hard it was for you to leave Oklahoma," Ricky said. "It would be perfectly understandable for you to want to go back. After all, you thought that was where your future was."
"I did think my future was there," Matthew admitted. "But that was then, and this is now. There's no way I

Leaving Justiceville: A Life Behind

would go back to Oklahoma. Unless we went back together, that is."
Ricky stared at him silently for a moment.
"So…you're not leaving?" he said uncertainly.
"Of course not," Matthew grinned. "The only reason he wanted me back was because I'm here with you. And because I was free help at the kennel. I mean, I think he truly believed he wanted me back, but deep down, he knew better, and so did I."
He raised an eyebrow impishly.
"Although I will admit that I did consider it for a while," he chuckled. "After all, the fact that you don't like onions was almost a deal breaker for me."
The two had argued with and teased each other about Ricky's dislike of onions since the first day they met. Matthew was a big fan of onions and was determined that if Ricky gave them a chance, he would like them too.
"Asshole," Ricky frowned. "Do you know how much it hurt me just knowing that you were talking to him? Especially since I knew what he wanted?"
Matthew's smile disappeared immediately.
"Ricky, I'm sorry," he said. "I was just kidding you. I wasn't going to go back."
"I…I thought you were going to leave me," Ricky said. This time he couldn't keep the tears from filling his eyes.
Matthew leaned forward and embraced him tightly.
"I'm not going anywhere," he whispered in his ear. "Not unless you're going with me."

Leaving Justiceville: A Life Behind

Ricky clung to him until he was able to bring his emotions under control. He was unaccustomed to showing vulnerability to the world. Over the years he had developed an emotional suit of armor to protect himself from the cruelty of other people. He had had no choice but to shield himself from the hostile world; otherwise he might never have survived. As it was, he had kept people at a distance, and there were very few who he had allowed into his personal space. In fact, there was really only Matthew, and the thought of being left or betrayed by the one person he cared for was unbearable.

He pulled away from Matthew and dried his eyes. "I'm sorry," he said, his face red with embarrassment. "Just don't ever tease me about something as important as this. I don't like it."

"I won't," Matthew said apologetically. "I didn't realize that you were so worried about this meeting with Ted. I should have known, and I'm sorry for being so insensitive. It won't happen again."

Matthew received a call from his mother one day. "Dad's having heart surgery," she said.

Matthew's father had had a bout of rheumatic fever as a boy, which had resulted in damage to the aortic valve in his heart. It had gotten progressively worse over his lifetime and was now at the point that it urgently needed repair.

She went on to give him all the details, and both he and Ricky could hear the worry in her voice. Bill and Betty had been married forty years and were

absolutely devoted to one another. In fact, the two had never been apart except for the time that Betty had had an emergency appendectomy at their small local hospital when Matthew was a child.

"He'll be fine," Matthew reassured his mother over the phone. "Don't worry. Heart surgery isn't nearly as big a deal as it used to be."

But Ricky knew that Matthew felt anything but confident in what he was saying. After all, Matthew had a nursing degree and knew enough about the medical field to be frightened of the potential outcomes to such a major surgery.

"He will be fine," he said after Matthew hung up the phone. He gave his partner a comforting hug. "Just wait and see."

Matthew's father had his surgery at University Hospital in Indianapolis, and he came through the procedure well. A few complications arose in the days following the operation, and Bill was kept in the hospital for a total of thirty days. Ricky and Matthew made the six hour trip to Indianapolis when they could but had to continue working as much as possible. There were bills to pay, and they had no benefits from an employer to help them out, so they did what they had to do.

Matthew's parents' home was located half way between Mossville and Harrington, two small towns in east central Illinois about three hours from Mount Morris. Ricky drove down with Matthew every Friday evening to help with mowing and other chores

Leaving Justiceville: A Life Behind

that needed to be done. They drove back on Sunday nights in time to go to bed so they could get up and go back to work the next morning.

Ricky had grown very fond of Matthew's mother, a gentle, sweet, maternal woman, who treated him with great kindness. He was to learn that she was loved dearly by all the children and young adults in their rural neighborhood, many of whom she had babysat for over the years. Matthew's father remained somewhat aloof with Ricky, but Matthew explained again that it was just his way and not to take it personally.

Ricky was glad to help out in any way that he could, so he and Matthew mowed the two acres of grass each weekend, trimmed the shrubs, took out the trash, did household repairs, and more. He wanted to make this ordeal as painless as possible for both Matthew and his mother.

"You don't have to come with me," Matthew said one night when they were lying in bed together. "If you want to stay home and relax on some of the weekends, that's okay."

"I'm not going to let you make that long trip all by yourself," Ricky said firmly. "There's too much for you to handle."

Matthew's father finally came home from the hospital to the old farmhouse in which Matthew had grown up. He was weak and a bit unsteady after his long hospital stay, so Ricky and Matthew took some

Leaving Justiceville: A Life Behind

time off from their work schedules to drive down and stay with him and Betty for a few days.

Bill was restless and somewhat unclear cognitively on his first night home, so Ricky and Matthew slept in the living room, next door to Bill and Betty's bedroom. Bill couldn't sleep and paced restlessly around the downstairs. Ricky sat up with him so that Betty and Matthew could sleep. Long hours and little sleep were no stranger to him, so this wasn't anything new; he could get by on very little shuteye since that was what he had done all of his life. Bill had little to say to him, but Ricky was only concerned with keeping him safe while Betty and Matthew got some rest.

A few weeks after Matthew's father had returned home and was back to something resembling his normal self, Ricky and Matthew spent the weekend at home in the trailer. They needed a few days to relax and catch up on some of their own chores, so one of Matthew's sisters looked after their parents. Bill's mind was completely clear now, but his body remained somewhat frail.

"I don't know how they're going to take care of that house anymore," Matthew said worriedly to Ricky that Sunday morning as they snuggled together in bed. "It's way too big for them, and Dad can't handle mowing two acres of grass every weekend. Plus, it's getting to be in bad shape."

"We'll just have to do it," Ricky shrugged. "We're only three hours away. I don't mind driving down

there. Besides, it would kill your mom to have to give up that house. She loves it there."

That was true enough, he realized. Betty had said more than once how much her home meant to her. She had told them how she used to drive by it when she was a girl and always admired it. And he had to agree that there was something especially homey about the big old house.

"I know," Matthew sighed. "I love it too. All of my memories there are happy ones."

He cuddled closer to Ricky and kissed his neck.

"You know, no matter how bad things would get at school, that was the one place that I was safe and happy."

He had told Ricky how badly he had been bullied all through school, both from students and even a few teachers.

"And at church, they were always telling me how evil gay people were and that we were all going to hell. That used to scare the daylights out of me when I was a kid. I mean, they're telling me that God hated me for something that was out of my control. It was awful. Oh, I know it was nothing compared to what you went through as a boy, but it was still traumatic for me.

"Anyway, all of the bad things I was trying to cope with out in the world disappeared when I was at home in that house," Matthew went on. "I knew I was loved, and I didn't have to be afraid of anyone or anything. So even though it's nothing special, that house has always been very important to me."

Leaving Justiceville: A Life Behind

It was the very next weekend that Matthew's parents told Ricky and Matthew that they were going to buy a small house in Mossville, the same town where Matthew and his siblings had gone to elementary and high school. Matthew's niece was visiting too, and the five of them were sitting at the dining room table.
"You're moving?" Matthew frowned.
"We have to," Betty told him regretfully. "This place is way too big for the two of us, and we can't afford to take care of it anymore."
That was obvious, Ricky thought. The old farmhouse was definitely looking shabby. He and Matthew had kept the grass mowed and neatly trimmed, but the house itself was in bad shape. There was broken and cracked stucco, rusty or missing downspouts, rotting eaves and window trim, and the roof was leaking and needed to be replaced. The plaster walls were badly cracked, the hardwood floors stained and worn, the furnace ancient, and the kitchen quite dated. There were two and a half bathrooms, but only one of them was functional. Two decrepit garages on the property as well as a ramshackle summer kitchen appeared beyond repair.
Bill and Betty had updated the property when they bought it when their family was very young, but little had been done to it since that time nearly thirty years ago. In spite of all of its shortcomings, the place still had a warm, welcoming atmosphere about it, and Ricky knew that the main reason for that was the house's inhabitants. They were genuinely good

people, the best he had ever known, and it was clear that they loved their children very much. True, Bill had never warmed up to him the way he would have liked, but he understood him and knew he was still a good man who had worked hard all of his adult life to provide for his family.

Leaving Justiceville: A Life Behind

CHAPTER TWENTY

By this time, Ricky had met the rest of Matthew's family, most of whom lived nearby. There was his brother, three sisters, their families, as well as a number of cousins and aunts and uncles. Farming was a big part of Matthew's heritage on both his father's and mother's sides; Bill himself had been a farmer before his health had forced him to retire.
"Where are you going to go?" Matthew asked his folks.
"There's a ranch house in town that Kenny built," Bill told him, referring to his cousin's husband who was an exceptional craftsman. "It's very solid and right on the highway, just north of the schools."
"It's only two bedrooms," Betty added, "but it has a full basement and an attached garage. It's very nice."
"What about this place?" Ricky frowned at them. "You love this house, and so does Matthew."
"So do I," Matthew's niece added.
"We're going to sell it," Bill said, looking uncomfortably at his wife. "We'll miss it, but we don't have any choice. You can see the shape it's in, and we can't afford to live here."
"Your father needs to be in town, what with his health and all," Betty said.
"But you've never lived in town," Matthew pointed out. "How will you like not living in the country?"
"It will be fine," Betty shrugged. "We'll adapt."

Leaving Justiceville: A Life Behind

"But who will buy this house?" their granddaughter asked them. "I don't want to see strangers living here."

"Me, neither," Matthew agreed. "I don't think I could handle that. I mean, this is where we grew up. And now strangers are going to live in it? They won't care about it."

"It's just a house, Matthew," his dad reminded him.

"I know," Matthew said. "But it means something to me."

"So why don't you buy it?" his niece suggested.

"Us?" Matthew said, startled by the suggestion. "We can't do that."

"Why not?" Ricky said.

"Yeah, why not?"

"Because…because we'd have to move again. We'd have to start all over," Matthew said. "There's the grooming and the piano lessons, and your job. We can't give all of that up."

That night, as Ricky and Matthew lay in bed in Matthew's boyhood bedroom, they talked the matter over.

"You love this house," Ricky said.

"I do love this house," Matthew admitted. "But it's in such bad shape. There'd be so much we'd have to do to it."

"So? We can do it," Ricky said. "A little paint, a few repairs, and it will be good as new."

"There are a lot of things I've always dreamed of doing to it," Matthew said. "Ever since I was a little

kid, I thought about how I would decorate this place if it was mine."

"Well, this could be your chance."

"But it would mean starting over again," Matthew frowned. "You love your job, and I've built up the grooming and lessons. Wouldn't it be foolish to give all of that up?"

"There are other jobs," Ricky said. "And if you can groom and give lessons in Mount Morris, you can do it here."

"But it's six miles from town. People won't drive all that way to get their dogs groomed."

"Sure they will."

"But –"

"Matthew, I know you want this house, and I want you to have it," Ricky said firmly. "And I'll do whatever is necessary to make that happen."

Matthew's parents bought a house on North Chicago Street in a nice neighborhood in the nearby small town. It was a lovely ranch style home with a breezeway and a big back yard.

Matthew's sister-in-law appraised the old farmhouse for them, and a deal was soon struck. Because Matthew had very little credit, all of the banks they talked to were reluctant to give them a loan. Fortunately, his parents' bank in Mossville took pity on Matthew and Ricky, mostly due to Bill and Betty's good standing in the community. The interest rate was rather high, but Ricky knew they couldn't be choosy at this point. They borrowed an extra few

thousand dollars, so they could redo the old kitchen and buy paint and other supplies.

Oh god, Ricky thought, what have we done? He stared up at the ramshackle farmhouse. It was in a more advanced state of decay than he had originally thought. The fifty foot porch across the front of the house needed some major repairs, window frames were rotting away, the roof and furnace desperately needed to be replaced, the outbuildings torn down, stucco repaired, and the list went on and on. Why on earth did I ever think this was a good idea?
Still, the house did have some good qualities. It had hardwood floors, a fireplace in the living room, large rooms, an enormous kitchen, pocket doors, and the big front porch.
It didn't matter anyway, he thought. This is what Matthew wanted, and nothing was so important to

him than to see his partner happy. He should just look at this as another challenge, an uphill climb like all the others he had conquered. This would be no different.

Over the next few months, Ricky and Matthew drove to Matthew's parents' house every weekend to help them get it ready to move into and to empty out the five bedroom farmhouse. It was a daunting task to condense a fifteen room house down to a place that was less than half that size. Once they were moved into their new house, Betty told Matthew and Ricky that they could keep whatever remained in the farmhouse since she had no where to put it.
For days, Ricky and Matthew cleaned, sorted, and threw away until they had cleared out every room of their new house. Now that it was empty of furniture, the old place looked even worse, Ricky thought unhappily. Wow, we are in way over our heads here! It's going to cost a fortune to make this place inhabitable, even if we do all the work ourselves.

Since money was clearly going to be an issue, Ricky and Matthew began applying for jobs. Matthew landed a job immediately as a nurse at the small local hospital in Harrington, six miles away, and Ricky accepted a position at a publishing company in another town twenty-five miles away. It published four different newspapers in the surrounding communities, including Harrington, and Ricky was hired to act as advertising manager. Once again, he

Leaving Justiceville: A Life Behind

would be working in a totally new field, but he wasn't concerned. He knew he would pick up on his duties quickly, just like he had done in the past at all of his previous jobs.

A year and a half after moving to Mount Morris, Ricky and Matthew loaded up another U-Haul truck with all of their belongings and made the move to their new home. Joyce and Charlotte drove up the day before the move to help load the truck and drive the cars down. Ricky ordered Ciminello's pizza for them late that evening just as the snow began. They were all exhausted, and all the dishes were packed away in the back of the truck. The four of them sat on the living room floor while they talked and ate before settling down to sleep for a few hours on their blankets.

The next morning when they got up, the lightly falling snow had turned into a full-fledged blizzard. Matthew climbed behind the wheel of the big truck while Ricky drove his car, Charlotte was in the Cadillac, and Joyce drove her own car. The roads were barely visible as their little convoy headed east on Route 64. They crept along at twenty miles an hour until they reached Interstate 39. The highway was drifted and visibility was near zero as they joined the other wary travelers.

Ricky was still a bit unfamiliar with the changeability of Illinois weather, so he was astonished when they abruptly drove out of the inclement weather. It was like a curtain had suddenly parted; the highway was

perfectly clear, the ground bare, the sky merely overcast. He looked in his rearview mirror and saw the wall of snow from which they had just emerged. How bizarre, he thought, to go in an instant from the worst weather to a merely calm, chilly day.

When they arrived at the farmhouse, the weather was clear and the temperature merely cold instead of blustery. Matthew's parents had arranged for some help in unloading the truck and setting up the piano. Several of the young people from the neighborhood for whom Betty had babysat were there to assist, and in less than an hour, the truck was empty.

Ricky and Matthew spent the next couple of days arranging furniture to make the drafty old place habitable. Matthew had come down on his own a few times in the past few weeks to paint and clean what he could, but there was still much to be done.

The kitchen had been completely gutted in preparation for new drywall and cabinets, so for the first several weeks, Ricky and Matthew had to make do with only a sink, a refrigerator, and a microwave. Once the drywall had been completed by a local contractor, Ricky and Matthew, Bill, and a few friends of Matthew's parents installed the new cabinets, countertops, and sink. Matthew had purchased a how-to book that explained how to do many household repairs, and it wasn't long before Ricky became annoyed with him whenever they started a new project.

"All you have to do is…" became Matthew's catchphrase, and Ricky would tease him about it.

Leaving Justiceville: A Life Behind

There were so many projects to be done, some of which were beyond their scope, such as installing a new furnace, water heater, holding tank, and new carpeting. But they were determined to do as many of them as possible themselves. So over the next few years, they installed new drywall, new windows, sided and roofed one of the old garages, built a deck on the back of the house, and so on.

"But we don't know how to install siding," Ricky reminded him.

"The book says all you have to do is…" Matthew would reply, causing Ricky to groan with exasperation.

And so they did many projects on the old house for which they had no training, and yet they did them anyway. Most of them turned out well, while a few had to be redone by professionals. God, Ricky sighed, and to think I used to own a brand new house in a nice neighborhood that didn't need any work done.

One of the most important jobs that needed to be done immediately was installing new windows. Matthew had told Ricky how, as a boy, he had woken one morning during a strong blizzard to find an outline of snow on the carpeting in front of the two west windows in his bedroom. Matthew's parents had had the old house insulated years before, but it had done little good since the windows were in such poor shape.

The upstairs bathroom had been gutted many years before Matthew's parents bought the house. The

previous owners had wintered in Florida one year and the pipes froze, causing extensive damage to the floor and the ceiling of the dining room below. Ricky hired a plumber to replace the broken pipes from the basement all the way to the second floor fixtures, and then he and Matthew put in the new floor and painted the walls. They also had to hire an electrician to do several projects, and a contractor to cover the outside eaves with aluminum. Little by little, the old house was beginning to come alive.

One of the biggest projects they faced, besides removing four layers of shingles from the leaky roof and replacing them with new, was repairing the fifty foot long front porch. The floor was rotten, the roof sagging, and the beams supporting the whole structure had more or less disintegrated.

"All we have to do…" Matthew began. Ricky held up a hand to stop him.

"No," he said. "Not this time. This is too big of a job, and we don't have the engineering skills to do it. We need help."

"But we can't afford to hire anyone to fix it," Matthew said.

"All right," Ricky conceded. "We'll do it, but you're going to call your brother and get his advice."

It just so happened that Matthew's brother was an excellent engineer who had graduated from the University of Illinois at the top of a class of nine hundred students. He and his wife lived about twenty miles away. For that entire summer, he drove up to the farmhouse every weekend and oversaw the

rebuilding of the porch from the foundation up. Other members of Matthew's family helped out too, until the whole porch had been completely reconstructed.

Matthew worked twelve hour shifts at the hospital and began grooming dogs on the side. At first, it was only for his family's pets, but his reputation began to grow swiftly. Soon he was grooming twenty dogs a week or so in the kitchen. It was hardly an ideal situation, but he made do the best he could. Meanwhile, Ricky left the publishing company and took a job as a general manager over five convenient stores scattered throughout Lafayette, Indiana, as well as the small towns of Brookston, Monon, and Delphi. It paid quite well, and he enjoyed the work and the responsibility, but once again he found himself working long hours. Sometimes he would have to leave home in the middle of the night to get to one of the stores in time for it to open. There was an hour's time difference between Illinois and Indiana, which made his schedule even more difficult.
As with all of his previous employment, Ricky had to learn the job from the ground up. There was no one to show him how to handle the books, the cash registers, the vendors, and so on; he was forced to figure it all out for himself. As a result, there was no task involved in the running of the stores that he didn't know and couldn't do. His employees, especially the managers, respected him for that. They knew he wasn't asking anything of them that he

Leaving Justiceville: A Life Behind

wasn't willing to do himself. Most of them worked hard for him, but of course there were always those few who merely wanted a paycheck and cared nothing about the job they were hired to do.

He had an assistant named Loretta, a middle-aged woman with a cheerful disposition and a quirky sense of humor. She was an enormous help to him as he struggled to take in the overwhelming amount of responsibility the job required.

Computers were becoming an integral part of his work, and he was a natural when it came to their operation. The owner of the stores, an attractive man named Greg, soon came to rely on Ricky, not only to manage the stores/gas stations, but to help oversee many of his other enterprises. Most things to do with computers were over Greg's head, so Ricky had to step in and help him out with his construction business and other financial endeavors. Greg was less than an ideal businessman, so he was fortunate to have Ricky to keep things running in the black. Thanks to Ricky, he was making more money than he ever had before, and he paid him a good wage.

Ricky soon befriended one of his store managers, a slightly older woman named Carol. She was always willing to help out when someone called in sick or when they were shorthanded at other stores. Sometimes the two of them would run a store for ten hours with no other help. The work was difficult and exhausting, but they always made it fun, laughing and joking and teasing each other and the customers.

Leaving Justiceville: A Life Behind

Carol and her boyfriend Al lived in the small town of Brookston, a few miles north of Lafayette. Al owned a concrete contracting business, and the two of them had converted a couple of bays of an old L-shaped loafing shed into an apartment. It wasn't fancy, but at least it was clean. Carol set up a cot in the small room they used as an office and told Ricky he was welcome to stay there at night when he was too tired to drive home, or if the roads were too snowy. There was an outside door in the office that led into the adjoining set of open bays, where Al stored some of his cement contracting equipment. Often times Ricky would have to keep the door slightly ajar since Al insisted on keeping the thermostat set at a stifling seventy-eight degrees.

One night, Ricky opened the door a few inches before dropping heavily onto the cot after working an eighteen hour shift at one of the Lafayette stores. He didn't even have the energy to undress, and within thirty seconds he was asleep. The rustling sound of an animal disturbed his slumber sometime later, and he reached over with alarm and switched on the bedside lamp. To his astonishment there was a large raccoon scratching at the door, trying to force it open a little farther. He started yelling at the wild animal, and it hastily retreated. From that point on, he knew he would just have to endure the heat rather than risk being attacked in his sleep by potentially ferocious beasts.

Leaving Justiceville: A Life Behind

There were times when Ricky didn't get home for days at a time. He would stay with Carol and her boyfriend, and they did their best to look after him. After a while, he felt as if all he did was work, that this job's responsibilities were becoming too much. He missed his home, he missed Matthew. He was tired of working eighty hours a week; it reminded him too much of working those kinds of hours when he was living in his car as a child.

Late one night, he decided to make the long drive home after work. It had been over a week since he had been home last, and he needed some fresh clothes and to see Matthew. He yawned as he started the company van and set out from the West Lafayette store. If he was smart, he told himself, he would have stayed with Carol. But he wanted desperately to go home. It was almost as if he was feeling homesick. They hadn't lived in the old farmhouse that long, but it had already become his home. Like Matthew had said to him once, it was the place where he was safe and loved. Everything he cared about was there. Something about those two acres in rural Illinois called to him, and he knew a big part of that was Matthew.

He struggled to keep his eyes open as he headed west on Rt. 352. He passed through the small town of Oxford and began to pick up speed once he was outside of the city limits. His eyelids drooped heavily as his foot pressed harder on the accelerator. Before he knew it, his eyes were closed, and he was asleep at the wheel. The van veered from the highway at a high

Leaving Justiceville: A Life Behind

rate of speed and crashed through the fence of the Oxford Cemetery. The jolt of that event brought Ricky to his senses, but it was too late. There was nothing he could do as the van careened into the graveyard, knocking over headstones in its path before it became airborne. It sailed over more grave markers before hitting the ground hard and flattening several more tombstones. It finally lurched to an abrupt stop against a tree, and Ricky took a moment to recover from the shock of the accident. He couldn't see out of the windshield because it was completely shattered, and the transmission was pushed up through the center console next to him. His legs were pinned into the small space below him, but they seemed uninjured.

Once he had collected himself, he attempted to open the driver's door, but it was jammed. After several attempts, he finally rolled the window down and crawled out through the opening. Yes, thank god, he was uninjured, it seemed. The van, however, was a different story; the entire front end of the vehicle was demolished.

"Hey!" a masculine voice called to him from somewhere nearby. "You okay?"

It was an older man, a semi truck driver who had witnessed the accident.

"I'm...I'm okay, I think," Ricky said shakily.

"That was some accident," the man whistled. "You took out a whole bunch of headstones."

"I...I should call the police, I suppose," Ricky said.

"Already done," the man said. He whistled and shook his head. "Will you look at this van? There ain't much left of it. You sure as hell won't be driving it again."

When the police arrived a few minutes later, Ricky gave them all of his information and the details of the crash. They wanted to take him to the hospital, but he refused, insisting that he was fine, just tired and that he wanted to go home. The policemen informed him that they could only take him as far as the state line.

"I'll get him home," the trucker drawled. "I'm headed that way anyhow."

Ricky climbed up in the passenger seat of the big rig. God, what was he going to tell Greg, he wondered? The business was insured, and at least he hadn't been hurt, so things could have been worse. He realized suddenly that his rescuer was talking to him.

"What was that?" he said tiredly.

"I was saying it's been a long time since I got any tail," the man repeated. "Sometimes I get so damn horny, I'd fuck just about anything. Ya know what I mean?"

"Um, yeah," Ricky said warily.

"A blow job would feel really good," the man said, watching Ricky out of the corner of his eye. "Wouldn't even matter to me who gave it. I just need something warm and wet to stick my dick into."

"Uh, yeah, I can understand that," Ricky said uneasily.

"You could always help me out," the man said nonchalantly. "If you wanted to."

Leaving Justiceville: A Life Behind

"I wish I could," Ricky said carefully. "But I'm, uh, not into that kind of thing."
"Oh, I ain't either," the man said hastily. "I'm one hundred percent straight. But there's times…"
"Maybe someone else could give you a hand," Ricky suggested uncomfortably.
"I got a wife," the man shrugged. "But she ain't no good at it, and she don't like to do it."
"That's too bad," Ricky said. "Uh, my house is down this next road."
He thanked the man for the ride and ran to the house and locked the door. He waited a moment until he heard the big semi drive away before he breathed a sigh of relief.

With Ricky still working so many hours at the stores and helping out with Greg's other businesses, Greg finally hired an IT person to help with the computerized cash registers, which were seemingly always crashing. He was a young guy named Neil, and Ricky took an instant dislike to him. The man seemed untrustworthy and even a little slimy to Ricky, so he kept his distance from him. He clearly didn't know his job since Ricky was still having to work on the registers frequently himself. After a few weeks of covering for Neil, Ricky complained to Greg, only to have his words ignored.
It was shortly after this that Ricky learned of a rumor that was being spread about him among the employees. He had heard some of the snide remarks about his sexuality being made behind his back, but

nothing that concerned him. People were petty and unkind; that was nothing new to him, and he could usually ignore their ignorance and nastiness.

A frequent customer came into the Brookston store one day while Ricky was there arranging a new shipment of magazines on the display rack. He was an older construction worker, the kind with a beer belly and a cocky attitude who thought he was god's gift to women.

"I'll bet you've never even looked at one of those," he snickered, pointing to one of the pornographic magazines that Greg insisted they carry.

"What's that supposed to mean?" Ricky frowned at him.

"Just that I heard you're not into girls," the man shrugged.

"Maybe you're into 'girls', but if I was straight, I'd be into women," Ricky said heatedly. "Just like I'm into men, not boys."

"I figured," the man snorted. "Greg said he thought…"

He hesitated as he realized he had just given away a confidence that he shouldn't have. Instead, he walked on to the register and paid for his gas before quickly leaving the store.

"Did you hear that?" Ricky said angrily to Carol. "Greg's been talking about me with the customers."

"Yes, I know," she said uncomfortably. "That guy is a friend of his."

Leaving Justiceville: A Life Behind

It turned out that Greg was also friends with Carol's boyfriend, which is how Carol had come to work for Greg in the first place.
"But it doesn't mean anything," she added. "No one cares."
"If they didn't care, they wouldn't be talking about it," Ricky said. His anger grew as he pondered the situation. "Well, I'm going to settle this right now!" He strode determinedly across the store toward the office.
"Ricky, what are you going to do?" Carol followed him worriedly.
"I'm going to fucking take care of this!" he said.
"You don't want to do that," she warned him. "Just let it go."
"No!" he snapped. "I've let it go my whole life, and I'm not going to put up with it now!"
He stepped into her office and closed the door and locked it.
"Ricky, don't do this," she cried, banging repeatedly on the door. "It won't do any good."
He ignored her and picked up the phone. When the office secretary answered, he demanded to talk to Greg.
"Ricky!" Carol called to him through the door.
"This is Greg."
"So I hear you have a problem with me being gay," Ricky said coldly.
"I...I don't have a problem," Greg sputtered, unprepared for this conversation. "I didn't even know for sure that you were...that way."

"But you've talked about it," Ricky said. "And I can tell you where it started. One of two places: either with Neil or Al!"

"I don't –"

"If I want to suck a dick, I'll suck a dick!" Ricky yelled into the phone. "What I do in my own time is none of your fucking business, and it has no place being discussed by you or the employees or the customers. It's none of your goddammed business!"

"I –"

"If you've got a problem with who I am, I'll quit this fucking job and you can do the goddamned work yourself!"

With that, he slammed down the phone and opened the door, breathing heavily as he struggled to contain his fury. He gazed around the store and was surprised to see several people standing perfectly still, looking back at him.

"Sorry, everyone," he said in a calmer voice. "I didn't mean for all of you to hear that."

"Ricky, you shouldn't have done that," Carol said. "You can't go talking to Greg like that. He'll fire you for sure."

"I don't care," Ricky said honestly. "I don't need this job. I can always find something else. And if Greg thinks he can replace me with all that I do for him, good luck to him. I'm the one who's kept his businesses going; I'm the one who's put up with his shit all this time. Just let him see if anyone else will do what I've done for him."

Leaving Justiceville: A Life Behind

He thought back to the time that Greg had bought out the contents of Piddle's grocery store at Indiana Beach, which had recently ceased operations. He and Carol had been given the task of cleaning out the store. They loaded everything into a big box truck and placed it all in a series of storage sheds located behind the Brookston store. It had been backbreaking work, but Ricky hadn't complained. Over the next few months, he gradually distributed the items to the various stores to be sold to the public. Talk about a headache, Ricky thought.

And there were countless other jobs he had done for Greg that no other general manager would have put up with: trying to fix broken freezers or deep fryers because Greg refused to call for professional help, reprogramming all the cash registers in the middle of the night because the entire system had gone down, doing personal errands for Greg, and even straight-catheterizing his invalid brother on a business trip to Indianapolis. For god's sake, enough was enough!

The store phone rang shortly after he had hung up on Greg, and Ricky answered it sharply.

"What?" he snapped.

"We need to talk about this," Greg said to him.

"Fine," Ricky said calmly. "I'm on my way."

"You're on your way where?" Greg said, confused.

"I'm on my way to your office so we can talk," Ricky said. "Because I want to tell you in person that I quit this fucking job so I can see the expression on your face."

Leaving Justiceville: A Life Behind

He slammed down the phone and headed out the door to the company truck.

When Ricky got to the office, Neil was sitting on the steps outside. He stood up as Ricky neared him.
"I'm sorry about this," he said.
"Sorry about what?"
"I shouldn't have been talking about this," Neil said.
"I knew you were part of it," Ricky said. "All you fucking straight guys have a problem with me. You all think I'm just dying to suck your dick."
"I don't have a problem with it," Neil said.
"Sure you do," Ricky said. "But it doesn't matter. I'm not here to be your friend. I'm here to do a job. So I'll do my job, and you do yours. Otherwise, just leave me the hell alone."
He walked on into the office building.

"I know you're upset about this," Greg said. "But there's no need to quit."
"There isn't?" Ricky said.
"No," Greg said. "None of what we were talking about matters."
"No, you're right," Ricky agreed. "All that matters is that you and your straight buddies think it's funny to make fun of the faggot that runs your businesses for you and keeps your fucking head above water."
"We weren't making fun."
"Sure you were," Ricky said. "You wouldn't be talking about it if you didn't have a problem with it. I know how all you straight guys think. You all believe

that every woman and every gay guy in the whole world desperately wants you, that we're all anxious to have you fuck us. Well, I've got news for you, boss. I don't want you. I've already got my guy and he's got a huge dick, so what the fuck would I want with you?"
"I'm just saying I don't want you to quit," Greg said.
"Fine," Ricky said. "I won't quit. But if I hear one more word from any employee or customer that happens to be a friend of yours, I'm done."

Leaving Justiceville: A Life Behind

CHAPTER TWENTY-ONE

That was the beginning of the end as far as Ricky was concerned. He had always taken great pride in his work; he knew he was at least partially responsible for keeping Greg's businesses afloat. It was a boost to his ego to have customers tell him how clean the stores were now that he was in charge, that the selection of merchandise was much improved, that the pizzas and fried chicken the stores sold were better than ever. It made him feel good to surprise an employee with a birthday cake or a small bonus for a job well done.

But now all of that was ruined for him. He could no longer look at this job the same way now that he knew he was the topic of conversation among Greg and his homophobic buddies. Because he wasn't naïve enough to think that Greg and Neil and Al had stopped gossiping about him behind his back. They were no different from all the other straight men he had known all his life, beginning with his own father. As far as he was concerned, the bastards were all alike!

He was to learn later from Carol that Neil was having an affair with one of the married female employees and was having sex with her in one of the stores. Eventually he went to jail for dealing drugs. Greg hired a man to take Ricky's place after Ricky quit, and it turned out the man stole a considerable amount of money from the stores to finance a restaurant he planned to open. Greg ended up selling all the stores

Leaving Justiceville: A Life Behind

to another convenience store chain and soon after filed bankruptcy.

Ricky received an unexpected call one day from a cousin back in Texas.
"Your dad's sick," she said.
"So?" he shrugged. "I don't care."
"I know," she said. "But he wants to see you before he dies."
"Why? He never wanted to see me before, and I sure as hell don't want to see him."
"I'm just calling to tell you what he said."
Ricky hung up the phone and turned to Matthew.
"My dad is sick and wants to see me," he said flatly.
"Really?" Matthew frowned. "That seems odd. You haven't seen him in nearly thirty years."
"I know," Ricky said. "He treated me like shit and beat me more times than I can count, and now he wants to see me?"
"Maybe he wants to make it up to you," Matthew suggested.
"More likely he's suddenly afraid of going to hell and thinks he can still get into heaven if he begs me to forgive him," Ricky said dryly.
"So what are you going to do?" Matthew asked him.
"Nothing," Ricky said. "I have no intention of ever seeing those sons of bitches again. They made my life a living hell, and they can all rot in hell as far as I'm concerned."
He thought a moment.

Leaving Justiceville: A Life Behind

"Well, except for my sister," he shrugged. "She was the one person who never treated me too bad."

"Maybe you should go," Matthew said. "If he does want to apologize to you, it might help you resolve the issues you have with him. It might be good for you."

"No way," Ricky said firmly. "I will never go back to Texas. The whole state and everyone in it sucks as far as I'm concerned!"

"Now, that isn't true," Matthew said. "There are plenty of good people there. You just said your sister was a good person. I know you feel bitter about how you were treated, but that's in the past. Maybe going back will help you see things differently."

A few days later, Matthew drove Ricky to the airport in Bloomington. It was easily accessible and had a direct flight to Fort Worth.

"I can't believe I let you talk me into doing this," Ricky said grimly as they walked toward the terminal.

"I think this will be a good thing for you," Matthew reiterated. "This is an opportunity to let you make peace with your dad and your childhood. Try to see it as a good thing."

"No. I can't."

"Sure you can. What if he dies and you never get this chance again?" Matthew said. "At least this way you can say you tried. That you were the bigger man. Right?"

Leaving Justiceville: A Life Behind

"Wrong," Ricky said wryly. "This isn't going to do any good."
"Maybe nothing good will come out of it," Matthew admitted. "I don't know. I just think you owe it to yourself to make the effort."
"I'm only doing it to make you happy," Ricky said. "I'm not doing it for them, and I'm not doing it for me."

Ricky's plane landed at DFW airport, and he gave his cousin a call.
"Why'd you come here?" his cousin said. "They don't live in Texas anymore."
"What?!" Ricky cried. "Why didn't you tell me that?"
"I didn't know you were coming," she said. "They live in Whitaker, Oklahoma."
With a sigh, Ricky rented a car at the airport and drove to Whitaker and the address his cousin had given him. It was a small, shabby brick ranch house located out on the dusty prairie. The grass and weeds around the house were tall and sparse. The whole property appeared uncared for, and there was a dirty pickup parked in the drive. A half dried up scum-covered pond sat to the left of the house with some mangy looking cattle grazing beside it.
What the hell am I doing here, he asked himself? This was a really bad idea. I despise these people. Nothing good can possibly come from this. He took a deep breath and knocked on the front door. A moment later, his mother came to the door. Wow, she

Leaving Justiceville: A Life Behind

has not aged well, he thought as he studied her forbidding face. She was wearing a faded housecoat and slippers.

"Well, you're here," she said as she stepped back to let him in.

"You shouldn't have gotten all dressed up just for me," Ricky said sarcastically.

"Watch yer mouth," she said. She gestured to a wide doorway. "Come on, yer dad's in here."

He followed her into the living room. The walls were unadorned, the flooring made of cheap linoleum throughout the entire house, and the furnishings were plain and shabby. At least it was clean, he noted with surprise. His father was sitting in a recliner with an oxygen tank beside him. He was unshaven and wearing a stained and torn tee shirt.

"Hello," Ricky said coolly.

"Your aunt said you was comin' down," his dad said. "You look older."

"Well, you haven't seen me since I was eleven," Ricky reminded him. "And you don't look so great yourself."

"Sit down and visit while I put dinner on the table," his mother said.

A few minutes later, she called them to the dining room. I'll be damned, Ricky thought, this is the same worn and battered table they had when I was a little kid. His mother cut him a slice of some unappetizing meatloaf that was an inch thick from a pan in the center of the table. That and a glass of water was their lunch. He took a few bites to be polite while he

Leaving Justiceville: A Life Behind

listened to his parents tell him all about what they had been doing since he had seen them last. Mostly it was about their failing health and the many financial adventures at which they had supposedly succeeded dramatically. If they're doing so well, he mused, why are they living in this dump?

As he listened to them go on and on, he wondered when they were going to ask him about his life. Just as that thought occurred to him, his mother brought up that very subject.

"So are there any grandkids runnin' around that we should know about?" she asked brusquely.

"No," Ricky said. "I'm not married."

"I ain't surprised," his father said.

"In fact, I brought a few pictures in case you wanted to see them," Ricky ignored him and pulled an envelope from his pocket.

"This your house?" his mother frowned.

"Yeah," Ricky nodded. He pointed out a few details, explaining some of the work he and Matthew had done to the old house, turning it into a showplace.

"Hmm," she said with an indifferent shrug. "Look at you, mister fancy-pants!"

"Who's this guy?" his dad asked. He pointed to an image of Matthew.

"That's Matthew," Ricky said. "He's my partner. We own the house together. It was the house he grew up in."

"Partner?" his dad said suspiciously. "What does that mean?"

Leaving Justiceville: A Life Behind

"He means business partner," his mother said to her husband. "They own this groomin' shop or whatever the hell it is."
"Uh, yeah, that's right," Ricky said.
"So no grandchildren?" his dad frowned.
As if I'd introduce any kids of mine to you two horrible human beings, Ricky thought. He merely shook his head, and the topic turned back to his parents. They didn't even look at all the pictures, he thought dourly. After a couple of hours with them, Ricky had seen enough. These two awful people were still the same. Not once since he had been here had they apologized, or even acknowledged in any way how terribly they had abused him as a child. They don't even know they did anything wrong, he thought with exasperation. As far as they're concerned, I was just a bratty kid that ran away in spite of their devoted parentage.
"Well, I've got to be going," he said, standing up from the table.
"Will you be comin' back?" his father asked.
"No, there's no reason to," Ricky shook his head. "You got to see me, and I saw everything I needed to see."
"I might not be around next time you come," his father reminded him. "Is there anything you want to say to me?"
"Nope," Ricky said. "Do you have anything to say to me?"
"Like what?" his parents said as one.

Leaving Justiceville: A Life Behind

"Never mind," Ricky said. "This was a waste of time, just like I knew it would be. Goodbye."
He walked to his car and never looked back.

"Well, at least you tried," Matthew said when he picked Ricky up at the airport.
"For all the good that it did," Ricky shrugged.
"It did some good," Matthew said. "It proved that you're a better person than them. No matter how awful they were or what they did to you as a child, you overcame it."
"I did?" Ricky said doubtfully.
"Yes, you did," Matthew said. "Don't you get it? You won. You beat them. They wanted you to fail, but you didn't."

Soon after Ricky returned from his anticlimactic visit with his parents, he got a call from Julie, the woman who had interviewed and hired Matthew at the hospital a few years before. She was a lovely young woman with a warm and enthusiastic personality. Since that time, she had left her job there and started her own business with the help of a number of investors. It was called Ascent Healthcare, and it provided oxygen and oxygen supplies, respiratory care, nurse consulting, and miscellaneous equipment to nursing homes in Illinois and Indiana. Ricky had sent her his resume and called her a few times ever since he had confronted Greg at the convenient stores. He had made up his mind that no matter how good the money he was earning was, it was time to

move on. He knew nothing about healthcare or oxygen equipment, but he wasn't deterred by that fact.
"I was wondering if you're still interested in coming to work for me?" she asked him.
"Sure," he said, surprised.
"I need a product support manager," she told him. "Someone to oversee what's going out to our customers."
"I can do that," he said confidently.
"I believe you can," she agreed. "I can't afford to pay a lot. At least not as much as you're making now."
"That's okay," he said. "When do you want me to start?"

Ricky met with Julie to finalize his employment before giving his two week notice to Greg, who tried in vain to get him to stay. He said goodbye to Carol and his other managers, cleaned out his office, and drove back to Illinois with a sense of relief. Instead of working sixty to eighty hours per week, including drive time, he would be working a forty to fifty hour work week six miles from home. Of course, he thought ruefully, he was starting over once more, but that wasn't going to be a problem. Money was going to be tight again, but at least this way, he would have time to enjoy his relationship and his home.

And so Ricky began another new job, although he knew in his heart that this one was going to be different. Julie already knew that he and Matthew

were a couple, so his sexuality wasn't going to be an issue. After all, she was the president of the company.

He threw himself into learning every aspect of the work, which included warehouse and inventory management, billing, accounting, payroll, on-site visits with hospitals and nursing homes, and so on. He also helped maintain the dozens of oxygen concentrators that were constantly being rented out. Ascent was a small company based in the former offices of a local canning company. It wasn't long before it outgrew that building, and they moved across town into a new structure that was more than double the size of the previous one. Ricky and Matthew took a weekend before the company moved and painted the entire interior of the building. Julie insisted that Ricky take the biggest office since he was taking on more and more responsibility.

Julie observed Ricky's hard work, and within a few months gave him a raise and a promotion. The two of them became good friends and worked well together. It wasn't long before Ricky had risen to the position of Vice-President/Chief Operating Officer. The company was growing by leaps and bounds, thanks in large part to his and Julie's hard work, and she immediately recognized his worth. In less than two years he was earning double the salary he had earned at the convenience stores. He was working some long hours, but still not as long as previous jobs. The work was enjoyable and important, which gave him a great

Leaving Justiceville: A Life Behind

deal of satisfaction. He knew that he was playing a crucial role in the success of this business.
As time passed, he and Julie became almost best friends. They worked hard, but they were able to laugh and joke and talk about any topic at all. Ricky was unaccustomed to having a boss like her; all of his previous bosses had either been tyrannical or indifferent or homophobic. But Julie was different. She was a smart businesswoman, and she knew that customer service was paramount to the success of her business, as well as employing the best staff she could find. That included Ricky, she knew, which was why she insisted on paying him well for all of his hard work.

Meanwhile, Matthew was grooming an average of forty dogs per week. He had an excellent reputation, and more and more people were vying for appointments. The business had long since outgrown the kitchen, and it was time for a proper shop. Matthew designed and planned a twenty-four foot by thirty-six foot two car garage with a nine foot by twenty-four foot grooming shop at one end.
"All we have to do…" Matthew began.
Ricky just sighed and nodded. After all, they had made many other improvements to the old house that had seemed beyond their scope. They had roofed it, installed kitchen cabinets and new windows, hung drywall, built a deck, sided and roofed a garage, and more. There was no reason they couldn't build a garage.

Leaving Justiceville: A Life Behind

He had kept in touch with his friend Carol from the convenience stores, and her boyfriend Al offered to pour the concrete for the new building, as well as the use of his skid-steer Bobcat. Over the course of a couple of weekends, the two of them came over and demolished the old summer kitchen and second garage. Matthew had had his brother examine the buildings and was assured that they were too far gone to try to salvage. Al showed Ricky how to drive the Bobcat, and soon he was operating the small vehicle like a pro. A huge hole was dug and the two buildings burned and then buried. Meanwhile, Al set the forms for the cement foundation and floor for the new building. Once the concrete was set, Ricky and Matthew began building the walls of the structure. They learned how to do this from one of Matthew's books and from advice they received from his brother. In a matter of a few days, they had the walls erected and braced. The plumbing and electrical work were handled by professionals, but otherwise Ricky and Matthew did most of the work entirely by themselves. It took a few months, but eventually the garage was finished, and more importantly, the new grooming shop was ready for business.

The local newspaper did an article on the new shop, and Matthew was flooded with business. He groomed dogs every day that he wasn't working twelve hour shifts at the hospital. Ricky helped him groom on Saturdays when he could. The two men felt like they were working nonstop, but it felt good and satisfying to both of them.

Leaving Justiceville: A Life Behind

The old house was becoming a real showplace, they were enjoying their work and their relationship, and they had a few friends with whom they associated on occasion. Things were good until they got a call one cold January morning.

They rushed to Lakeview Hospital, twenty-five miles away. Matthew's father had woken that morning with a severe headache. By the time he arrived at the hospital by ambulance, he was comatose and on a ventilator. The rest of the family arrived, including Bill's brothers, sisters-in-law, nieces, nephews, children, and grandchildren. They all spent the day sitting with him in the ICU or visiting with one another in the waiting room.

That evening, the nurses sent them all home to get some sleep. They were reluctant to leave the hospital, but the staff assured them that if there was any change during the night, they would notify them immediately. It was a twenty mile trip to Mossville through heavy snow and wind to Matthew's parents'

Leaving Justiceville: A Life Behind

house, and they formed a convoy behind a family member's big four wheel drive SUV.
No sooner had they arrived at his parents' house when the phone rang. The doctor informed them that they were unable to keep Bill's blood pressure up and that they should return immediately. Back into their vehicles they climbed and made the treacherous trek to the hospital. Ricky held Matthew's hand on the slow drive, sensing his sorrow and apprehension.

A few minutes after they said their goodbyes to Matthew's father, the doctors turned off the ventilator, and Bill died. Ricky did his best to comfort Matthew and his mother, but they, along with the rest of the family, were overcome with grief and disbelief.

A few days later, the funeral was held. Matthew sat in a chair by himself at the funeral home.
"How are you doing?" Ricky asked him, sitting down beside him and giving him a little kiss on the cheek. He put an arm around him protectively.
"I'm okay," Matthew sighed sadly. "I can't believe this is happening."
"I know," Ricky nodded. "But at least you got to give him his birthday present."
"That's true," Matthew said tearfully.
The birthday present he was talking about had been a special project of Matthew's. He had taken a letter written by his dad's beloved father before Bill had ever been born. It was a particularly beautiful letter in

which he professed his love for Bill's mother. He had been her schoolteacher and then gone off to fight in France in WWI. She had grown into a lovely young woman, and it was her letters to him that kept him going, he claimed. In the letter, he spoke eloquently of his feelings for her, and he even proposed to her at the end of it.

Matthew wrote a short story to go with the letter and then submitted it to 'Reminisce' magazine. They printed the story along with pictures of Bill's parents. An advance copy of the magazine was sent to Matthew a few months before it was to be published, and he was excited to show it to his father. Bill's birthday was coming up in February, and Matthew decided that it would make the perfect gift for the occasion.

"You're just itching to show it to him, aren't you?" Ricky teased him a few days before Bill's hospitalization.

"I am," Matthew said. "He's going to love it."

"Why don't you go ahead and show it to him now?" Ricky suggested. "You can get him something else for his birthday."

"You think so?" Matthew said uncertainly.

"I do," Ricky said. "Just go ahead and give it to him now and let him enjoy it."

Matthew had taken the copy of the magazine in to his parents' house the next morning. Typical of his father, his reaction was pleased, but subdued. Betty told him later that Bill had spent that entire day

calling family and friends and telling them all about the article that featured his dear father.
"He was so thrilled with it," she said tearfully. "It's all he could talk about all day."

It was the very next day that he died.

Nine years after Ricky had started work at Ascent Healthcare, Julie received an offer from a big corporation to buy her out. The company had gone from a fledgling local operation to one worth millions of dollars, due almost entirely to Ricky and Julie's tireless dedication. Julie and her investors agreed to a deal, and the business was sold. She and Ricky agreed to stay on with the new company with the understanding that nothing would change. This was a new direction for the corporation, they were told, and they wanted to leave everything alone so that they could observe the day to day operation.
Ricky knew better than to believe that, and sure enough, everything changed almost immediately. A big truck showed up the very next day, filled with all new computers.
"What's this?" Ricky frowned at the delivery driver.
"Your new computers," the man said as he chomped his gum and held out an electronic pad for Ricky to sign.
"I can see that," Ricky said dryly. "But why didn't someone tell us about this? Who's supposed to switch everything out? Are they sending people to help?"

Leaving Justiceville: A Life Behind

"Nope," the driver shrugged. "I was told it's up to you."

Being the whiz with computers that he was, Ricky began the arduous task of replacing all the computers in the offices and warehouse. He had wisely kept a backup of every program and every file.

Where service had been Ricky's primary concern in the past, the new owners had a different approach. With their corporate mentality, they believed that the customer would take what they had to offer and be happy about it, while Ricky had always put the customer's needs first. For instance, one nursing home asked him to get them a lawn mower. Rather than tell them that that wasn't his job, he did some research and delivered a brand new lawn mower with their order.

After about a year of being forced to endure seeing more and more accounts lost, despite their best efforts, Julie and Ricky had had enough. Julie decided to quit as CEO, and Ricky soon followed suit.

By now the grooming business had grown to approximately fifty dogs per week, which was too much for Matthew to handle alone. The two of them talked, and it was decided that Ricky would retire from the workforce and come home to groom fulltime. They had saved up some money in preparation for this day, so they weren't too worried about finances. Of course, there were still projects

they wanted to do to the house, but none were pressing, and they could do those a little at a time.
"You see," Matthew said one evening while they sat on their luxurious patio behind the house. "You did it."
"I did what?" Ricky frowned.
The flicker of light from several patio torches gave the space a cozy, intimate feeling.
"You made a success of your life."
"I'm a dog groomer," Ricky said dryly.
"That's what you are now, but look at all you've done," Matthew said. "You've succeeded at everything you've ever done, from working in fast-food, to the publishing business, to managing five convenience stores and whatever else Greg had you doing. And you just retired from being a vice-president and chief operating officer of a multi-million dollar business. Do you not see how impressive that is? There's no way I could have done what you've done, and you did it all on your own, with no help from anyone. You should be proud of yourself."
"Are you proud of me?"
"Did you not listen to what I just said?" Matthew teased him. He gave him a kiss on the cheek. "I'm very, very proud of you. If it wasn't for you, this house wouldn't look like it does, and we wouldn't be driving a Mercedes and a Lincoln Navigator. You, Ricky Blain, are the most successful man in the world as far as I'm concerned. Don't ever forget that!"

Leaving Justiceville: A Life Behind

EPILOGUE

NOVEMBER 2013

"Same sex marriage is legal in Illinois!" Matthew shouted excitedly as the announcement came over the television. The two were sitting together on the sofa in front of the fireplace.
"It's hard to believe," Ricky said, grinning at his partner's exuberance.
"I know, right?" Matthew said. "Who would have ever believed that gay marriage would be legal in our lifetime?"

Leaving Justiceville: A Life Behind

"Not me, that's for sure."
"So do you want to?" Matthew turned to him.
"Do I want to what?" Ricky said.
"Do you want to get married?" Matthew said.
"Married?" Ricky looked confused. "Who would I marry?"
"Look, do you want to get married or not?" Matthew raised an eyebrow, knowing that Ricky was being purposely obtuse.
"This is how you ask me? 'Do you want to get married or not?' That's not much of a proposal," Ricky chuckled. "Besides, we already have commitment rings. What do we need with a wedding?"
He was referring to the beautiful matching one-carat diamond rings they had bought for each other several years before.
"But there are benefits to being married," Matthew said. "Legal and tax benefits."
"So this is about practicality," Ricky said.
"Well, yes…but no," Matthew said hesitantly.
Ricky slid down onto one knee and took Matthew's hand in his own. He removed the diamond ring on Matthew's left hand and looked up into Matthew's eyes.
"I love you more now than when we met, all these years later," he said. "Will you marry me?"
"I'll marry you," Matthew grinned down at him. "Who else would have me?"
"Probably just about every gay guy out there," Ricky said wryly.

"Well, that's a big fat lie," Matthew laughed. He held out his hand. "Give me your ring."
"Why?"
"Just give it here."
Ricky handed him his ring, and Matthew dropped to one knee in front of him.
"Will you marry me?" he asked.
"I already asked you," Ricky protested.
"And I said yes," Matthew said. "Now I'm asking you. Will you marry me?"
"I will," Ricky grinned mischievously. "I've already stuck around this long. I might as well stay for the duration."
"You romantic dog, you," Matthew rolled his eyes. He slipped the ring back onto Ricky's finger and stood up. They kissed for a moment and then sat back down on the sofa. "Of course, it will probably be a very small wedding. Just you and me and a witness or two; no one else would want to come. That is, if we can even find someone to perform a gay wedding around here."
"Someone will do it," Ricky said confidently.
"Maybe we could do it here in front of the fireplace," Matthew said thoughtfully. "Or out on the patio. Maybe next summer some time."
"It doesn't matter to me," Ricky shrugged. "Now let's go to bed."
"I'm not tired."
"Who said you're going to sleep?" Ricky growled with one raised eyebrow.

Leaving Justiceville: A Life Behind

And so the whirlwind of wedding planning began. Ricky wanted Matthew to have the wedding of his dreams, so he let him do most of the planning. It was obvious that he was having a ball deciding the hows and wheres and whens of the event. He searched Pinterest and other websites for ideas and collected as much information as he could. Ricky listened to him indulgently as he prattled on about the wedding. Ricky happened to mention their plan to wed to a few grooming customers. The next thing he knew, people were calling or stopping by, asking if they could come. One of their customers, a dear friend and schoolteacher in Mossville named Lynn, eagerly offered her services as officiant. She could go online, she said, and get ordained in no time. Ricky had to laugh because it seemed she was more excited about their nuptials than they were!

One day in January, Ricky and Matthew did some necessary shopping over in Champaign-Urbana, about sixty miles away.

"Hey, there's a Men's Wearhouse store over there," Matthew pointed across the parking lot from the grocery store they had just visited. "Let's go look at tuxedos."

The two men entered the store and began eying the various tuxedos on display.

"Oh my god," Ricky frowned as he examined a price tag. "This Vera Wang is nine hundred dollars!"

"Wow," Matthew whispered, disappointed. "We can't afford that."

"Can I help you?" a male clerk approached them.

Leaving Justiceville: A Life Behind

"We were just looking at tuxedos," Matthew said.
"For a wedding?" the man asked them, peering over his half-glasses.
"Uh, yeah," Matthew said warily.
Both Ricky and Matthew knew better than to reveal too much about their planned wedding. There were many people in central Illinois who were decidedly homophobic. At the very least, most people in the area were very conservative, so the two men had learned to be cautious. They had never tried to hide their relationship, but they hadn't flaunted it, either.
"I see," the salesman said. "And will you both be needing a tuxedo?"
"Yes," Ricky said.
"Well, we are having a buy-one-get-one-free sale this week."
"Even so," Matthew said ruefully. "This is more than we can afford right now."
There was only one other customer in the store, so a few of the other clerks gathered around them to help point out some cheaper options. Many of the tuxedos were expensive, but there were a few that were a bit less costly. Ricky noticed that one of the salesladies walked away with a frown on her face. Hmm, she must have figured out we're a gay couple and has decided she doesn't want any part of it.
"We'll think about it," he said to the others. "Maybe we'll come back."
As the salespeople were wishing them well, the saleswoman who had left them before returned carrying a tuxedo in her arms.

Leaving Justiceville: A Life Behind

"If money is an issue," she said, "we do have these."
She held up the beautiful, finely made tuxedo and
Ricky and Matthew examined it admiringly. Five
hundred dollars, Ricky noted the tag on the sleeve.
"They're last year's, of course," the woman went on.
"But if you don't care about that…"
Why on earth would they care about that, Ricky
thought?
"It's beautiful," Matthew said. "But how much is it?"
"Thirty-five dollars," she said.
Ricky and Matthew just stared at her with wide eyes.
Finally Ricky spoke.
"What did you say?"
"Thirty-five dollars," the woman repeated.
"Did you say thirty-five dollars?" he asked
disbelievingly.
The other clerks chuckled at their reaction.
"I did," she smiled warmly at them. "I just need to
see if I can get two of them from some of the other
stores."
She made some quick calls and returned with good
news. They could get the tuxedos in question in their
sizes from another store and would have them in a
few days.
"Meanwhile," she suggested, "we are having our
half-price sale. Why don't you go ahead and pick out
the other things you'll need: shoes, shirts,
cummerbunds, cufflinks, and so on."
She and several of the other clerks guided the two
dazed men through the store, helping them select
shiny black shoes, elegant cufflinks and studs,

pleated shirts, bowties, and more. By the time they had chosen their complete outfits, what would have cost them a couple of thousand dollars had totaled less than two hundred fifty!

Both of them walked out of the store an hour later feeling exhilarated. Well, one more thing to check off the list, Ricky thought. And look how excited Matthew is.

Over the next few months, more of Matthew's plans fell into place. One of their grooming customers, a friend named Sherry, offered to cater the event as soon as she learned of it. Matthew insisted that it all be comfort food: various kinds of meatballs, wings, and finger sandwiches, plus bacon wrapped Smokies, vegetable platters, and wraps.

Matthew called the daughter of one of his ex-coworkers, who happened to be a skilled photographer. When he hesitantly asked her if she would be interested in handling the wedding and reception, her exact words were, "I'd be honored." She even gave them a special discount since it was her first gay wedding to photograph.

It was the same response when it came to the bakery. "I'd be honored to do the cake for you," the woman smiled at them. "You just tell me what you want."

The Men's Wearhouse had another surprise for Ricky and Matthew when they went back to be fitted for their tuxedos.

Leaving Justiceville: A Life Behind

"Everything in the store is discounted," the clerk smiled as he rang them up. "That brings the cost of each tuxedo down to thirty dollars instead of thirty-five!"

(A few weeks after the wedding that summer, Matthew sent an email to the CEO of the Men's Wearhouse, thanking him and the staff of the Champaign store for their kindness. He added that not all salespeople were as kind as his staff had been, and that he and Ricky appreciated it. To their surprise, the CEO wrote back and asked to talk to them by phone. A time was agreed upon, and the shop phone rang at the designated hour. The man was very nice and insisted on hearing every detail of the ceremony and their experiences leading up to it, including how they met and how long they had been a couple. When Ricky and Matthew had explained their entire wedding journey, the CEO insisted on sending them an extremely generous wedding gift in the form of a gift certificate to their favorite restaurant.)

Ricky and Matthew had planned on a few friends attending the wedding followed by a small party afterwards. However, as the months went by, the guest list grew to include well over one hundred people, much to their amazement.
"That's because people love you," Lynn, their friend and officiant, told Ricky one day. "They want to support you and be here for you."

Leaving Justiceville: A Life Behind

And it turned out that she was right. Even family members that Matthew was certain would have no interest in attending were planning on coming.
One day, the couple asked one of their friends and grooming customers a favor. He was a distinguished and world-renowned eye surgeon, who Matthew had worked with for many years. His name was Dave, and he owned two enormous and gentle Newfoundland males that Ricky and Matthew groomed every two weeks.
"I have a favor to ask you," Matthew said to him one day in the grooming shop. "Or, I should say, we have a favor."
"Okay," Dave said. "Just name it."
"You have to feel free to say no," Matthew added hastily. "I don't want you to feel obligated."
"Matthew, he won't say no," Ricky said. "Just ask him."
"Would you consider letting Angus and Murphy be the ring bearers at the wedding?"
"Oh, my goodness," Dave said, taken aback for a moment. "I'd be honored – thrilled – to have them act as ring bearers! Thank you so much for asking."

Leaving Justiceville: A Life Behind

Ricky asked Carol and Julie to stand up with him at the wedding, and Matthew asked his dear friend and coworker Kelly to stand up with him. He also asked his favorite cousin, who also happened to be named Kellie. All four of the women told them how pleased they were to do this for them.

A huge open air tent was rented to stand over the blacktopped driveway. One hundred fifty white folding chairs were set up in a semi-circle, and Kelly attached purple ribbons and bows to each of them. Ricky and Matthew had become very interested in growing flowers for their patio over the years, and they decided on yellow marigolds, purple wave petunias, and mossy green ivy to go with the wedding's color scheme this year. Ricky's and Matthew's bowties, suspenders, and boutonnières

were purple, while the other wedding participants' boutonnière and corsages were yellow.

Ricky and Matthew had worked unceasingly on preparations for the big day for weeks now. They had designed invitations, programs, and hand fans printed with purple ink, drawn purple and yellow chalk hearts on the blacktop, bought gifts for each participant, come up with funny props for a photo booth, bought cases of beer, soft drinks, and wine, and lots more.

Matthew rented two refrigerators from a local appliance store that they had done business with a few times over the years. They told Kent, the owner, that it was for a party, but didn't mention anything about the wedding.

"What kind of party is it?" Kent asked them curiously when he delivered the two used refrigerators.

"Oh, just a party for friends," Matthew said evasively.

"I see," Kent said.

When he came back a few days after the wedding to pick up the appliances, he scolded the two of them.

"Why didn't you tell me this was for your wedding?" he frowned at them.

"We've learned to keep our mouths shut," Ricky shrugged. "You never know how people around here are going to react."

"I suppose that's true," Kent said. He handed Ricky a package.

"What's this?" Ricky asked him.

Leaving Justiceville: A Life Behind

"It's a wedding present," Kent grinned. "Nothing fancy, just something I thought you could use."

Matthew sat down and wrote out an email to his brother and sisters and niece when he mailed out the invitations:

I'm sending each of you an invitation to our wedding. I love you all, and Ricky and I would love nothing more than to have you all here. But I'll remind you now that this is a gay wedding. So if you decide to attend on the twelfth of July, please remember that I want only positive energy here that day. This will be a once in a lifetime moment in our lives, and I don't want anything negative anywhere near this property. If you can do that, then I look forward to seeing each of you.

"Don't let it bother you if they don't come," Ricky told him. "You don't need them."
"I know," Matthew nodded. "I have you, so what else do I need?"
As it turned out, Matthew received a response from his brother, who planned to attend with his wife as long as he wasn't expected to kiss the groom, and one sister who said they couldn't attend because of the long distance trip.

July twelfth, the day of the wedding, finally arrived. Ricky and Matthew awoke early that morning to the

sound of thunder and heavy rain hitting the bedroom windows.

"Oh my god!" Matthew cried. "It's raining! Everything's going to be ruined!"

He groaned and put his head back under the covers.

"It'll be fine," Ricky said soothingly.

"No, it won't," Matthew mumbled. "We should just call the whole thing off."

"We can't call it off," Ricky chuckled. "There are over a hundred people coming here this evening, plus the cake and all the food. The tent will keep the driveway dry even if it rains during the ceremony."

"No, it's all ruined," Matthew moaned.

"Come on," Ricky pulled the covers down. "People are going to be here any minute to help set up."

The two men threw on some shorts and tee shirts and headed downstairs. Their friends and Matthew's niece arrived to help. They all huddled in the garage and listened to the thunder and pouring rain while they blew up balloons, set out tablecloths and decorations, and so on.

The rain stopped around noon that day, but the weather remained hot and extremely humid. Matthew walked around the perimeter of the tent and pushed up on the canvas where the rain had collected in deep pockets. The water splattered to the pavement below.

"Oh god, this is never going to work," he moaned. "Everything's going to be wet and muddy."

"No, it's going to be perfect," Ricky said. "It's our day, and nothing is going to spoil it, especially not some heat or humidity."

Leaving Justiceville: A Life Behind

"How can you not be worried about this?"

"Rain on a wedding day is good luck," Ricky said. "It means that the knot we're tying is wet and hard to unravel."

"But it's my wedding day," Matthew said. "What if it rains during the ceremony? I don't want it to rain."

"Well, it's my wedding day too, and I say it's good luck," Ricky insisted. "So let it rain!"

Matthew grinned at him and sighed. Ricky always knew what to say to make him feel better.

And he was right, of course. The sky cleared, the pavement dried, and a gentle breeze helped alleviate a bit of the heat and humidity. The guests arrived and found their seats, using the homemade fans to cool themselves. The music began, and Ricky and Matthew made their entrances. Lynn spoke

eloquently for a few minutes about true love, and then it was time for the vows. Ricky went first:

"Matthew, when we met twenty-three years ago, we started our life's journey together. I never guessed that the day would come that we would be able to marry and make our commitment to each other complete. Over the years we've had good times and bad, and that won't change.
"You make my heart warm, you make me smile when I feel I cannot, you are always here to support me. Even when we were dirt poor and had to buy lunch with a Phillips 66 gas card, we were still happy. I still remember how we used the car mats to slide down snowy hills at White Pines Park, hoping we didn't end up in the river. We lived on canned corn and Mountain Dew because we couldn't afford hamburger. No matter what we had to do, we survived. We laughed together so many times over the crazy things that have happened. We've cried over the sad times, but we never gave up. We stuck it out and now here we are today."
The guests laughed and teared up as he continued.

"I guess I'm a little weird, and life is even weirder, and when we find someone whose weirdness is compatible with ours, we get together and put our weirdness all together. And that is what we call love.
"I promise that I will always love you unconditionally, I will support you, honor and respect

Leaving Justiceville: A Life Behind

you, laugh with you, and cherish you with all my heart. I love you."

There was a collective "awww" from the assembly. "Matthew?" Lynn turned to him.

"Ricky, in spite of the heat and humidity, and the threat of storms, it was important to do all of this here at home, because this house is a symbol to me. Growing up, it was the one place where I fit in, where I was safe and accepted, and loved.
"At church they told me I was going to hell, and school *was* hell, but not here. Then twenty-three years ago I met you, and for whatever reason, from Texas to Oklahoma to Illinois, we ended up back here.
"And because of you, it's still the one place on earth where I know I am safe and accepted and loved. You've been my best friend for those twenty-three years, and I love you and I'll always be here for you, just like I know that you'll always be here for me.
"There is a quote I really like that I wish I could take credit for, but it's by a woman named Barbara Alpert. I've paraphrased it and adapted it here for you:
"You are my mirror, shining back at me with a world of possibilities. You are my witness, who sees me at my best and worst, and loves me anyway. You are my partner in crime, my midnight companion. You know when I am smiling, even in the dark. You are my soulmate, and my home."

Leaving Justiceville: A Life Behind

Matthew and Ricky were unaware of it, but there was scarcely a dry eye among the guests. The only thing Ricky could see was his beloved Matthew's tear stained face looking back at him. He waited until Lynn pronounced them husband and husband, and then leaned forward and kissed Matthew gently on the lips. He was startled by the loud cheers and applause that erupted from their friends and family. Soon they were surrounded by dozens of people offering their hugs, pats on the back, and words of congratulations.

A little later, Ricky took to the microphone as the guests were enjoying the scrumptious food that their friend had prepared for them. There had been numerous toasts to honor the newly married couple, including Dave, Matthew's niece Cara, and their wonderful friend and emcee, Angelena.
"Thank you all for being here," he said. "I have a few things I'd like to say to you all. First of all, I want you to know that I've heard the rumors that have been floating around here this evening. And I think it's time to set the record straight, once and for all. Matthew and I…" he paused dramatically, never cracking a smile, "…are gay."
The audience practically howled with laughter.
"So that rumor is put to rest," he grinned at them when they had quieted. "Secondly, some of you have asked which of us is the husband and which is the wife. Well, it doesn't really work like that in a gay marriage."

Leaving Justiceville: A Life Behind

Matthew stood up next to him and snatched the microphone out of his hand.

"All I can tell you is that Ricky does everything I tell him to do."

More laughter.

"Sure he does," someone called out sarcastically.

Ricky took back the microphone.

"Matthew's right. I'm not sure if that makes me the husband or the wife," he chuckled. "I'll let you all figure that one out.

"And then lastly, I just want to tell you that never in my life…" his throat tightened a bit, "never in my life have I felt such an atmosphere of genuine love. That's something I've never experienced anywhere else, and it's because of all of you, and because of Matthew. I love you all."

"And we love you!" the crowd shouted back at him.

And so Ricky and Matthew lived happily ever after.

THE END

Leaving Justiceville: A Life Behind

ACKNOWLEDGEMENTS

This is a novel, but it is based on fact. All of the events portrayed here actually happened, although the names and places have been changed to protect the innocent, and more importantly, the guilty. The character of Ricky is a real person, and he really did survive the horrific childhood that is described here. Fortunately, he and Matthew found one another and their weirdness – their love – has kept them together for nearly thirty years.

Ricky is the author of two cookbooks of recipes that he and Matthew have experimented with over the years and changed to make their own. Matthew is the author of nineteen gay romance novels. The two of them still live in the old farmhouse that Matthew grew up in, and no, they are not finished remodeling it. Their main hobby, and most expensive one, is buying and trading automobiles. Over the years they've owned just about every type of car, SUV, and pickup, from Mercedes to Lincoln to Fiat, and everything in between. Currently they are driving a BMW and a Chevy pickup, but that could change from now to whenever this book is published!

Made in the USA
Columbia, SC
20 April 2022